D0512886

Security+ Practice Questions

Hans Sparbel

CERTIFICATION

Security+ Practice Questions Exam Cram 2

Copyright © 2004 by Que Publishing

International Standard Book Number: 0-7897-3151-7

Library of Congress Catalog Card Number: 2003115742

Printed in the United States of America

First Printing: March 2004

07   06   05   04   4   3   2   1

Trademarks

All terms mentioned in this book that are known to be trademarks or service marks have been appropriately capitalized. Que Publishing cannot attest to the accuracy of this information. Use of a term in this book should not be regarded as affecting the validity of any trademark or service mark.

Warning and Disclaimer

Every effort has been made to make this book as complete and as accurate as possible, but no warranty or fitness is implied. The information provided is on an "as is" basis. The author and the publisher shall have neither liability nor responsibility to any person or entity with respect to any loss or damages arising from the information contained in this book or from the use of the CD or programs accompanying it.

Bulk Sales

Que Publishing offers excellent discounts on this book when ordered in quantity for bulk purchases or special sales. For more information, please contact

U.S. Corporate and Government Sales

1-800-382-3419

corpsales@pearsontechgroup.com

For sales outside of the U.S., please contact

International Sales

1-317-428-3341

international@pearsontechgroup.com

Publisher
Paul Boger

Executive Editor
Jeff Riley

Development Editor
Steve Rowe

Managing Editor
Charlotte Clapp

Project Editor
Dan Knott

Copy Editor
Linda Seifert

Technical Editor
Robert Shimonski

Publishing Coordinator
Pamalee Nelson

Multimedia Developer
Dan Scherf

Interior Designer
Anne Jones

Cover Designer
Anne Jones

Page Layout
Kelly Maish

CERTIFICATION

Que Certification • 800 East 96th Street • Indianapolis, Indiana 46240

A Note from Series Editor Ed Tittel

You know better than to trust your certification preparation to just anybody. That's why you, and more than two million others, have purchased an Exam Cram book. As Series Editor for the new and improved Exam Cram 2 series, I have worked with the staff at Que Certification to ensure you won't be disappointed. That's why we've taken the world's best-selling certification product—a finalist for "Best Study Guide" in a CertCities reader poll in 2002—and made it even better.

As a two-time finalist for the "Favorite Study Guide Author" award as determined by CertCities readers, I know the value of good books. You'll be impressed with Que Certification's stringent review process, which ensures the books are high-quality, relevant, and technically accurate.

We've also added MeasureUp, a powerful, full-featured test engine, which is trusted by certification students throughout the world.

As a 20-year-plus veteran of the computing industry and the original creator and editor of the Exam Cram series, I've brought my IT experience to bear on these books. During my tenure at Novell from 1989 to 1994, I worked with and around its excellent education and certification department. This experience helped push my writing and teaching activities heavily in the certification direction. Since then, I've worked on more than 70 certification-related books, and I write about certification topics for numerous Web sites and for *Certification* magazine.

In 1996, while studying for various MCP exams, I became frustrated with the huge, unwieldy study guides that were the only preparation tools available. As an experienced IT professional and former instructor, I wanted "nothing but the facts" necessary to prepare for the exams. From this impetus, Exam Cram emerged in 1997. It quickly became the best-selling computer book series since "...*For Dummies*," and the best-selling certification book series ever. By maintaining an intense focus on subject matter, tracking errata and updates quickly, and following the certification market closely, Exam Cram was able to establish the dominant position in cert prep books.

You will not be disappointed in your decision to purchase this book. If you are, please contact me at etittel@jump.net. All suggestions, ideas, input, or constructive criticism are welcome!

Ed Tittel

Expand Your Certification Arsenal!

Security+
Exam Cram 2
(Exam SY0-101)

Kirk Hausman, Diane Barrett, and Martin Weiss

ISBN 0-7897-2910-5

$39.99 US/$60.99 CAN/£28.99 Net UK

- Key terms and concepts highlighted at the start of each chapter

- Notes, Tips, and Exam Alerts advise what to watch out for

- End-of-chapter sample Exam Questions with detailed discussions of all answers

- Complete text-based practice test with answer key at the end of each book

- The tear-out Cram Sheet condenses the most important items and information into a two-page reminder

- A CD that includes PrepLogic Practice Tests for complete evaluation of your knowledge

- Our authors are recognized experts in the field. In most cases, they are current or former instructors, trainers, or consultants— they know exactly what you need to know!

About the Author

Hans Sparbel is a Licensed Vocational Networking Trainer by the State of California. He has been in this position since 1999. He is also a computer science educator, adjunct college professor, and guest speaker. Hans is certified in multiple computer programs, including MCSE in Windows 2000 and NT 4.0, MCT, MCP + Internet, Microsoft Office applications, Linux and Novell Administration, Hubbell Wiring, and A+ Hardware Technician. Hans also has one year of experience as a technical school director overseas. Lastly, Hans is an experienced supervisor, planner, analytical evaluator, and published technical writer.

Hans has a variety of educational backgrounds: music composition in Germany, vocational nursing with the military, educational degrees in vocational education and sociology at the master's level and many computer certifications. In his spare time, Hans plays piano, writes music, and is continuing his education in the medical field.

What's fascinating about this author is his uniquely positive and helpful attitude about nearly every aspect of life. I have heard him say on more than one occasion to students and friends alike, "The more you do, the more you can do." His belief that "With God all things are possible" is a proven testimony throughout his life.

It's hard to imagine that someone who escaped from East Germany without a cent could have accomplished so many things.

Comments from Esther, his loving wife.

We Want to Hear from You!

As the reader of this book, *you* are our most important critic and commentator. We value your opinion and want to know what we're doing right, what we could do better, what areas you'd like to see us publish in, and any other words of wisdom you're willing to pass our way.

As an executive editor for Que Publishing, I welcome your comments. You can email or write me directly to let me know what you did or didn't like about this book—as well as what we can do to make our books better.

Please note that I cannot help you with technical problems related to the topic of this book. We do have a User Services group, however, where I will forward specific technical questions related to the book.

When you write, please be sure to include this book's title and author as well as your name, email address, and phone number. I will carefully review your comments and share them with the author and editors who worked on the book.

Email: feedback@quepublishing.com

Mail: Jeff Riley
          Executive Editor
          Que Publishing
          800 East 96th Street
          Indianapolis, IN 46240 USA

For more information about this book or another Que Publishing title, visit our Web site at www.examcram2.com. Type the ISBN (excluding hyphens) or the title of a book in the Search field to find the page you're looking for.

Contents at a Glance

Table of Contents

. . . .

Introduction

. . . .

What Is This Book About?

Welcome to the *Security+ Practice Questions Exam Cram 2*! The aim of this book is to provide you with practice questions complete with answers and explanations that will help you learn, drill, and review for the Security+ certification exam.

Who Is This Book For?

If you have studied the Security+ exam's content and feel you are ready to put your knowledge to the test, but not sure you want to take the real exam yet, then this book is for you! Maybe you have answered other practice questions or unsuccessfully taken the real exam, reviewed, and want to do more practice questions before going to take the real exam; then this book is for you too!

What Will You Find in This Book?

As mentioned before, this book is all about practice questions! This book is separated according to the topics you will find in the Security+ exam. Each chapter represents an exam topic and in each chapter you will find three elements:

➤ *Practice Questions* These are numerous questions that will help you learn, drill, and review topics based on the Security+ objectives.

➤ *Quick Check Answer Section* After you have finished answering the questions, you can quickly grade your exam from this section. Only correct answers are given here. No explanations are offered, yet!

➤ *Answers and Explanations*   This section offers you the correct answers, as well as further explanation about the content posed in that question. Use this information to learn why an answer is correct and to reinforce the content in your mind for exam day.

You will also find a CramSheet at the beginning of this book specifically written for this exam. This is a very popular element that is also found in the corresponding *Security+ Exam Cram 2* study guide (ISBN: 0-7897-2910-5). This item condenses all the necessary facts found in this exam into one, easy-to-handle tear card. The CramSheet is something you can carry with you to the exam location and use as a last second study aid. Beware that you can't take it into the exam room, though!

Hints for Using This Book

Because this book is a paper practice product, you might want to complete your exams on a separate piece of paper so you can reuse the questions over and over without having previous answers in your way. Also, a general rule of thumb across all practice question products is to make sure you are scoring well into the high 80 to 90 percent range in all topics before attempting the real exam. The higher percentages you score on practice question products, the better your chances for passing the real exam. Of course, we can't guarantee a passing score on the real exam, but we can offer you plenty of opportunities to practice and assess your knowledge levels before entering the real exam.

Need Further Study?

Are you having a hard time correctly answering these questions? If so, you probably need further review. Be sure to see the sister product to this book, the *Security+ Exam Cram 2*, by Que Publishing, (ISBN:0-7897-2910-5) for further review. If you need even further study, check out Que's *Security+ Training Guide* (ISBN: 0-7897-2836-2).

General Security Concepts

1. There are many security concepts that have turned into well-known acronyms. Which of the following refer to the security acronym AAA? (Select all that apply.)

   - ❑ a. Access Control
   - ❑ b. Authentication
   - ❑ c. Auditing
   - ❑ d. Accountability

2. There are many security concepts that have turned into well-known acronyms. Which of the following refer to the security acronym CIA? (Select the best answer.)

   - ❑ a. Central Intelligence Agency
   - ❑ b. Confidentiality, Integrity, and Availability
   - ❑ c. Confidence, Intelligence, and Accountability
   - ❑ d. Confidentiality, Integrity, and Authentication

Objective 1.1: Access Control

1. Which of the following is the best example of what access control is similar to?

   - ❑ a. A floor
   - ❑ b. A wall
   - ❑ c. A key
   - ❑ d. A room

2. Which of the following are reasonable examples of denying access to network resources? (Select all that apply.)

   - ❑ a. Domain names
   - ❑ b. Computer IP addresses
   - ❑ c. Computer names
   - ❑ d. Brute force

. . . .

3. When dealing with data or file security, which of the following establishes what a user has the privilege to change or examine?

   ❑   a. Folder Authentication

   ❑   b. Data Integrity

   ❑   c. Access Control

   ❑   d. Corporate Confidentiality

4. Which of the following items determine what a user can change or view?

   ❑   a. Data integrity

   ❑   b. Data confidentiality

   ❑   c. Data authentication

   ❑   d. Access control

Objective 1.1.1: MAC

1. Which of the following are examples of access control methods? (Select all that apply.)

   ❑   a. Mandatory Access Control

   ❑   b. Rule-Based Access Control

   ❑   c. Role-Based Access Control

   ❑   d. Discretionary Access Control

2. Mandatory Access Control (MAC) places sensitivity labels on both subjects and objects. Which of the following would be identified as subjects on a network using Mandatory Access Control? (Select all that apply.)

   ❑   a. People

   ❑   b. Folders

   ❑   c. Computer programs

   ❑   d. Computer processes

3. What access control method is used for the system to determine which users or groups access files or folders?

   ❑   a. Role-Based Access Control

   ❑   b. Mandatory Access Control

   ❑   c. Discretionary Access Control

   ❑   d. List Based Access Control

4. What are the choices based upon when using Mandatory Access Control?

Quick Answer: **40**
Detailed Answer: **44**

- ❑ a. Sensitivity labels
- ❑ b. Group membership
- ❑ c. Individual status
- ❑ d. File ownership

5. Which one of the following access control methods involves defining the specific classification for objects?

Quick Answer: **40**
Detailed Answer: **44**

- ❑ a. Object-Based Access Control
- ❑ b. Identity-Based Access Control
- ❑ c. Mandatory Access Control
- ❑ d. Discretionary Access Control

6. What kind of access control method is needed when a user does *not* have the ability to control access to the files and folders they own?

Quick Answer: **40**
Detailed Answer: **44**

- ❑ a. Mandatory Access Control
- ❑ b. Discretionary Access Control
- ❑ c. Role-Based Access Control
- ❑ d. Unknown Access Control

7. What are access decisions based on when using Mandatory Access Control (MAC)?

Quick Answer: **40**
Detailed Answer: **44**

- ❑ a. Access control lists
- ❑ b. File / folder ownership
- ❑ c. Group membership
- ❑ d. Sensitivity labels

8. Which access control method is in use when the system makes all determinations about which processes can access a device?

Quick Answer: **40**
Detailed Answer: **44**

- ❑ a. Kernel Access Control
- ❑ b. Discretionary Access Control
- ❑ c. Total Access Control
- ❑ d. Mandatory Access Control

9. Which one of the following access control methods necessitates security clearance for subjects?

Quick Answer: **40**
Detailed Answer: **45**

- ❑ a. Identity-based Access Control
- ❑ b. Military Access Control
- ❑ c. Role-Based Access Control
- ❑ d. Mandatory Access Control

10. In reference to Mandatory Access Control, which of the following statements is true?

Quick Answer: **40**
Detailed Answer: **45**

    ❑   a. A user may establish file permissions

    ❑   b. The system establishes group membership, but a user may decide which individuals may access their files

    ❑   c. The system mandates which users can create files, but users may establish group membership

    ❑   d. The system establishes which users or groups may access a file

11. Which of the following is a type of Mandatory Access Control?

Quick Answer: **40**
Detailed Answer: **45**

    ❑   a. Lattice-Based Access Control

    ❑   b. Role-Based Access Control

    ❑   c. Control-Based Access Control

    ❑   d. Rule-Based Access Control

12. There are several models that relate to network security. Which of the following is generally *not* associated with Mandatory Access Control (MAC)?

Quick Answer: **40**
Detailed Answer: **45**

    ❑   a. The Biba Model

    ❑   b. The Bell La-Padula Model

    ❑   c. The Clark Wilson Model

    ❑   d. Sensitivity labels

13. Which of the following access control concepts pertain to the use of MAC? (Select all that apply.)

Quick Answer: **40**
Detailed Answer: **45**

    ❑   a. MAC is based on sensitivity labels of objects and subjects

    ❑   b. MAC is lattice-based access control

    ❑   c. MAC is used in organizations with Secret and Top Secret classified data

    ❑   d. MAC means Modified Access Control

Objective 1.1.1: DAC

1. Which of the following are true statements about Discretionary Access Control methods? (Select all that apply.)

Quick Answer: **40**
Detailed Answer: **45**

    ❑   a. The network administrator or superuser takes ownership of each object

    ❑   b. Each file or object has its own owner

    ❑   c. The network is based on a centralized authority or policy that determines object access

    ❑   d. Object owners have complete power over their files to control or limit access

2. Which access control measure allows data owners to create and manage access to their own files?

- ❏ a. Discretionary Access Control
- ❏ b. Rule-Based Access Control
- ❏ c. Lattice-Based Access Control
- ❏ d. Mandatory Access Control

Quick Answer: **40**
Detailed Answer: **45**

3. Which of the following statements is true about Discretionary Access Control methods? (Select all that apply.)

- ❏ a. They are more flexible than Mandatory Access Control
- ❏ b. They are concerned with the flow of information
- ❏ c. They use security labels
- ❏ d. They are widely used in commercial environments

Quick Answer: **40**
Detailed Answer: **45**

4. Which of the following terms allows a user to protect information as they deem necessary?

- ❏ a. DAC
- ❏ b. RBAC
- ❏ c. PAC
- ❏ d. MAC

Quick Answer: **40**
Detailed Answer: **45**

5. Which of the following is a type of Discretionary Access Control?

- ❏ a. Identity-Based Access Control
- ❏ b. Task-Based Access Control
- ❏ c. Rule-Based Access Control
- ❏ d. Role-Based Access Control

Quick Answer: **40**
Detailed Answer: **45**

6. Which one of the following access control methods is a type of Discretionary Access Control?

- ❏ a. Role-Based Access Control
- ❏ b. User-Directed Access Control
- ❏ c. Mandatory Access Control
- ❏ d. Rule-Based Access Control

Quick Answer: **40**
Detailed Answer: **45**

7. Which one of the following statements is true regarding Discretionary Access Control?

- ❏ a. Files that don't have an owner *cannot* be modified
- ❏ b. The administrator of the system is an owner of each object
- ❏ c. The operating system is an owner of each project
- ❏ d. Each object has an owner, which has full control over that object

Quick Answer: **40**
Detailed Answer: **45**

8. Access controls that are created and managed by the data owner are considered:

- ❑ a. Mandatory Access Control (MAC)
- ❑ b. Role-Based Access Control (RBAC)
- ❑ c. List-Based Access Control (LBAC)
- ❑ d. Discretionary Access Control (DAC)

Quick Answer: **40**
Detailed Answer: **45**

Objective 1.1.1: RBAC

1. Which of the following key terms apply to Role-Based Access Control methods? (Select all that apply.)

- ❑ a. Each user's roles are assigned privileges
- ❑ b. Access rights are based on an Access Control List
- ❑ c. Access rights link to an organizational structure
- ❑ d. Users have full control over their own objects

Quick Answer: **40**
Detailed Answer: **45**

2. Which of the following best describes Role-Based Access Control (RBAC)?

- ❑ a. A central authority makes the decisions for individual users in an organization
- ❑ b. A local authority or network administrator makes the decisions for individual users in an organization
- ❑ c. Access control options are based on an individual's responsibility within the organization
- ❑ d. Access control options are tied to the security clearance of individuals within the organization

Quick Answer: **40**
Detailed Answer: **45**

3. Which of the following terms refers to a user or authorized worker that attempts to access areas of the network that are considered restricted or off-limits?

- ❑ a. Remote logon
- ❑ b. Unauthorized login
- ❑ c. Logon abuse
- ❑ d. Unauthorized logon

Quick Answer: **40**
Detailed Answer: **46**

4. Which of the following access control methods is a type of Non-Discretionary Access Control?

- ❑ a. Discretionary Access Control
- ❑ b. Identity-Based Access Control
- ❑ c. Mandatory Access Control
- ❑ d. Role-Based Access Control

Quick Answer: **40**
Detailed Answer: **46**

5. Which of the following access control methods are based on jobs that a user has within an organization?

Quick Answer: **40**
Detailed Answer: **46**

- ❏ a. Mandatory Access Control
- ❏ b. Role-Based Access Control
- ❏ c. Discretionary Access Control
- ❏ d. User-Directed Access Control

6. Hans created a file while working in the Accounting Group. Sean is also in the Accounting Group and Jessie is working in the Finance Department. The Access Rights and Access Control Lists indicate that the object owner has Read, Write, Execute permissions; Finance Department has No Access; and Accounting Group has Read permissions. What permissions does Hans have?

Quick Answer: **40**
Detailed Answer: **46**

- ❏ a. No Access
- ❏ b. Read
- ❏ c. Read and Write
- ❏ d. Read, Write, and Execute

7. Sam created a file while working in the Accounting Group. Chuck is also in the Accounting Group. Joan is working in the Finance Department. The Access Rights and Access Control Lists indicate that the object owner has Read, Write, Execute permissions; Finance Department has No Access; and Accounting Group has Read permissions. What permissions does Joan have?

Quick Answer: **40**
Detailed Answer: **46**

- ❏ a. No Access
- ❏ b. Read
- ❏ c. Read and Write
- ❏ d. Read, Write, and Execute

8. Sam created a file while working in the Accounting Group. Bill is also in the Accounting Group. Joan is working in the Finance Department. The Access Rights and Access Control Lists indicate that the object owner has Read, Write, Execute permissions; Finance Department has No Access; and Accounting Group has Read permissions. What permissions does Bill have?

Quick Answer: **40**
Detailed Answer: **46**

- ❏ a. No Access
- ❏ b. Read
- ❏ c. Read and Write
- ❏ d. Read, Write, and Execute

9. Access control decisions are based on responsibilities that an individual user or process has within an organization. This is best known as:

- ❑ a. Mandatory Access Control (MAC)
- ❑ b. Role-Based Access Control (RBAC)
- ❑ c. Discretionary Access Control (DAC)
- ❑ d. Rule-Based Access Control (RBAC)

Quick Answer: **40**
Detailed Answer: **46**

10. A management team has established an organizational chart and security policy that uses a central authority to institute which subjects have access to specific objects. This is known as:

- ❑ a. Mandatory Access Control
- ❑ b. Rule-Based Access Control
- ❑ c. Non-Discretionary Access Control
- ❑ d. Discretionary Access Control

Quick Answer: **40**
Detailed Answer: **46**

11. Which of the following uses a central authority to determine which subjects can have access to which objects?

- ❑ a. Domain Access Control
- ❑ b. Non-Discretionary Access Control
- ❑ c. Mandatory Access Control
- ❑ d. Discretionary Access Control

Quick Answer: **40**
Detailed Answer: **46**

Objective 1.2: Authentication

1. What substantiates that a user's claimed identity is valid and is normally applied through a user password at time of logon?

- ❑ a. Confidentiality
- ❑ b. Integrity
- ❑ c. Authentication
- ❑ d. Identification

Quick Answer: **40**
Detailed Answer: **46**

2. Which of the following are methods of authenticating yourself to computer security software? (Select all that apply.)

- ❑ a. Something you know
- ❑ b. Something you have
- ❑ c. Something you want to be
- ❑ d. Something you are

Quick Answer: **40**
Detailed Answer: **46**

3. Which one of the following is a method of authenticating yourself to computer security software?

Quick Answer: **40**
Detailed Answer: **46**

- ❑   a.   Something you read about
- ❑   b.   Something you do
- ❑   c.   Something you will become
- ❑   d.   Something you are

4. Which of the following are methods of authenticating yourself to computer security software? (Select all that apply.)

Quick Answer: **40**
Detailed Answer: **46**

- ❑   a.   Something you understand
- ❑   b.   Something you know
- ❑   c.   Something you like
- ❑   d.   Something you have

5. Which of the following is *not* related to authenticating yourself to computer security software?

Quick Answer: **40**
Detailed Answer: **47**

- ❑   a.   Something you know
- ❑   b.   Something you have
- ❑   c.   Something you do
- ❑   d.   Something you are

6. When considering authenticating network computers, "to Allow" and "to Deny" directives authenticate using which of the following? (Select all that apply.)

Quick Answer: **40**
Detailed Answer: **47**

- ❑   a.   Host name
- ❑   b.   Host IP address
- ❑   c.   Machine name
- ❑   d.   User name

7. What is the term in security operations that describes a server's function to verify that someone's logon truly is that claimed identity?

Quick Answer: **40**
Detailed Answer: **47**

- ❑   a.   Password verification
- ❑   b.   User recognition
- ❑   c.   Login
- ❑   d.   Authentication

Objective 1.2.1: Kerberos

1. Which of the following best describes what Kerberos offers?

Quick Answer: **40**
Detailed Answer: **47**

- ❑   a.   Communication between users and servers
- ❑   b.   Mutual authentication and encrypted communication
- ❑   c.   Security tokens and single sign-on
- ❑   d.   Single user password authentication

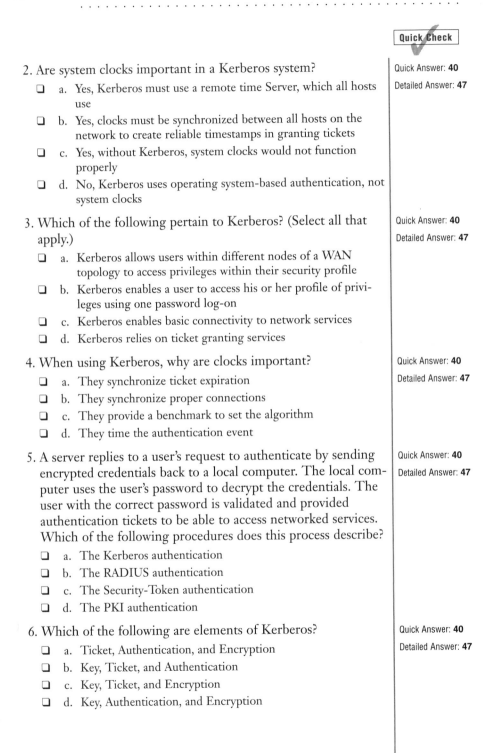

2. Are system clocks important in a Kerberos system?

   ❑ a. Yes, Kerberos must use a remote time Server, which all hosts use

   ❑ b. Yes, clocks must be synchronized between all hosts on the network to create reliable timestamps in granting tickets

   ❑ c. Yes, without Kerberos, system clocks would not function properly

   ❑ d. No, Kerberos uses operating system-based authentication, not system clocks

Quick Answer: **40**
Detailed Answer: **47**

3. Which of the following pertain to Kerberos? (Select all that apply.)

   ❑ a. Kerberos allows users within different nodes of a WAN topology to access privileges within their security profile

   ❑ b. Kerberos enables a user to access his or her profile of privileges using one password log-on

   ❑ c. Kerberos enables basic connectivity to network services

   ❑ d. Kerberos relies on ticket granting services

Quick Answer: **40**
Detailed Answer: **47**

4. When using Kerberos, why are clocks important?

   ❑ a. They synchronize ticket expiration

   ❑ b. They synchronize proper connections

   ❑ c. They provide a benchmark to set the algorithm

   ❑ d. They time the authentication event

Quick Answer: **40**
Detailed Answer: **47**

5. A server replies to a user's request to authenticate by sending encrypted credentials back to a local computer. The local computer uses the user's password to decrypt the credentials. The user with the correct password is validated and provided authentication tickets to be able to access networked services. Which of the following procedures does this process describe?

   ❑ a. The Kerberos authentication

   ❑ b. The RADIUS authentication

   ❑ c. The Security-Token authentication

   ❑ d. The PKI authentication

Quick Answer: **40**
Detailed Answer: **47**

6. Which of the following are elements of Kerberos?

   ❑ a. Ticket, Authentication, and Encryption

   ❑ b. Key, Ticket, and Authentication

   ❑ c. Key, Ticket, and Encryption

   ❑ d. Key, Authentication, and Encryption

Quick Answer: **40**
Detailed Answer: **47**

7. Which of the following abbreviations are elements of Kerberos?

   ❑ a. KDC, AS, and EN

   ❑ b. KDC, TGS, and EN

   ❑ c. KDC, TGS, and AS

   ❑ d. TGS, AS, and EN

Quick Answer: **40**
Detailed Answer: **47**

8. Which of the following is true about Kerberos?

   ❑ a. Kerberos makes use of public key cryptography

   ❑ b. Kerberos uses passwords in clear text

   ❑ c. Kerberos is a third-party encryption protocol

   ❑ d. Kerberos requires symmetric ciphers

Quick Answer: **40**
Detailed Answer: **47**

9. When you think of information integrity and confidentiality, which of the following would apply?

   ❑ a. Single Sign-On

   ❑ b. Kerberos

   ❑ c. Kryptonight

   ❑ d. KryptoLock

Quick Answer: **40**
Detailed Answer: **47**

10. Which of the following is an improvement over Kerberos, because it uses public key cryptography for the circulation of secret keys and offers additional access control defense?

   ❑ a. TACACS+

   ❑ b. SESAME

   ❑ c. KryptoKnight

   ❑ d. RADIUS

Quick Answer: **40**
Detailed Answer: **47**

11. What are some of the weaknesses in Kerberos? (Select all that apply.)

   ❑ a. Weak public key cryptography

   ❑ b. Weak Access control

   ❑ c. No Symmetric keys

   ❑ d. Weak Authentication

Quick Answer: **40**
Detailed Answer: **47**

12. Kerberos can prevent which one of the following attacks?

   ❑ a. Tunneling

   ❑ b. Progressive attack

   ❑ c. Process attack

   ❑ d. Playback attack

Quick Answer: **40**
Detailed Answer: **47**

Objective 1.2.2: CHAP

1. What is Challenge-Handshake Authentication Protocol (CHAP) primarily used for?

   ❏   a. Network Layer encryption

   ❏   b. Remote Access

   ❏   c. LAN server configuration

   ❏   d. WAN ISDN connection

Quick Answer: **41**
Detailed Answer: **48**

2. Which of the following protocols are used for authentication? (Select all that apply.)

   ❏   a. PAP

   ❏   b. MAP

   ❏   c. CHAP

   ❏   d. RAP

Quick Answer: **41**
Detailed Answer: **48**

3. Which of the following uses regular intervals when requesting authentication?

   ❏   a. CHAP

   ❏   b. PAP

   ❏   c. SAP

   ❏   d. RAP

Quick Answer: **41**
Detailed Answer: **48**

4. A common security tool used for Remote Access is CHAP. What do the letters CHAP stand for?

   ❏   a. Cryptographic Hashing Application Protocol

   ❏   b. Common Hacking Application Program

   ❏   c. Challenge Handshake Authentication Protocol

   ❏   d. Comprehensive Hashing Access Protocol

Quick Answer: **41**
Detailed Answer: **48**

Objective 1.2.3: Certificates

1. In reference to computer and network security, what do certificates provide?

   ❏   a. System security

   ❏   b. System authentication

   ❏   c. User authentication

   ❏   d. Group policy

Quick Answer: **41**
Detailed Answer: **48**

2. Which of the following is true concerning digital certificates?

   ❏   a. They are available only from Verisign

   ❏   b. They are identical to digital signatures

   ❏   c. They make use of a security credential

   ❏   d. They can't contain geography data

Quick Answer: **41**
Detailed Answer: **48**

3. There are several business levels of assurance for digital certificates. Which of the following items does Level 2 verify
when using a credit bureau database? (Select all that apply.)

   ❏ a. User's name

   ❏ b. User's address

   ❏ c. User's mother's maiden name

   ❏ d. User's social security number

Quick Answer: **41**
Detailed Answer: **48**

4. When considering digital certificates, which of the following
statements is generally true?

   ❏ a. Public keys encrypt and private keys decrypt

   ❏ b. Private keys encrypt and public keys decrypt

   ❏ c. There are no public keys used

   ❏ d. There are no public or private keys used

Quick Answer: **41**
Detailed Answer: **48**

5. Which one of the following is usually managed by a third
party and is used to issue and manage security credentials?

   ❏ a. Certificate Authorization

   ❏ b. Digital Signature

   ❏ c. Digital Certificate

   ❏ d. Certificate Authority

Quick Answer: **41**
Detailed Answer: **48**

Objective 1.2.4: Username/Password

1. Which of the following is considered to be the best example of
a strong user password?

   ❏ a. One that has at least four characters, including small and
large caps along with numbers and symbols

   ❏ b. One that has at least six characters, including large caps along
with numbers

   ❏ c. One that has at least eight characters, including small and
large caps along with numbers and symbols

   ❏ d. One that has at least twelve characters, including numbers
and symbols

Quick Answer: **41**
Detailed Answer: **48**

2. When choosing a password, you want to use your street
address with all the vowels in uppercase. What is true about
your password? (Select the best answer.)

   ❏ a. It is considered a good password because it mixes numbers
with upper- and lowercase letters

   ❏ b. It is considered a good password because it is longer than 10
characters

   ❏ c. It is considered a poor password because everyone knows
your address

   ❏ d. It is considered a poor password because it's predictable

Quick Answer: **41**
Detailed Answer: **48**

3. What are the advantages of using password synchronization? (Select all that apply.)

❑ a. Increased security

❑ b. Decreased cost

❑ c. Decreased intrusion

❑ d. Increased detection

Quick Answer: **41**
Detailed Answer: **48**

4. Which of the following is the best example of a good password?

❑ a. MyPassword

❑ b. mYpA55w0rd

❑ c. mY?a5%w0rD

❑ d. MyPa55w0RD

Quick Answer: **41**
Detailed Answer: **48**

5. Which of the following should you decrease to increase security?

❑ a. Encryption strength

❑ b. Password expiration period

❑ c. Number of characters in your password

❑ d. Number of characters in your username

Quick Answer: **41**
Detailed Answer: **48**

6. What are some technical methods to protect passwords from discovery? (Select all that apply.)

❑ a. Authentication

❑ b. Smart cards

❑ c. Encryption

❑ d. Protocols

Quick Answer: **41**
Detailed Answer: **48**

Objective 1.2.5. Tokens

1. When discussing computer and network security, which of the following functions relates to tokens?

❑ a. ID authentication

❑ b. Security at the login level

❑ c. Authentication of DNS

❑ d. Verification of keys

Quick Answer: **41**
Detailed Answer: **49**

2. When creating passwords, which of the following is actually a physical device that can be used to generate passwords?

❑ a. Certificates

❑ b. Tokens

❑ c. Keys

❑ d. Kerberos

Quick Answer: **41**
Detailed Answer: **49**

3. Which of the following devices is used only a single time for physical authentication and generates a unique password for each use?

❑   a. Smart Card

❑   b. Token

❑   c. Flash Card

❑   d. Private Key

4. Which of the following is true of authentication tokens?

❑   a. They produce one-time passwords

❑   b. You can use them to automatically log on

❑   c. They work well in large networks because of their cost

❑   d. They are easy to replicate for various employees

5. Some tokens make use of time synchronizations. Which of the following is such a token?

❑   a. Asynchronous dynamic password tokens

❑   b. Synchronous dynamic password tokens

❑   c. Asynchronous static password tokens

❑   d. Synchronous static password tokens

6. When does an owner authenticate himself/herself to a token?

❑   a. When using an active password token

❑   b. When using a passive password token

❑   c. When using a static password token

❑   d. When using a dynamic password token

Objective 1.2.6: Multi-Factor

1. When should Multi-Factor be used as a type of authentication? (Select all that apply.)

❑   a. When you have a group of users

❑   b. When stored keys are not strong enough

❑   c. When memorized passwords are not strong enough

❑   d. When additional security layers are needed

2. You have found that your password security is lacking. You have stored keys and memorized password, but this is not strong enough and additional layers of security are needed. What should you use to improve authentication?

❑   a. Mutual Authentication

❑   b. Biometric Authentication

❑   c. Tokens for Authentication

❑   d. Multi-Factor Authentication

Objective 1.2.7: Mutual Authentication

1. Which of the following describes a method to verify the identity of both a client and server in direct communication?

   ❑ a. Multi-Factor Authentication

   ❑ b. Mutual Authentication

   ❑ c. Biometric Authentication

   ❑ d. Client-Server Authentication

Quick Answer: **41**
Detailed Answer: **49**

2. Which of the following is *not* a condition of mutual authentication?

   ❑ a. Servers must be able to authenticate clients

   ❑ b. Clients must be able to authenticate servers

   ❑ c. Servers and Clients must be in communication with each other in order to prove each other's identities

   ❑ d. Servers and Clients must trust each other in order to prove each other's identities

Quick Answer: **41**
Detailed Answer: **49**

Objective 1.2.8: Biometrics

1. Which of the following depends solely on Biometric Authentication to control access to secure areas? (Select all that apply.)

   ❑ a. Voice patterns

   ❑ b. Retinal scans

   ❑ c. Strong passwords

   ❑ d. Fingerprints

Quick Answer: **41**
Detailed Answer: **49**

2. You have decided to use biometrics as part of your network security system. Which of the following options is a locking system for access control that relies only on biometric authentication?

   ❑ a. Username and password

   ❑ b. Fingerprint, retinal scans, PIN numbers, and facial characteristics

   ❑ c. Voice patterns, fingerprints, and retinal scans

   ❑ d. Strong password, PIN numbers, and digital imaging

Quick Answer: **41**
Detailed Answer: **49**

3. Which of the following describes an automated process of identifying someone based on the physiological characteristics of that person?

   ❑ a. Biology

   ❑ b. Biogenetics

   ❑ c. Biometrics

   ❑ d. Microbiology

Quick Answer: **41**
Detailed Answer: **49**

4. When dealing with biometric authentication, results can sometimes be False Positive or False Negative. Which of the following relate to a False Positive? (Select all that apply.)

Quick Answer: **41**
Detailed Answer: **49**

- ❑ a. An authorized person is attempting to gain access
- ❑ b. An unauthorized person is attempting to gain access
- ❑ c. Access is wrongfully approved
- ❑ d. Access is wrongfully denied

5. When dealing with biometric authentication, results can sometimes be False Positive or False Negative. Which of the following relate to False Negative? (Select all that apply.)

Quick Answer: **41**
Detailed Answer: **50**

- ❑ a. An authorized person is attempting to gain access
- ❑ b. An unauthorized person is attempting to gain access
- ❑ c. Access is wrongfully approved
- ❑ d. Access is wrongfully denied

Objective 1.3: Nonessential Services and Protocols

1. Any TCP request received on port 23 is considered a:

Quick Answer: **41**
Detailed Answer: **50**

- ❑ a. Mail service
- ❑ b. Telnet session
- ❑ c. Web service
- ❑ d. FTP session

2. Any TCP request received on port 21 is considered a:

Quick Answer: **41**
Detailed Answer: **50**

- ❑ a. Mail service
- ❑ b. Telnet session
- ❑ c. Web service
- ❑ d. FTP session

3. Any TCP request received on port 25 is considered a:

Quick Answer: **41**
Detailed Answer: **50**

- ❑ a. Mail service
- ❑ b. Telnet session
- ❑ c. Web service
- ❑ d. FTP session

4. The Internet Assigned Numbers Authority (IANA) has reserved which of the following ports for most well-known services?

Quick Answer: **41**
Detailed Answer: **50**

- ❑ a. Ports 0-255
- ❑ b. Ports 0-1023
- ❑ c. Ports 512-1023
- ❑ d. Ports 1024-7200

5. Which of the following UDP ports relates to a NetBIOS session?

Quick Answer: **41**
Detailed Answer: **50**

- ❑   a. Port 23
- ❑   b. Port 68
- ❑   c. Port 139
- ❑   d. Port 169

6. Which of the following UDP ports relates to use of the Simple Network Management Protocol (SNMP)?

Quick Answer: **41**
Detailed Answer: **50**

- ❑   a. Port 23
- ❑   b. Port 25
- ❑   c. Port 119
- ❑   d. Port 161

7. Which of the following UDP ports relates to use of the bootp server service?

Quick Answer: **41**
Detailed Answer: **50**

- ❑   a. Port 23
- ❑   b. Port 25
- ❑   c. Port 67
- ❑   d. Port 119

8. Which of the following TCP ports relates to use of the Network News Transfer Protocol?

Quick Answer: **41**
Detailed Answer: **50**

- ❑   a. Port 25
- ❑   b. Port 68
- ❑   c. Port 119
- ❑   d. Port 123

9. Which of the following TCP ports relates to the use of the Post Office Protocol V.3 (POP3) service?

Quick Answer: **41**
Detailed Answer: **50**

- ❑   a. Port 25
- ❑   b. Port 110
- ❑   c. Port 123
- ❑   d. Port 161

10. Which of the following UDP ports relates to DNS zone transfers?

Quick Answer: **41**
Detailed Answer: **50**

- ❑   a. Port 23
- ❑   b. Port 53
- ❑   c. Port 123
- ❑   d. Port 139

11. Which of the following TCP ports is used when communicating between Web browsers and Web servers?

    ❑ a. Port 20
    ❑ b. Port 69
    ❑ c. Port 80
    ❑ d. Port 119

12. Which of the following UDP ports relates to access to remote file systems using Network File System (NFS)?

    ❑ a. Port 123
    ❑ b. Port 139
    ❑ c. Port 1246
    ❑ d. Port 2049

13. Which of the following TCP ports relates to group access via Internet Message Access Protocol (IMAP)?

    ❑ a. Port 110
    ❑ b. Port 143
    ❑ c. Port 159
    ❑ d. Port 2049

14. Which of the following protocols listens on ports 6667–7000 and allows clients to communicate in real time?

    ❑ a. Internet Message Access Protocol (IMAP)
    ❑ b. Internet Relay Chat (IRC)
    ❑ c. Network News Transfer Protocol (NNTP)
    ❑ d. Post Office Protocol V.3 (POP3)

15. Which of the following TCP ports is used to transfer actual files and data?

    ❑ a. Port 11
    ❑ b. Port 20
    ❑ c. Port 21
    ❑ d. Port 137

16. Which of the following services transmits data using clear text? (Select all that apply.)

    ❑ a. FTP
    ❑ b. SMTP
    ❑ c. HTTP
    ❑ d. Telnet

17. Which of the following services transmits data using clear text? (Select all that apply.)

- ❏   a.   FTP
- ❏   b.   S/FTP
- ❏   c.   SMTP
- ❏   d.   SNMP v1

18. Which of the following ports is used to transfer data using Secure Sockets Layer (SSL)?

- ❏   a.   Port 22
- ❏   b.   Port 119
- ❏   c.   Port 323
- ❏   d.   Port 443

19. Which of the following is the correct port for Secure Shell (SSH)?

- ❏   a.   12
- ❏   b.   22
- ❏   c.   32
- ❏   d.   62

20. Which of the following is true regarding network services? (Select the best answer.)

- ❏   a.   Running nonessential services poses a security risk
- ❏   b.   Running essential services poses an unwarranted security risk
- ❏   c.   Turn off all services before connecting to the Internet
- ❏   d.   Turning off all nonessential services is a security risk

Objective 1.4: Attacks

1. There are many different types of attacks. Which of the following terms applies to a network intrusion?

- ❏   a.   Unauthorized personal use of the Internet
- ❏   b.   Breaking into a computer via a dial-up connection
- ❏   c.   Breaking into a network from an external source
- ❏   d.   Authorized users right to use networked services

2. There are many different types of attacks.

Which of the following terms applies to probing?

- ❏   a.   Allows an attacker to find different ways into the network
- ❏   b.   Frees network connections for cracker intervention
- ❏   c.   Makes available all network resources
- ❏   d.   Tricks users into taking the wrong action

3. Network attacks may occur from inside the LAN. Which of the following security violations is a type of eavesdropping?

Quick Answer: **42**
Detailed Answer: **51**

- ❑ a. Unapproved use of the Internet
- ❑ b. Unauthorized sharing of information with an external partner after monitoring the LAN
- ❑ c. Authorized sharing of information with an internal partner after monitoring the LAN
- ❑ d. Actively listening to your employer's instructions

4. In security operations, which of the following is *not* a type of attack?

Quick Answer: **42**
Detailed Answer: **51**

- ❑ a. Polymorphic Spoofing
- ❑ b. Buffer Overflow
- ❑ c. DDOS
- ❑ d. Man in the Middle

5. What kind of attack is designed to capture sensitive pieces of information passing through the network?

Quick Answer: **42**
Detailed Answer: **51**

- ❑ a. Searching
- ❑ b. Sniffing
- ❑ c. Spoofing
- ❑ d. Spamming

Objective 1.4.1: DOS/DDOS

1. You are receiving oversized ICMP request packets. What could be the cause? (Select all that apply.)

Quick Answer: **42**
Detailed Answer: **51**

- ❑ a. A Ping of Death attack
- ❑ b. A Spoofing attack
- ❑ c. A Birthday attack
- ❑ d. A Dictionary attack

2. Which of the following correlates to a Denial of Service attack?

Quick Answer: **42**
Detailed Answer: **51**

- ❑ a. A cracker listens to network transmissions, waiting for passwords in clear text
- ❑ b. A cracker tricks a user into shutting down all services
- ❑ c. A cracker uses up all a target's resources
- ❑ d. A cracker is denied access into the network

3. Digital signatures and token technologies do *not* protect networks from which of the following threats?

Quick Answer: **42**
Detailed Answer: **51**

   - ❏ a. Denial of Service
   - ❏ b. Password compromise
   - ❏ c. Replay attacks
   - ❏ d. Spoofing

4. There are several types of computer attacks that usually result in theft of information or loss of data. Which of the following is a type of attack that does *not* have that purpose, but instead, results in the inability to use the system?

Quick Answer: **42**
Detailed Answer: **51**

   - ❏ a. TCP
   - ❏ b. DOS
   - ❏ c. SYN
   - ❏ d. UDP

5. The target of a Distributed Denial of Service (DDOS) is:

Quick Answer: **42**
Detailed Answer: **51**

   - ❏ a. One domain is being attacked
   - ❏ b. Multiple servers are being attacked
   - ❏ c. One server is being attacked
   - ❏ d. Multiple clients are being attacked

6. What are some of the basic characteristics of a Distributed Denial of Service (DDOS) attack? (Select all that apply.)

Quick Answer: **42**
Detailed Answer: **51**

   - ❏ a. One server is being attacked
   - ❏ b. Many workstations are being attacked
   - ❏ c. Remote attacks are simultaneously triggered from many places at once
   - ❏ d. Local attacks are sequentially triggered from many places at once

7. A Distributed Denial of Service (DDOS) is generally accomplished by:

Quick Answer: **42**
Detailed Answer: **52**

   - ❏ a. Simultaneously sending worm infiltrations on many Web sites
   - ❏ b. Triggering remote attacks from thousands of infiltrated systems at one host
   - ❏ c. Local internal users who are frustrated with the current working conditions
   - ❏ d. IP spoofing due to vulnerabilities within IPv4

. . . .

8. Which steps should be taken to prevent Distributed Denial of Service (DDOS) attacks? (Select all that apply.)

❑ a. Filter select packets coming into and out of a network

❑ b. Adjust routers to enable logging

❑ c. Ensure routers are broadcast amplifiers

❑ d. Use routers only on WAN connections

9. Which of the following actions may help prevent a Distributed Denial of Service? (Select all that apply.)

❑ a. Use digital signatures

❑ b. Set routers to be broadcast amplifiers

❑ c. Enable routers to perform logging

❑ d. Use Ingress and Egress packet filtering

10. Which of the following actions may help prevent a DDOS? (Select all that apply.)

❑ a. Use tokens for authentication

❑ b. Check to ensure that routers are *not* set to be broadcast amplifiers

❑ c. Do *not* allow routers to perform logging

❑ d. Use Ingress and Egress packet filtering

11. Which of the following is another name for ICMP storms?

❑ a. Smurf attack

❑ b. Spoofing attack

❑ c. Special attack

❑ d. Socket attack

12. Which of the following is another name for ICMP storms?

❑ a. UDP flooding

❑ b. TCP flooding

❑ c. Data Link Layer storms

❑ d. Broadcast storms

13. Broadcast storms are also known as

❑ a. ICMP storms

❑ b. TCP flooding

❑ c. UDP broadcasting

❑ d. SYN attack

14. What type of attack could be used against a client to disable the client from communicating with a server connection?

Quick Answer: **42**
Detailed Answer: **52**

- ❑ a. Back Door
- ❑ b. Brute Force
- ❑ c. Dictionary
- ❑ d. ICMP Flood

15. What is the name of the attack that is characterized by routers creating a DOS via ICMP storms?

Quick Answer: **42**
Detailed Answer: **52**

- ❑ a. Smurf attack
- ❑ b. Spoofing attack
- ❑ c. Special attack
- ❑ d. Socket attack

16. What kind of DOS attack uses PING and a spoofed address?

Quick Answer: **42**
Detailed Answer: **52**

- ❑ a. Social Engineering attack
- ❑ b. Brute Force attack
- ❑ c. Smurf attack
- ❑ d. DNS attack

17. What kind of attack is a Smurf attack?

Quick Answer: **42**
Detailed Answer: **52**

- ❑ a. A DOS attack
- ❑ b. A Mathematical attack
- ❑ c. A SYN attack
- ❑ d. A Blue attack

18. In what way is a Smurf attack unlike a Fraggle attack?

Quick Answer: **42**
Detailed Answer: **52**

- ❑ a. A Smurf uses UDP
- ❑ b. A Smurf uses IP
- ❑ c. A Smurf uses TCP
- ❑ d. A Smurf uses ICMP

19. When considering DOS attacks, which statement best compares a Smurf to a Fraggle attack?

Quick Answer: **42**
Detailed Answer: **52**

- ❑ a. A Smurf attack is an identical, but more current name for a Fraggle attack
- ❑ b. A Smurf attack is ICMP-based and a Fraggle attack is UDP-based
- ❑ c. A Smurf attack cannot be spoofed
- ❑ d. A Smurf attack is UDP-based and a Fraggle attack is ICMP-based

20. You are receiving oversized ICMP request packets. What could be the cause? (Select all that apply.)

  □ a. A Ping of Death attack
  □ b. A Dictionary attack
  □ c. A Birthday attack
  □ d. A Dictionary attack

Objective 1.4.2: Back Door

1. Software developers have occasionally included access programs within their software, or back doors, to be able to provide technical support to users who employ their software. Do network administrators generally find such hidden back doors useful to their organizations?

  □ a. Yes
  □ b. No
  □ c. Yes, as long as programmers inform administrators about the code
  □ d. No, because administrators must first inform programmers about the code

2. Which of the following terms generally refer to a Back Door attack? (Select all that apply.)

  □ a. Intrusions may occur via dial-up connections
  □ b. Intrusions may occur via synchronous external network connections
  □ c. Intrusions may occur via asynchronous external network connections
  □ d. Intrusions may occur via asynchronous internal network connections

3. Which of the following are benefits to maintaining a hidden back door into your network?

  □ a. Network administrators can prevent Logic Bombs
  □ b. Network administrators are able to see the entire network
  □ c. Network administrators can secure their positions
  □ d. Network administrators generally find no benefit to hidden back doors

4. How can Back Door attacks be implemented? (Select all that apply.)

    ❑   a. Remote access using dial-up or asynchronous external network connections

    ❑   b. Trojan Horses

    ❑   c. Root kits

    ❑   d. Sniffing

Quick Answer: **42**
Detailed Answer: **53**

5. Which of the following programs are designed as malicious Back Door programs? (Select all that apply.)

    ❑   a. SubSeven

    ❑   b. PC Anywhere

    ❑   c. Virtual Network Computing

    ❑   d. Back Orifice

Quick Answer: **42**
Detailed Answer: **53**

Objective 1.4.3: Spoofing

1. Which of the following gives false information about the source of an attack?

    ❑   a. Smurf attack

    ❑   b. Spoofing

    ❑   c. SYN attack

    ❑   d. Back Door

Quick Answer: **42**
Detailed Answer: **53**

2. What does Spoofing do? (Select all that apply.)

    ❑   a. It disguises the source of communication

    ❑   b. It disguises the communication destination

    ❑   c. It tricks the user into continuing to communicate

    ❑   d. It ties up the response of a SYN communication

Quick Answer: **42**
Detailed Answer: **53**

3. IP Spoofing is what kind of attack?

    ❑   a. Host-Based

    ❑   b. Network-Based

    ❑   c. Client-Based

    ❑   d. IDS-Based

Quick Answer: **42**
Detailed Answer: **53**

4. A network cracker has posed as one of your ISP DNS servers to redirect LAN naming requests. What kind of attack is this?

    ❑   a. Server Sniffing

    ❑   b. Server Spamming

    ❑   c. Server Renaming

    ❑   d. Server Spoofing

Quick Answer: **42**
Detailed Answer: **53**

5. If an IP address is spoofed, backtracking a packet is no longer possible. (Select the best answer.)

   ❑ a. True

   ❑ b. False

   ❑ c. True, because the link is no longer visible

   ❑ d. True, because the link is clearly visible

Quick Answer: **42**
Detailed Answer: **53**

6. You get a phone call from your Internet Service Provider (ISP) that one of the DNS servers has been under a Spoofing attack. What are some possible results or symptoms? (Select all that apply.)

   ❑ a. A type of Denial of Service is attacking your network

   ❑ b. Your network may be misdirecting Internet traffic

   ❑ c. Your ISP DNS server may be misdirecting Internet traffic

   ❑ d. Your network is only being spoofed and no serious harm can come of it

Quick Answer: **42**
Detailed Answer: **53**

7. Which of the following results in a Domain Name Server resolving the domain name to a different network and thus misdirecting Internet traffic?

   ❑ a. DOS (Denial of Service)

   ❑ b. Spoofing

   ❑ c. Brute Force attack

   ❑ d. Reverse Domain Name Service (R-DNS)

Quick Answer: **42**
Detailed Answer: **53**

8. What is known as an attack that impersonates a user or a system?

   ❑ a. Spamming

   ❑ b. Sniffing

   ❑ c. Smurfing

   ❑ d. Spoofing

Quick Answer: **42**
Detailed Answer: **53**

9. What is it called when a cracker obtains the MAC address of a target machine and configures his or her machine with that MAC address?

   ❑ a. Spoofing

   ❑ b. Smacking

   ❑ c. Spoiling

   ❑ d. Smurfing

Quick Answer: **42**
Detailed Answer: **53**

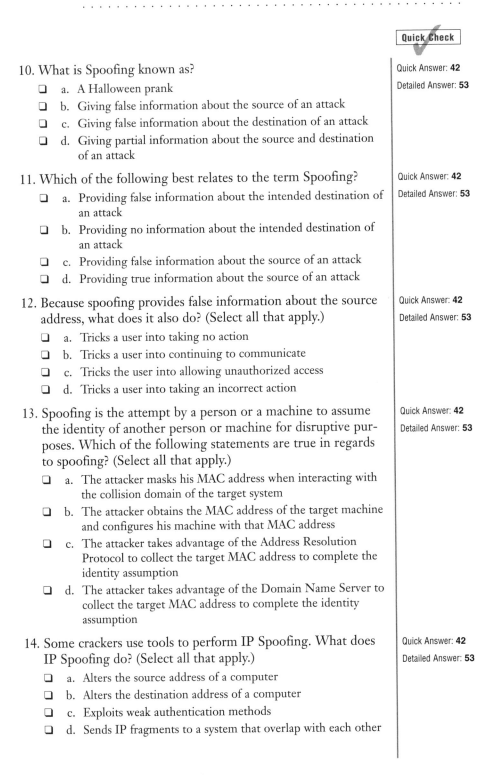

Quick Answer: **42**
Detailed Answer: **53**

10. What is Spoofing known as?

    ❑ a. A Halloween prank

    ❑ b. Giving false information about the source of an attack

    ❑ c. Giving false information about the destination of an attack

    ❑ d. Giving partial information about the source and destination of an attack

Quick Answer: **42**
Detailed Answer: **53**

11. Which of the following best relates to the term Spoofing?

    ❑ a. Providing false information about the intended destination of an attack

    ❑ b. Providing no information about the intended destination of an attack

    ❑ c. Providing false information about the source of an attack

    ❑ d. Providing true information about the source of an attack

Quick Answer: **42**
Detailed Answer: **53**

12. Because spoofing provides false information about the source address, what does it also do? (Select all that apply.)

    ❑ a. Tricks a user into taking no action

    ❑ b. Tricks a user into continuing to communicate

    ❑ c. Tricks the user into allowing unauthorized access

    ❑ d. Tricks a user into taking an incorrect action

Quick Answer: **42**
Detailed Answer: **53**

13. Spoofing is the attempt by a person or a machine to assume the identity of another person or machine for disruptive purposes. Which of the following statements are true in regards to spoofing? (Select all that apply.)

    ❑ a. The attacker masks his MAC address when interacting with the collision domain of the target system

    ❑ b. The attacker obtains the MAC address of the target machine and configures his machine with that MAC address

    ❑ c. The attacker takes advantage of the Address Resolution Protocol to collect the target MAC address to complete the identity assumption

    ❑ d. The attacker takes advantage of the Domain Name Server to collect the target MAC address to complete the identity assumption

Quick Answer: **42**
Detailed Answer: **53**

14. Some crackers use tools to perform IP Spoofing. What does IP Spoofing do? (Select all that apply.)

    ❑ a. Alters the source address of a computer

    ❑ b. Alters the destination address of a computer

    ❑ c. Exploits weak authentication methods

    ❑ d. Sends IP fragments to a system that overlap with each other

15. Which of the following describes Spoofing? (Select all that apply.)
    - ❏ a. It is used to falsify the source address
    - ❏ b. It uses falsely addressed packets to disguise the source of the communication
    - ❏ c. It is used to falsify the destination address
    - ❏ d. It uses falsely addressed packets to disguise the destination address

Quick Answer: **42**
Detailed Answer: **53**

16. What is another name for Server Spoofing?
    - ❏ a. Man in the Middle
    - ❏ b. Back Door
    - ❏ c. Weak Keys
    - ❏ d. Dictionary

Quick Answer: **42**
Detailed Answer: **54**

17. Which of the following are related to symptoms of Spoofing? (Select all that apply.)
    - ❏ a. Crackers take advantage of clear text Server Message Block (SMB) messages
    - ❏ b. Crackers make use of client's username and password
    - ❏ c. Crackers pretend to be clients
    - ❏ d. Crackers initiate a virus attack

Quick Answer: **42**
Detailed Answer: **54**

18. What is another name for Session Hijacking?
    - ❏ a. Dictionary
    - ❏ b. ICMP Flood
    - ❏ c. Server Spoofing
    - ❏ d. Back Door

Quick Answer: **42**
Detailed Answer: **54**

19. Clients that log on to a Server Message Block (SMB) LAN Manager (LANMAN) server can only be authenticated in clear text.

    Some hackers have taken advantage of this fact to gain the client logon name and password information. This is an example of what kind of attack?
    - ❏ a. Back Door
    - ❏ b. Dictionary
    - ❏ c. ICMP Flood
    - ❏ d. Server Spoofing

Quick Answer: **42**
Detailed Answer: **54**

Objective 1.4.4: Man in the Middle

1. What type of attack uses an application to capture and manipulate your network packets?

   ❑ a. DDOS

   ❑ b. Server Spoofing

   ❑ c. Spoofing

   ❑ d. Man in the Middle

Quick Answer: **42**
Detailed Answer: **54**

2. Does using "secure" sites prevent Man in the Middle attacks?

   ❑ a. Yes

   ❑ b. No

   ❑ c. Yes, for LAN networks only

   ❑ d. No, for WAN networks only

Quick Answer: **42**
Detailed Answer: **54**

3. Is it true that when you receive a download from a trusted site you will avoid the Man in the Middle attack? (Select the best answer.)

   ❑ a. Yes

   ❑ b. No

   ❑ c. Only if the trusted site uses different operating systems

   ❑ d. Only if the trusted site uses the same network protocols

Quick Answer: **42**
Detailed Answer: **54**

4. If you decided to download data from a secure site, what will be your network security defense against attacks?

   ❑ a. You will prevent Man in the Middle attacks

   ❑ b. You will stop DOS attacks

   ❑ c. You will stop Server Sniffing attacks

   ❑ d. You will not be able to absolutely prevent attacks

Quick Answer: **42**
Detailed Answer: **54**

5. Using routers to segment traffic at the Network Layer of the Open System Interconnection (OSI) model can help reduce the threat of which of the following types of attack?

   ❑ a. Man in the Middle attacks

   ❑ b. Man on the Router attacks

   ❑ c. Man on the LAN attacks

   ❑ d. Man on the Network attacks

Quick Answer: **42**
Detailed Answer: **54**

6. How do Man in the Middle attacks work?

   ❑ a. They use a script program to find new networks and attack them

   ❑ b. They use an application to obtain and change network packets

   ❑ c. They use UDP to spoof client packet addresses

   ❑ d. They use ICMP to spoof server packet addresses

Quick Answer: **42**
Detailed Answer: **54**

Objective 1.4.5: Replay

1. Which of the following is used to prevent Replay or Playback attacks?

   ❑ a. Network Monitor
   ❑ b. Protocol Analyzer
   ❑ c. Hot fixes
   ❑ d. Kerberos

Quick Answer: **42**
Detailed Answer: **54**

2. Which of the following attack mechanisms are prevented by using Kerberos authentication?

   ❑ a. SYN
   ❑ b. SYN/ACK
   ❑ c. ACK
   ❑ d. Replay

Quick Answer: **42**
Detailed Answer: **54**

Objective 1.4.6: TCP/IP Hijacking

1. A user's Web-based connections involve open sessions. What are these sessions susceptible to?

   ❑ a. SSL encryption
   ❑ b. TCP/IP Hijacking
   ❑ c. Spamming
   ❑ d. Smurfing

Quick Answer: **42**
Detailed Answer: **54**

2. Which of the following terms relates to attacks that re-route data traffic from a network device to a personal machine?

   ❑ a. Network Address Analyzing
   ❑ b. Network Address Hijacking
   ❑ c. Network Address Subnetting
   ❑ d. Network Address Translation

Quick Answer: **42**
Detailed Answer: **54**

3. Which of the following apply to Session Hijacking? (Select all that apply.)

   ❑ a. Removes authorized users or at least shares logins
   ❑ b. Permits the monitoring of network data
   ❑ c. Permits the takeover of network connections
   ❑ d. Changes the computer's destination address to gain access to network servers

Quick Answer: **42**
Detailed Answer: **54**

4. Which of the following should you use to minimize TCP/IP hijacking?

    ❑   a. Encoding

    ❑   b. Decoding

    ❑   c. Encryption

    ❑   d. Decryption

Quick Answer: **42**
Detailed Answer: **54**

Objective 1.4.7: Weak Keys

1. What is the term that demonstrates vulnerability when patterns are frequently seen in an algorithm, for example in Data Encryption Standard (DES) some portion of the encryption is identical to the decryption?

    ❑   a. PKI

    ❑   b. Weak Keys

    ❑   c. Mathematical

    ❑   d. Public Keys

Quick Answer: **42**
Detailed Answer: **55**

2. When many users use the same password this causes vulnerability. Which one of the following types of attacks is best suited to exploit this situation?

    ❑   a. Weak Keys

    ❑   b. DOS

    ❑   c. SYN attack

    ❑   d. Back Door

Quick Answer: **42**
Detailed Answer: **55**

Objective 1.4.8: Mathematical

1. Which of the following attack methods relates to the cryptanalysis of algorithms?

    ❑   a. Mathematical

    ❑   b. Weak Keys

    ❑   c. Social Engineering

    ❑   d. Back Door

Quick Answer: **43**
Detailed Answer: **55**

2. Some highly intelligent crackers use a process of statistical analysis to interpret network activity and weaknesses in algorithms. What kind of process is this?

    ❑   a. Weak Keys

    ❑   b. Social Engineering

    ❑   c. Quantum Physics

    ❑   d. Mathematical

Quick Answer: **43**
Detailed Answer: **55**

Objective 1.4.9: Social Engineering

1. A close friend is curious about your job at work. He convinces
   you to invite him over to see the operation and test out your
   high-speed Internet connection. Next week, your boss tells
   you that your computer has a virus. Which of the following
   methods is the root cause for the virus in this situation?

   ❑ a. DDOS

   ❑ b. DOS

   ❑ c. Social Engineering

   ❑ d. IP Spoofing

Quick Answer: **43**
Detailed Answer: **55**

2. What is the security term that describes the following condition? A worker has been tricked into providing confidential or
   restricted data about the network or organization.

   ❑ a. Social Engineering

   ❑ b. Social Pioneering

   ❑ c. Sabotage

   ❑ d. Espionage

Quick Answer: **43**
Detailed Answer: **55**

Objective 1.4.10: Birthday

1. Which of the following statements are true about Birthday
   Attacks? (Select all that apply.)

   ❑ a. They are based on the likelihood of user passwords being
         known celebrated events

   ❑ b. They refer to a type of brute force attack

   ❑ c. They refer to a type of mathematical attack

   ❑ d. They are used to reveal mathematical weaknesses of hash
         algorithms

Quick Answer: **43**
Detailed Answer: **55**

2. Message Digest 5 (MD5) has a probability weakness of similar
   keys. Which of the following attacks exploit this weakness?

   ❑ a. Social Engineering

   ❑ b. Birthday attack

   ❑ c. Dictionary attack

   ❑ d. SYN attack

Quick Answer: **43**
Detailed Answer: **55**

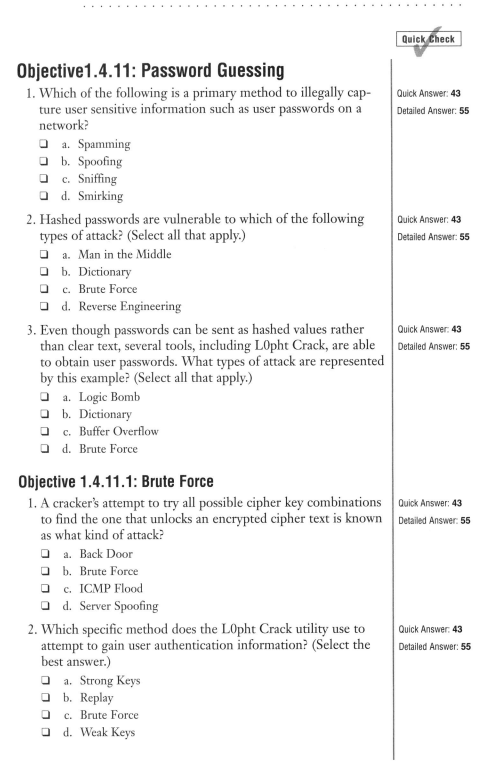
Objective 1.4.11: Password Guessing

1. Which of the following is a primary method to illegally capture user sensitive information such as user passwords on a network?

  ❑   a. Spamming

  ❑   b. Spoofing

  ❑   c. Sniffing

  ❑   d. Smirking

Quick Answer: **43**
Detailed Answer: **55**

2. Hashed passwords are vulnerable to which of the following types of attack? (Select all that apply.)

  ❑   a. Man in the Middle

  ❑   b. Dictionary

  ❑   c. Brute Force

  ❑   d. Reverse Engineering

Quick Answer: **43**
Detailed Answer: **55**

3. Even though passwords can be sent as hashed values rather than clear text, several tools, including L0pht Crack, are able to obtain user passwords. What types of attack are represented by this example? (Select all that apply.)

  ❑   a. Logic Bomb

  ❑   b. Dictionary

  ❑   c. Buffer Overflow

  ❑   d. Brute Force

Quick Answer: **43**
Detailed Answer: **55**

Objective 1.4.11.1: Brute Force

1. A cracker's attempt to try all possible cipher key combinations to find the one that unlocks an encrypted cipher text is known as what kind of attack?

  ❑   a. Back Door

  ❑   b. Brute Force

  ❑   c. ICMP Flood

  ❑   d. Server Spoofing

Quick Answer: **43**
Detailed Answer: **55**

2. Which specific method does the L0pht Crack utility use to attempt to gain user authentication information? (Select the best answer.)

  ❑   a. Strong Keys

  ❑   b. Replay

  ❑   c. Brute Force

  ❑   d. Weak Keys

Quick Answer: **43**
Detailed Answer: **55**

· ·

Objective 1.4.11.2: Dictionary

1. Which specific method does the L0pht Crack utility use to attempt to gain user authentication information? (Select the best answer.)

   ❑   a. Strong Keys
   ❑   b. Replay
   ❑   c. Brute Strength
   ❑   d. Dictionary

Quick Answer: **43**
Detailed Answer: **56**

2. Mary's computer passwords are simple pet names and birthdays so she won't forget them. These passwords are vulnerable to attacks. What kind of attack exploits common passwords?

   ❑   a. Dictionary attack
   ❑   b. Brute Force attack
   ❑   c. Birthday attack
   ❑   d. Replay attack

Quick Answer: **43**
Detailed Answer: **56**

3. Bruce has a hard time remembering things, so he decides to use his mother's birthday as a password on one machine and his wife's first name on another machine. What are his machines vulnerable to?

   ❑   a. Birthday attack
   ❑   b. Weak Keys
   ❑   c. Dictionary attack
   ❑   d. Mathematical attack

Quick Answer: **43**
Detailed Answer: **56**

4. Crackers use several techniques to obtain weak passwords. Which of the following will most likely provide crackers multiple passwords to authenticate onto a system?

   ❑   a. Dictionary attack
   ❑   b. Password Spoofing
   ❑   c. Dumpster Diving
   ❑   d. Weak Keys

Quick Answer: **43**
Detailed Answer: **56**

5. Martha's computer passwords are simple pet names and Bill uses his birthday so that neither of them will forget their passwords. These passwords are vulnerable to what kind of attack? (Select the best answer.)

   ❑   a. Dictionary attack
   ❑   b. Brute Name attack
   ❑   c. Birthday attack
   ❑   d. Replay attack

Quick Answer: **43**
Detailed Answer: **56**

Objective 1.4.12: Software Exploitation

1. Which of the following is the best explanation of Software Exploitation?

   ❑ a. Distribution of new software

   ❑ b. Distribution of software patches

   ❑ c. Attacks on software vulnerabilities

   ❑ d. Attacks on software patches

Quick Answer: **43**
Detailed Answer: **56**

2. Some crackers use improperly formatted packets to perform Software Exploitation and Denial of Service attacks. Which of the following answers pertains to the delivery of such unexpected packets? (Select all that apply.)

   ❑ a. It possibly involves one or two improperly formatted packets

   ❑ b. The damage should be limited to the crash of one computer system

   ❑ c. Prevent this by using current, proven patches or updates

   ❑ d. A vendor product error may be the source

Quick Answer: **43**
Detailed Answer: **56**

Objective 1.4.12: SYN attack

1. What action does a cracker take to make the target system crash in a SYN attack?

   ❑ a. Uses a virus attack to shut down the system

   ❑ b. Uses ACK messages to overflow the buffer space

   ❑ c. Uses a logic bomb to provide a timely disconnection of services

   ❑ d. Uses patience, waits without responding to connection requests

Quick Answer: **43**
Detailed Answer: **56**

2. What does a SYN attack take advantage of?

   ❑ a. The TCP/IP buffer space used during a handshake exchange

   ❑ b. The IPX/SPX frame relay used during a initial connection

   ❑ c. The UDP header frame used during a handshake exchange

   ❑ d. The ICMP echo connection used during connectivity checks

Quick Answer: **43**
Detailed Answer: **56**

3. Which of the following describes what the SYN attack accomplishes?

   ❑ a. It manipulates the acknowledgement of the SYN dialogue

   ❑ b. It modifies or removes the extensions of all office executable programs

   ❑ c. It opens port 80

   ❑ d. It manipulates the subnet mask address

Quick Answer: **43**
Detailed Answer: **56**

4. Which of the following takes advantage of the way sessions are established between TCP clients and servers?

❑   a.   TCP SYN attack

❑   b.   TCP ACK attack

❑   c.   DCHPDiscovery packet attack

❑   d.   DNS Lookup attack

Quick Answer: **43**
Detailed Answer: **56**

5. What type of attack is it when a network cracker targets and overwhelms a system with floods of initial connection requests and then fails to complete the connection, resulting in the target system becoming unstable?

❑   a.   Spoofing attack

❑   b.   SYN attack

❑   c.   Smurf attack

❑   d.   Subtle attack

Quick Answer: **43**
Detailed Answer: **56**

6. TCP/IP session connection between a network client and a server requires a small buffer space for a hand-shaking exchange. What kind of attack can exploit this exchange? (Select the best answer.)

❑   a.   Smurf attack

❑   b.   Buffer overflow

❑   c.   SYN attack

❑   d.   Birthday attack

Quick Answer: **43**
Detailed Answer: **56**

7. Which of the following seizes an advantage in the way a TCP session is established between two computers?

❑   a.   Buffer Overflow

❑   b.   SYN attack

❑   c.   Spoofing attack

❑   d.   Passive attack

Quick Answer: **43**
Detailed Answer: **57**

8. What does a SYN attack accomplish?

❑   a.   It changes TCP port numbers

❑   b.   It changes gateway addresses

❑   c.   It changes the response to the ACK exchange

❑   d.   It changes the response to the SYN exchange

Quick Answer: **43**
Detailed Answer: **57**

9. Which of the following describes the situation when your Website continues to be flooded by half-open requests?

❑   a.   DOS attack

❑   b.   SYN attack

❑   c.   Man in the Middle

❑   d.   Weak Keys

Quick Answer: **43**
Detailed Answer: **57**

. . . .

Objective 1.4.12: Buffer Overflow

1. Which of the following could be considered Software
   Exploitation? (Select all that apply.)
   - ❑ a. Buffer Overflow
   - ❑ b. Dictionary attack
   - ❑ c. Birthday attack
   - ❑ d. SYN attack

Quick Answer: **43**
Detailed Answer: **57**

2. Which of the following are primary causes for a Denial of
   Service (DOS) because of Software Exploitation? (Select all
   that apply.)
   - ❑ a. Buffer Overflow
   - ❑ b. SYN attack
   - ❑ c. ACK attack
   - ❑ d. Spoofing attack

Quick Answer: **43**
Detailed Answer: **57**

3. Which of the following statements are characteristics of a
   Buffer Overflow attack? (Select all that apply.)
   - ❑ a. A large string of data is sent to a buffer
   - ❑ b. A small string of data is sent to a buffer
   - ❑ c. Data sent is larger than the buffer was designed to handle
   - ❑ d. Data sent is smaller than the buffer was designed to handle

Quick Answer: **43**
Detailed Answer: **57**

4. Which of the following is considered both a kind of DOS
   attack, because it sends more traffic than expected, and
   Software Exploitation, because it is programmed code that
   exploits a target?
   - ❑ a. Buffer Overflow
   - ❑ b. Smart Card
   - ❑ c. Logic Bomb
   - ❑ d. Spam

Quick Answer: **43**
Detailed Answer: **57**

5. Your network is being exploited by more traffic than expected.
   What kind of attack may be occurring?
   - ❑ a. Ping of Broadcasts
   - ❑ b. Violent Death
   - ❑ c. Overflow of Logic
   - ❑ d. Buffer Overflow

Quick Answer: **43**
Detailed Answer: **57**

6. In security operations, which of the following is both a type of DOS and Software Exploitation attack?

  ❑   a. Strategic dialing

  ❑   b. Buffer Overflow

  ❑   c. Modem monitoring

  ❑   d. Sam Spade

Quick Answer: **43**
Detailed Answer: **57**

7. In security operations, which of the following is a type of attack due to Software Exploitation?

  ❑   a. Known plain text

  ❑   b. Polymorphic

  ❑   c. Buffer Overflow

  ❑   d. Strong Keys

Quick Answer: **43**
Detailed Answer: **57**

8. What occurs when a string of data is sent to a buffer that is larger than the buffer was designed to handle.

  ❑   a. Brute Force attack

  ❑   b. Buffer Overflow

  ❑   c. Man in the Middle attack

  ❑   d. Blue Screen of Death

Quick Answer: **43**
Detailed Answer: **57**

9. Which of the following apply to a Buffer Overflow? (Select the best answer.)

  ❑   a. A string of data is sent to a buffer that is too plain for the buffer to manage

  ❑   b. A string of data is sent to a buffer that is too large for the buffer to manage

  ❑   c. A string of data is sent to a buffer that is too small for the buffer to manage

  ❑   d. A string of data is sent to a buffer that is too foreign for the buffer to manage

Quick Answer: **43**
Detailed Answer: **57**

10. Which of the following is an example of an exploited string value of 90 90 90 90 …?

  ❑   a. Dictionary Attack

  ❑   b. Brute Force Attack

  ❑   c. Buffer Overflow

  ❑   d. Memory Loss

Quick Answer: **43**
Detailed Answer: **57**

Quick Check Answer Key

1. a, b, and c.

2. b.

Objective 1.1: Access Control

1. c.

2. a, b, and c.

3. c.

4. d.

Objective 1.1.1: Mandatory Access Control (MAC)

1. a, b, c, and d.

2. a, c, and d.

3. b.

4. a.

5. c.

6. a.

7. d.

8. d.

9. d.

10. d.

11. d.

12. c.

13. a and c.

Objective 1.1.1: Discretionary Access Control (DAC)

1. b and d.

2. a.

3. a and d.

4. a.

5. a.

6. b.

7. d.

8. d.

Objective 1.1.1: Role-Based Access Control (RBAC)

1. a, b, and c.

2. c.

3. c.

4. d.

5. b.

6. d.

7. a.

8. b.

9. b.

10. c.

11. b.

Objective 1.2: Authentication

1. c.

2. a, b, and d.

3. d.

4. b and d.

5. c.

6. a, b, and c.

7. d.

Objective 1.2.1: Kerberos

1. b.

2. b.

3. a, b, c, and d.

4. a.

5. a.

6. b.

7. c.

8. d.

9. b.

10. b.

11. a and b.

12. d.

Quick Check Answer Key

Objective 1.2.2: Challenge-Handshake Authentication Protocol (CHAP)

1. b.

2. a and c.

3. a.

4. c.

Objective 1.2.3: Certificates

1. c.

2. c.

3. a, b, and d.

4. a.

5. d.

Objective 1.2.4: Username/Password

1. c.

2. d.

3. a, b, and c.

4. c.

5. b.

6. b, c, and d.

Objective 1.2.5: Tokens

1. a.

2. b.

3. b.

4. a.

5. b.

6. c.

Objective 1.2.6: Multi-Factor

1. b, c, and d.

2. d.

1.2.7 Mutual Authentication

1. b.

2. d.

Objective 1.2.8: Biometrics

1. a, b, and d.

2. c.

3. c.

4. b and c.

5. a and d.

Objective 1.3: Nonessential Services and Protocols

1. b.

2. d.

3. a.

4. b.

5. c.

6. d.

7. c.

8. c.

9. b.

10. b.

11. c.

12. d.

13. b.

14. b.

15. b.

16. a, b, c, and d.

17. a, c, and d.

18. d.

19. b.

20. a.

Quick Check Answer Key

Objective 1.4: Attacks

1. c.

2. a.

3. b.

4. a.

5. b.

Objective 1.4.1: DOS/DDOS

1. b and c.

2. c.

3. a.

4. b.

5. c.

6. a and c.

7. b.

8. a and b.

9. c and d.

10. b and d.

11. a.

12. d.

13. a.

14. d.

15. a.

16. c.

17. a.

18. d.

19. b.

20. a.

Objective 1.4.2: Back Door

1. b.

2. a and b.

3. d.

4. a, b, and c.

5. a and d.

Objective 1.4.3: Spoofing

1. b.

2. a and c.

3. b.

4. d.

5. b.

6. b and c.

7. b.

8. d.

9. a.

10. b.

11. c.

12. a, b, c, and d.

13. b and c.

14. a and c.

15. a and b.

16. a.

17. a, b, and c.

18. c.

19. d.

Objective 1.4.4: Man in the Middle

1. d.

2. b.

3. b.

4. d.

5. a.

6. b.

Objective 1.4.5: Replay

1. d.

2. d.

Objective 1.4.6: TCP/IP Hijacking

1. b.

2. b.

3. a and c.

4. c.

Objective 1.4.7: Weak Keys

1. b.

2. a.

Quick Check Answer Key

Objective 1.4.8: Mathematical

1. a.

2. d.

Objective 1.4.9: Social Engineering

1. c.

2. a.

Objective 1.4.10: Birthday

1. b, c, and d.

2. b.

Objective 1.4.11: Password Guessing

1. c.

2. b and c.

3. b and d.

Objective 1.4.11.1: Brute Force

1. b.

2. c.

Objective 1.4.11.2: Dictionary

1. d.

2. a.

3. c.

4. a.

5. a.

Objective 1.4.12: Software Exploitation

1. c.

2. a, c, and d.

Objective 1.4.12: SYN attack

1. d.

2. a.

3. a.

4. a.

5. b.

6. c.

7. b.

8. d.

9. b.

Objective 1.4.12: Buffer Overflow

1. a and d.

2. a and b.

3. a and c.

4. a.

5. d.

6. b.

7. c.

8. b.

9. b.

10. c.

Answers and Explanations

1. **a, b, and c.** The security acronym, AAA, stands for Access Control, Authentication, and Auditing.

2. **b.** The security acronym, CIA, stands for Confidentiality, Integrity, and Availability.

Objective 1.1: Access Control

1. **c.** Controlling access into a computer network is like holding a valid key for a door or building.

2. **a, b, and c.** You can deny access from Internet sources, domain names, or specific computer names or IP addresses that are known to be a threat to the welfare or well being of a company.

3. **c.** Access control is the best term to describe a user's right to change or examine data or files.

4. **d.** Access control determines what a user can change or view.

Objective 1.1.1: Mandatory Access Control (MAC)

1. **a, b, c, and d.** Mandatory Access Control, Rule-Based Access Control (which is a type of MAC), Role-Based Access Control (which is a type of Non-Discretionary Access Control), and Discretionary Access Control are all examples of access control methods.

2. **a, c, and d.** MAC places sensitivity labels on both subjects and objects.

3. **b.** Mandatory Access Control is the method in use when the system determines which users or groups may access files or directories.

4. **a.** When Access Control is mandatory, sensitivity labels are used as a basis for determining access.

5. **c.** Mandatory Access Control involves defining the specific classification for objects.

6. **a.** Mandatory Access Control is the method in use when the system determines which users or groups may access files or directories.

7. **d.** When using Mandatory Access Control (MAC), the access decisions are based on sensitivity labels.

8. **d.** Mandatory Access Control is the method in use when the system determines which processes can access a device.

9. **d.** Mandatory Access Control necessitates security clearance for subjects. The capability of a subject to access an object depends on sensitivity labels, which verify the subject's clearance.

10. **d.** The system establishes which users or groups may access a file under Mandatory Access Control.

11. **d.** With one type of MAC, known as Rule-Based Access Control, access may also be determined by rules as well as by the identity of the subjects and objects.

12. **c.** The Clark Wilson Model is not generally associated with Mandatory Access Control.

13. **a and c.** MAC is based on sensitivity labels of objects and subjects and is used in organizations with classified data.

Objective 1.1.1: Discretionary Access Control (DAC)

1. **b and d.** Each file or object has an owner, which has complete control over that file or object.

2. **a.** Discretionary Access Control allows data owners to create and manage access to their own files.

3. **a and d.** Discretionary Access Controls are very flexible and frequently used in commercial environments because of their flexibility.

4. **a.** Discretionary Access Control (DAC) allows users to protect information as they desire.

5. **a.** Identity-Based Access Control is a type of Discretionary Access Control.

6. **b.** User-Directed Access Control is a type of Discretionary Access Control.

7. **d.** With Discretionary Access Control (DAC) each object has an owner, which has full control over that object.

8. **d.** Discretionary Access Control is a type of Access Control that is created and managed by the data owner.

Objective 1.1.1: Role-Based Access Control (RBAC)

1. **a, b, and c.** With Role-Based Access Control methods access rights link to an organizational structure. Each user's roles are assigned privileges and access rights are based on an Access Control List.

2. **c.** When access control options are based on an individual's responsibility within the organization, this method is best described as Role-Based Access Control.

3. **c.** Logon abuse refers to a user or authorized worker that attempts to access areas of the network that are regarded as off-limits to that user.

4. **d.** A Role-Based Access Control is a type of Non-Discretionary Access Control.

5. **b.** Role-Based Access Control methods are based on jobs that a user has within an organization.

6. **d.** Hans has the right to read, write, and execute since he created the file and is a member of the Accounting group. If he were a member of the Finance Department, he would have no access.

7. **a.** Joan has no access to the file, because she is a member of the Finance Department and not the Accounting Group.

8. **b.** Bill has the right to read the file, because he is a member of the Accounting group. If he were a member of the Finance Department, he would have no access.

9. **b.** Role-Based Access Control (RBAC) is used to make access control decisions, which are based on responsibilities that an individual user or process has within an organization.

10. **c.** Non-Discretionary Access Control is described by this situation. For more information about this question refer to (Objective 1.1.1) section "RBAC" in Chapter 1.

11. **b.** Non-Discretionary Access Control uses a central authority to determine which subjects can have access to which objects.

Objective 1.2: Authentication

1. **c.** Authentication confirms that a user's claimed identity is valid and is usually applied through a user password at time of logon.

2. **a, b, and d.** Generally speaking, authenticating yourself to the computer security software requires verification, including these methods: something you know, something you have, and something you are.

3. **d.** Generally speaking, authenticating yourself to the computer security software requires verification, including these methods: something you know, something you have, and something you are.

4. **b and d.** Generally speaking, authenticating yourself to the computer security software requires verification, including these methods: something you know, something you have, and something you are.

5. **c.** Generally speaking, authenticating yourself to the computer security software requires verification, including these methods: something you know, something you have, and something you are, not something you do or your vocation.

6. **a, b, and c.** Host name, host IP address, and machine name can be used by authentication systems to allow or deny network computers access.

7. **d.** Authentication describes a server's function to verify that someone's logon truly is that claimed identity.

Objective 1.2.1: Kerberos

1. **b.** Kerberos provides mutual authentication and encrypted communication for users accessing services.

2. **b.** Each network client must have a clock that is synchronized to the time of the other network clients. Synchronization reduces network security concerns by limiting relay.

3. **a, b, c, and d.** Kerberos works inside of LANs and WANs to provide single-password access to users' privileges, as they pertain to certain profiles and relies on ticket granting services.

4. **a.** When using Kerberos, clocks synchronize ticket expiration.

5. **a.** This process is known as Kerberos authentication.

6. **b.** Kerberos-trusted Key Distribution Center (KDC), Kerberos Ticket Granting Service (TGS), and Kerberos Authentication Service (AS) are the components of Kerberos.

7. **c.** Kerberos-trusted Key Distribution Center (KDC), Kerberos Ticket Granting Service (TGS), and Kerberos Authentication Service (AS) are the components of Kerberos.

8. **d.** Kerberos requires the use of symmetric ciphers.

9. **b.** Kerberos relates to information confidentiality and integrity.

10. **b.** SESAME addresses some of the weaknesses in Kerberos. SESAME uses public key cryptography for the circulation of secret keys and offers additional access control defense.

11. **a and b.** SESAME was developed to address some of the weaknesses in Kerberos. SESAME uses public key cryptography for the circulation of secret keys and offers additional access control defense.

12. **d.** Kerberos can prevent a "replay" or playback attack.

Objective 1.2.2: Challenge-Handshake Authentication Protocol (CHAP)

1. **b.** Challenge-Handshake Authentication Protocol (CHAP) is used for Remote Access.

2. **a and c.** PAP and CHAP are used for authentication.

3. **a.** CHAP uses regular intervals when requesting authentication.

4. **c.** CHAP stands for Challenge Handshake Authentication Protocol.

Objective 1.2.3: Certificates

1. **c.** Certificates provide for user authentication.

2. **c.** Digital certificates make use of an electronic security credential, given that the certificate holder is who they said they are.

3. **a, b, and d.** Level 2 verifies a user's social security number, a user's name, and a user's address using a credit bureau database.

4. **a.** Public keys encrypt and Private keys decrypt. Note the vowels and consonants: PU = E and PR = d.

5. **d.** Third parties generally issue a Certificate Authority.

Objective 1.2.4: Username/Password

1. **c.** A truly strong user password is one that has at least eight characters, including small and large caps along with numbers and symbols.

2. **d.** If you want to use your street address with all the vowels in uppercase as a password this would be considered a poor password because it's predictable.

3. **a, b, and c.** Increased security, decreased cost, and decreased intrusion are advantages for using password synchronization.

4. **c.** Of the items listed, MyPassword, mYpA55w0rd, mY?a5%w0rD, and MyPa55w0RD, the answer mY?a5%w0rD is the best example of a good password.

5. **b.** You should reduce the password expiration period to increase security.

6. **b, c, and d.** Encryption, smart cards, and protocols are some technical methods to protect passwords from discovery.

Objective 1.2.5: Tokens

1. **a.** Tokens provide for ID authentication.

2. **b.** Physical devices such as tokens and smart cards may be used to generate passwords.

3. **b.** A token is used only a single time for physical authentication and generates a unique password for each use.

4. **a.** A token is used a single time for physical authentication and generates a unique password for each use.

5. **b.** Synchronous dynamic password tokens make use of time synchronizations. Note the similarity between synchronous and synchronization.

6. **c.** The owner authenticates himself/herself to a token with Static password tokens.

Objective 1.2.6: Multi-Factor

1. **b, c, and d.** Multi-Factor should be used as a type of authentication when additional security layers are needed, or when stored keys and memorized passwords are not sufficient.

2. **d.** Multi-Factor Authentication should be used to improve authentication.

Objective 1.2.7: Mutual Authentication

1. **b.** Mutual Authentication describes a method to verify the identity of both a client and server in direct communication.

2. **d.** Servers and Clients do not need to trust each other to prove each other's identities, but all the other statements are true.

Objective 1.2.8: Biometrics

1. **a, b, and d.** Voice patterns, retinal scans, and fingerprints are examples of tools within Biometric Authentication.

2. **c.** Of the choices listed, only voice patterns, fingerprints, and retinal scans are used for biometric authentication.

3. **c.** Biometrics can be described as an automated process of identifying someone based on the physiological characteristics of that person.

4. **b and c.** A false positive is when an unauthorized person is attempting to gain access and that access is wrongfully approved.

5. **a and d.** A false negative is when an authorized person is attempting to gain access and that access is wrongfully denied.

Objective 1.3: Nonessential Services and Protocols

1. **b.** Any TCP request received on port 23 is considered a Telnet session. Telnet is made up of two (2) syllables, each having three (3) letters.

2. **d.** Any TCP request received on port 21 is considered an FTP session. A capital F is made with two (2) horizontal lines and one (1) vertical line.

3. **a.** Any TCP request received on port 25 is considered a mail service. Port 25 is reserved for Simple Mail Transfer Protocol (SMTP).

4. **b.** The Internet Assigned Numbers Authority (IANA) has reserved the following ports for most well-known services: Ports 0-1023.

5. **c.** Port 139 is the common UDP port that relates to a NetBIOS session.

6. **d.** Port 161 is the common UDP port that relates to use of the Simple Network Management Protocol.

7. **c.** Port 67 is the common UDP port that relates to use of the bootp server service. Port 68 is the common UDP port that relates to the bootp client service.

8. **c.** Port 119 is the common TCP port that relates to use of the Network News Transfer Protocol.

9. **b.** Port 110 is the common TCP port that relates to use of Post Office Protocol V.3 (POP3) service.

10. **b.** Port 53 is the common UDP port that relates to DNS zone transfers.

11. **c.** Port 80 is the common TCP port used to communicate HTTP between Web browsers and Web servers.

12. **d.** Port 2049 is the UDP port that relates to access to remote file systems using Network File System (NFS). Note that the number 2049 is very "Remote" from frequently used TCP port numbers.

13. **b.** Port 143 is the TCP port that relates to group access via Internet Message Access Protocol (IMAP).

14. **b.** Internet Relay Chat (IRC) listens on ports 6667-7000 and allows clients to communicate in real time.

15. **b.** Port 20 is the common TCP port used to transfer actual files and data.

16. **a, b, c, and d.** All of them transmit data using clear text.

17. **a, c, and d.** FTP, SMTP, HTTP, Telnet, and SNMP v1 transmit using clear text.

18. **d.** Port 443 is used to transfer data using Secure Sockets Layer (SSL). Note the similarity between "44" and "SS".

19. **b.** Port 22 is the correct port for SSH. Note the similarity between "22" and "SS".

20. **a.** Running nonessential services poses a security risk.

Objective 1.4: Attacks

1. **c.** Network intrusion means breaking into a network primarily from an external source.

2. **a.** Probing allows an attacker to find ways into the network. It is a cracker's scan of the network to create a network map for possible intrusion sometime later.

3. **b.** Eavesdropping may occur from inside the LAN, where an employee conducts unauthorized sharing of information with an external partner using the network.

4. **a.** Polymorphic Spoofing is a fictitious term.

5. **b.** Sniffing is designed to capture sensitive pieces of information passing through the network.

Objective 1.4.1: DOS/DDOS

1. **b and c.** Characteristics of a DOS attack results in an inability to use a system, but does not primarily result in theft of information.

2. **c.** The goal of a DOS is to use up all of a target's resources with bogus connections so that legitimate connections cannot use them.

3. **a.** Digital signatures and token technologies do not protect networks from DOS.

4. **b.** DOS is a type of attack that denies service to a system without resulting in theft or loss of data.

5. **c.** DDOS is achieved when one server is being attacked.

6. **a and c.** In a DDOS remote attacks are simultaneously triggered from many places at once to attack one server.

7. **b.** A Distributed Denial of Service (DDOS) is accomplished by triggering remote attacks from thousands of infiltrated systems at one host.

8. **a and b.** To prevent Distributed Denial of Service (DDOS) attacks, take these actions: Adjust routers to enable logging, filter select packets coming into (Ingress) and out of (Egress) a network, and ensure routers are *not* broadcast amplifiers.

9. **c and d.** Enabling routers to perform logging and using Ingress and Egress packet filtering may help prevent a DDOS.

10. **b and d.** Checking to ensure that routers are *not* set to be broadcast amplifiers and using Ingress and Egress packet filtering may help prevent a DDOS.

11. **a.** A Smurf attack is an example of a flooding Denial of Service attack that relies on routers to send ICMP broadcast messages to the computers they serve.

12. **d.** Broadcast storm is another name for ICMP storm.

13. **a.** ICMP storms and broadcasts storms are similar terms.

14. **d.** An ICMP flood could be used against a client to disable the client from communicating with a server.

15. **a.** A Smurf attack is an example of a flooding Denial of Service attack that relies on routers to send ICMP broadcast messages to the computers they support.

16. **c.** Smurf is a kind of DOS attack that uses PING and a spoofed address.

17. **a.** Smurf is a kind of DOS attack that uses ICMP and a spoofed address.

18. **d.** A Smurf attack uses ICMP, whereas a Fraggle attack uses UDP.

19. **b.** A Smurf attack is based on ICMP packets. But a Fraggle attack is based on UDP packets.

20. **a.** A Ping of Death attack could be causing you to receive oversized ICMP request packets.

Objective 1.4.2: Back Door

1. **b.** Having hidden back doors are generally *not* beneficial to organizations.

2. **a and c.** A Back Door attack may be an intrusion that occurs via dial-up or asynchronous external network connections.

3. **d.** Network administrators generally find no benefit to hidden back doors.

4. **a, b, and c.** Back Door attacks can be implemented by Remote access using dial-up or asynchronous external network connection, through Trojan Horses and Root kits.

5. **a and d.** SubSeven and Back Orifice are designed as malicious Back Door programs.

Objective 1.4.3: Spoofing

1. **b.** Spoofing gives false information about the source of an attack.

2. **a and c.** Spoofing gives false information about the source of an attack and tricks the user into continuing to communicate.

3. **b.** IP Spoofing is a network-based attack.

4. **d.** This is an example of a Server Spoofing attack, which is also known as a Man in the Middle attack.

5. **b.** Even if an IP address is spoofed, backtracking a packet is possible.

6. **b and c.** When the ISP DNS server is under a Spoofing attack, your ISP DNS server may be misdirecting Internet traffic or your network may be misdirecting Internet traffic.

7. **b.** When the ISP DNS server is under a Spoofing attack, your ISP DNS server may be misdirecting Internet traffic and your network may be misdirecting Internet traffic.

8. **d.** Spoofing is known as an attack that impersonates a user or a system.

9. **a.** During Spoofing, a cracker obtains the MAC address of a target machine and configures his or her own machine with that MAC address.

10. **b.** Spoofing is giving false information about the source of an attack.

11. **c.** Spoofing provides false information about the source of an attack.

12. **a, b, c, and d.** Since spoofing provides false information about the source address, it is used to gain unauthorized access and tricks the user to continue to communicate which is both "no action" and "an incorrect action."

13. **b and c.** Spoofing requires the attacker to capture and configure his computer with the captured target address.

14. **a and c.** IP spoofing alters the source address of a computer and exploits weak authentication methods.

15. **a and b.** Spoofing is used to falsify the source address. In essence it uses falsely addressed packets to disguise the source of the communication.

16. **a.** Man in the Middle is also known as Server Spoofing or Session Hijacking.

17. **a, b, and c.** Spoofing occurs when crackers take advantage of clear text Server Message Block (SMB) usernames and passwords and pretend to be the client.

18. **c.** Session Hijacking may also be referred to as Server Spoofing or Man in the Middle.

19. **d.** Server Spoofing may also be referred to as Session Hijacking or Man in the Middle.

Objective 1.4.4: Man in the Middle

1. **d.** Man in the Middle, also known as Server Spoofing, uses an application to capture and manipulate your network packets.

2. **b.** Using "secure" sites does not prevent Man in the Middle attacks.

3. **b.** Just because you receive a download from a trusted site doesn't mean that you will avoid the Man in the Middle attack.

4. **d.** Just because you receive a download from a trusted site doesn't mean that you will avoid the Man in the Middle attack.

5. **a.** Routers can help reduce the threat of Man in the Middle attacks.

6. **b.** Man in the Middle attacks use an application to obtain and change network packets.

Objective 1.4.5: Replay

1. **d.** Kerberos can be used to prevent a Playback (Replay) attack.

2. **d.** Kerberos prevents Replay attacks.

Objective 1.4.6: TCP/IP Hijacking

1. **b.** Web-based connections that involve open sessions using user's cookies are susceptible to TCP/IP Hijacking.

2. **b.** Network Address Hijacking enables the intruder to re-route data traffic from a network device to a personal machine.

3. **a and c.** Session Hijacking takes over network connections, by either stopping an authorized user or sharing an authorized login.

4. **c.** Encryption should be used to minimize TCP/IP Hijacking.

Objective 1.4.7: Weak Keys

1. **b.** Weak Keys is a vulnerability term that refers to patterns that are frequently seen in an algorithm.

2. **a.** Weak Keys exploits common passwords.

Objective 1.4.8: Mathematical

1. **a.** A Mathematical attack relates to the cryptanalysis of algorithms.

2. **d.** A Mathematical attack relates to the cryptanalysis or statistical analysis of algorithms.

Objective 1.4.9: Social Engineering

1. **c.** Social Engineering could be the cause in this situation.

2. **a.** Social Engineering is a term that relates to workers being tricked into providing confidential or restricted data about the network or organization.

Objective 1.4.10: Birthday

1. **b, c, and d.** Birthday Attacks refer to a type of Brute Force attack. They do *not* reference celebrated events. Birthday Attacks do refer to a type of mathematical attack and are used to reveal mathematical weaknesses of hash algorithms.

2. **b.** Birthday attack exploits the fact that MD5 uses similar keys.

Objective 1.4.11: Password Guessing

1. **c.** Sniffing is used to capture sensitive pieces of information, such as user passwords, as they pass through the network.

2. **b and c.** Hashed passwords are vulnerable to Dictionary and Brute Force attacks.

3. **b and d.** Dictionary and Brute Force attacks use tools to guess user passwords.

Objective 1.4.11.1: Brute Force

1. **b.** Brute Force attack is a cracker's attempt to try all possible cipher key combinations to find the one that unlocks an encrypted cipher text.

2. **c.** L0pht Crack essentially uses Brute Force and Dictionary files to attempt all possible values to authenticate a system.

Objective 1.4.11.2: Dictionary

1. **d.** L0pht Crack essentially uses Brute Force and Dictionary files to attempt all possible values to authenticate a system.

2. **a.** Simple passwords are vulnerable to a Dictionary attack.

3. **c.** Dictionary attack works against poorly chosen passwords such as dates and common names.

4. **a.** A Dictionary attack is the most likely technique to obtain multiple passwords from a source using weak passwords.

5. **a.** Simple passwords such as pet names are extremely vulnerable to a Dictionary attack.

Objective 1.4.12: Software Exploitation

1. **c.** Attacks on software vulnerabilities is the best explanation of Software Exploitation.

2. **a, c, and d.** The use of improperly formatted packets may exploit software and perform a Denial of Service. A vendor product error may be the source. It possibly involves only one or two improperly formatted packets. The damage may be unlimited throughout the system. Prevent this by using current, proven patches or updates.

Objective 1.4.12: SYN attack

1. **d.** By refusing to respond to a target system request, the cracker makes that system unstable, causing it to crash. This is because the SYN attack causes the system to time-out while waiting for a response.

2. **a.** A SYN attack takes advantage of the TCP/IP buffer space used during a handshake exchange.

3. **a.** The SYN attack manipulates the acknowledgement of the SYN dialogue.

4. **a.** A TCP SYN attack takes advantage of the way sessions are established between TCP clients and servers.

5. **b.** In a SYN attack, the cracker makes that system unstable by refusing to respond to a target system request. The SYN attack causes the system to time-out while waiting for a response.

6. **c.** A SYN attack can exploit the TCP/IP exchange.

7. **b.** A SYN attack seizes an advantage in the way a TCP session is established. It takes advantage of the TCP/IP buffer space used during the handshake exchange.

8. **d.** The SYN attack changes the response to the SYN exchange.

9. **b.** A SYN attack can create a situation where your Web site continues to be flooded by half-open requests.

Objective 1.4.12: Buffer Overflow

1. **a and d.** Buffer Overflow and SYN attacks could be considered Software Exploitation.

2. **a and b.** Both Buffer Overflow and SYN attack are kinds of DOS that exploit your network by sending more traffic than expected.

3. **a and c.** Characteristics of a Buffer Overflow attack include the fact that a large string of data is sent to a buffer and that the data sent is larger than the buffer was designed to handle.

4. **a.** Buffer Overflow is both a DOS attack and considered Software Exploitation.

5. **d.** A Buffer Overflow is a kind of DOS that exploits your network by exploiting software sending more traffic than expected.

6. **b.** Buffer Overflow is a type of attack due to Software Exploitation that can also cause DOS.

7. **c.** Buffer Overflow is a type of attack due to Software Exploitation.

8. **b.** Buffer Overflow is a type of DOS attack that occurs when a string of data is sent to a buffer that is larger than the buffer was designed to handle.

9. **b.** When a string of data is sent to a buffer that is too large for the buffer to manage, this is called a Buffer Overflow.

10. **c.** Buffer Overflow is an example of an exploited string value of 90 90 90 90.

Communication Security

Objective 2.1: Remote Access

1. What are some valid methods you can use to apply security when using remote access? (Select all that apply.)

   ❏ a. Restricted Address
   ❏ b. Callback
   ❏ c. Caller ID
   ❏ d. POP

Quick Answer: **91**
Detailed Answer: **95**

2. John is working at a branch office and has made an initial authorized connection to his headquarters. Which of the following remote access protection methods limits connections by returning John's call on the number he specified?

   ❏ a. Call forward
   ❏ b. Call forwarding
   ❏ c. Call again
   ❏ d. Callback

Quick Answer: **91**
Detailed Answer: **95**

3. Which of the following is a centralized access control method for remote users?

   ❏ a. Hang up
   ❏ b. Callback
   ❏ c. Deny Access
   ❏ d. Backup

Quick Answer: **91**
Detailed Answer: **95**

Objective 2.1.1: 802.1x

1. The IEEE 802.1x is a standard for remote access. Which of the following items would the 802.1x standard be concerned with? (Select all that apply.)

   ❏ a. Authentication for remote access to a centralized LAN
   ❏ b. Simple Network Management Protocol (SNMP)
   ❏ c. RADIUS Server
   ❏ d. Extensive Authentication Protocol (EAP)

Quick Answer: **91**
Detailed Answer: **95**

2. Which of the following standards governs Extensible Authentication Protocol (EAP)?

Quick Answer: **91**
Detailed Answer: **95**

- ❑   a.   802.11
- ❑   b.   802.11a
- ❑   c.   802.11b
- ❑   d.   802.1x

Objective 2.1.2: VPN

1. IPSec is integrated with Cisco routers and uses both public and private key encryption. Which of the following is a remote access tool that is also used with IPSec?

Quick Answer: **91**
Detailed Answer: **95**

- ❑   a.   SSH
- ❑   b.   RADIUS
- ❑   c.   VPN
- ❑   d.   PPTP

2. You want to have a secure connection. You decide on establishing a VPN. Which of the following protocols can be used to accomplish your goal? (Select all that apply.)

Quick Answer: **91**
Detailed Answer: **95**

- ❑   a.   S/MIME
- ❑   b.   TACACS
- ❑   c.   IPSec
- ❑   d.   L2TP

3. You want to have a secure connection. You decide on establishing a Virtual Private Network (VPN). Which of the following can be used to accomplish your goal?

Quick Answer: **91**
Detailed Answer: **95**

- ❑   a.   SSL/TLS
- ❑   b.   IDS
- ❑   c.   IPSec
- ❑   d.   PKCS#10

4. You want to have a secure connection. You decide on establishing a VPN. Which of the following can be used to accomplish your goal? (Select all that apply.)

Quick Answer: **91**
Detailed Answer: **95**

- ❑   a.   X.509
- ❑   b.   TLS
- ❑   c.   S/MIME
- ❑   d.   L2TP

5. VPN can be used for remote access. Which of the following are tunneling protocols that work with VPN? (Select all that apply.)

- ❏ a. PPTP
- ❏ b. L2F
- ❏ c. L2FP
- ❏ d. TCP

6. A Virtual Private Network (VPN) can be used for remote access. Which of the following are tunneling protocols that work with VPN? (Select all that apply.)

- ❏ a. PPTP
- ❏ b. L2F
- ❏ c. UDP
- ❏ d. TCP

Objective 2.1.3: RADIUS

1. Which of the following remote authentication methods uses a central server for all remote client network access, transports with UDP, and can be used with firewalls?

- ❏ a. TACACS/+
- ❏ b. 802.1x
- ❏ c. RADIUS
- ❏ d. VPN

2. Which of the following methods is a good choice for authenticating remote users but not as secure as TACACS+? (Select the best answer.)

- ❏ a. RADIUS
- ❏ b. MS-CHAP
- ❏ c. DSL
- ❏ d. ISP

Objective 2.1.4: TACACS/+

1. There are several ways to authenticate remote users. Which of the following is a CISCO proprietary improvement?

- ❏ a. TACACS+
- ❏ b. MS-CHAP
- ❏ c. TACACS
- ❏ d. RADIUS

2. Which of the following remote authentication servers enables a user to change passwords, enables two-factor authentication, and uses and resynchronizes security tokens?

❏ a. DNS Server

❏ b. TACACS+

❏ c. RADIUS

❏ d. PROXY Server

Quick Answer: **91**
Detailed Answer: **96**

3. When users log on remotely to a Terminal Access Controller Access Control System (TACACS), what is used for authentication?

❏ a. A user ID and biometric password

❏ b. A user ID and static password

❏ c. A user ID and dynamic password

❏ d. A biometric user ID and symmetric password

Quick Answer: **91**
Detailed Answer: **96**

Objective 2.1.5: L2TP/PPTP

1. Many more companies are using remote access, looking for ways to establish a Virtual Private Network (VPN) connection. Which of the following protocols directly support VPN? (Select all that apply.)

❏ a. STP

❏ b. L2TP

❏ c. PPTP

❏ d. PPP

Quick Answer: **91**
Detailed Answer: **96**

2. Remote users need to be authenticated and frequently need their data to be encrypted. Which of the following protocols are used together to meet both needs? (Select the two that apply.)

❏ a. L2TP

❏ b. PPTP

❏ c. IPSec

❏ d. AES

Quick Answer: **91**
Detailed Answer: **96**

3. Which of the following Virtual Private Network (VPN) protocols uses Transmission Control Protocol (TCP) port 1723?

❏ a. L2F

❏ b. L2TP

❏ c. PPTP

❏ d. PPP

Quick Answer: **91**
Detailed Answer: **96**

4. Which of the following Virtual Private Network (VPN) protocols uses Transmission Control Protocol (TCP) port 1721?

- ❏ a. L2F
- ❏ b. L2TP
- ❏ c. PPTP
- ❏ d. MPPE

Objective 2.1.6: SSH

1. Which of the following protocols is used to transport Secure Shell (SSH)?

- ❏ a. User Datagram Protocol
- ❏ b. Transmission Control Protocol
- ❏ c. Internet Control Message Protocol
- ❏ d. Internet Protocol

2. Which of the following applies to the correct port for Secure Shell?

- ❏ a. UDP Port 16
- ❏ b. TCP Port 22
- ❏ c. UDP Port 25
- ❏ d. TCP Port 136

3. Secure Shell (SSH) is used on Port 22 to encapsulate which of the following clear text sessions? (Select all that apply.)

- ❏ a. Telnet
- ❏ b. HTTP authentication
- ❏ c. FTP authentication
- ❏ d. Gopher authentication

4. John and Bill need to communicate clear text data between two locations. But they need to provide security to the data, because the network is not secure. What should they use?

- ❏ a. Telnet
- ❏ b. SSH
- ❏ c. Rexec
- ❏ d. RSH

5. What protocol is used to secure data transmission between two sites over a nonsecure network?

- ❏ a. FTP
- ❏ b. UDP
- ❏ c. SSH
- ❏ d. HTTP

6. Clients on your network are using SSH for authentication. Which of the following offers a digital certificate exchange when clients use SSH?

- ❏ a. DES
- ❏ b. AES
- ❏ c. SSL
- ❏ d. RSA

Quick Answer: **91**
Detailed Answer: **96**

7. Telnet is used frequently for remote login, but it offers little security. Which of the following should be used instead?

- ❏ a. SSH
- ❏ b. Secure Telnet
- ❏ c. SSL
- ❏ d. Secure Rlogin

Quick Answer: **91**
Detailed Answer: **96**

Objective 2.1.7: IPSec

1. Which of the following conditions are best suited to configure IPSec in tunnel mode? (Select all that apply.)

- ❏ a. The router at the main office is the only router needing tunnel configuration
- ❏ b. The router at the branch office is the only router needing tunnel configuration
- ❏ c. Secure connections are needed over a public network
- ❏ d. The routers at both locations need tunnel configuration

Quick Answer: **91**
Detailed Answer: **97**

2. Which of the following are functions of IPSec? (Select all that apply.)

- ❏ a. Data Integrity
- ❏ b. User Authentication
- ❏ c. Data Confidentiality
- ❏ d. User Non-Repudiation

Quick Answer: **91**
Detailed Answer: **97**

3. What does IPSec use to maintain data integrity?

- ❏ a. Authentication Header (AH)
- ❏ b. Encapsulation Security Payload (ESP)
- ❏ c. Non-Repudiation Header (NH)
- ❏ d. Secure Shell (SSH)

Quick Answer: **91**
Detailed Answer: **97**

4. What does IPSec use to maintain data confidentiality?

- ❏ a. Authentication Header (AH)
- ❏ b. Encapsulation Security Payload (ESP)
- ❏ c. Non-Repudiation Header (NH)
- ❏ d. Internet Protocol (IP)

Quick Answer: **91**
Detailed Answer: **97**

5. Remote users need to be authenticated and frequently need their data to be encrypted. Which of the following protocols are used together to meet both needs? (Select the two that apply.)

- ❏ a. L2TP
- ❏ b. DES
- ❏ c. IPSec
- ❏ d. PPTP

6. IPSec is very popular with organizations that have remote business connections. What type of algorithm does IPSec use?

- ❏ a. 40-bit DES
- ❏ b. 56-bit DES
- ❏ c. 128-bit DES
- ❏ d. 256-bit DES

7. Computers are readily identified by their numerical IP addresses. Which of the following is able to authenticate and encrypt an IP address?

- ❏ a. Host-Based IDS
- ❏ b. IPSec
- ❏ c. SSL
- ❏ d. DES

8. Which of the following are benefits of using IPSec? (Select all that apply.)

- ❏ a. Authentication
- ❏ b. Expense
- ❏ c. Non-Repudiation
- ❏ d. Privacy

9. Which of the following protocols apply to IPSec?

- ❏ a. Authentication Header (AH) for destination IP integrity
- ❏ b. Encrypted Security Payload (ESP) for secure authentication
- ❏ c. Authentication Header (AH) for IP source authentication
- ❏ d. Encrypted Security Payload (ESP) for confidentiality

10. Which of the following standards is used to encrypt private data so that it can move securely through the public Internet?

- ❏ a. ISAKMP
- ❏ b. IPSec
- ❏ c. IDEA
- ❏ d. IETF

11. IPSec works at the network layer in two modes: Transport mode and Tunnel mode. What is encrypted in the Transport mode?

Quick Answer: **91**
Detailed Answer: **97**

- ❑ a. Data only
- ❑ b. IP Header only
- ❑ c. Data and IP Header
- ❑ d. No encryption occurs with IPSec

12. IPSec works at the network layer in two modes: Transport mode and Tunnel mode. What is encrypted in the Tunnel mode?

Quick Answer: **91**
Detailed Answer: **97**

- ❑ a. Data only
- ❑ b. IP Header only
- ❑ c. Data and IP Header
- ❑ d. No encryption occurs with IPSec

13. You want to establish a VPN connection from one computer to another using IPSec. What IPSec mode should you use?

Quick Answer: **91**
Detailed Answer: **97**

- ❑ a. Tunnel mode
- ❑ b. Transfer mode
- ❑ c. Transport mode
- ❑ d. Timed mode

14. You want to establish a VPN connection from one computer through a router to another network group using IPSec. What IPSec mode should you use?

Quick Answer: **91**
Detailed Answer: **97**

- ❑ a. Tunnel mode
- ❑ b. Transfer mode
- ❑ c. Transport mode
- ❑ d. Trust mode

15. You decided to create a secure connection between two of your newly created offices. Which of the following would be the best way to configure IPSec to accomplish this goal?

Quick Answer: **91**
Detailed Answer: **97**

- ❑ a. A workstation at each location should be configured to use IPSec in Transport mode
- ❑ b. A router at each location should be configured to use IPSec in Transport mode
- ❑ c. A router at each location should be configured to use IPSec in Tunnel mode
- ❑ d. A workstation at each location should be configured to use IPSec in Tunnel mode

16. When using IPSec, one of your goals is to ensure data integrity. Which of the following components of IPSec will meet your goal?

   ❑   a. Internet Protocol (IP)
   ❑   b. Authentication Header (AH)
   ❑   c. Encapsulation Security Payload (ESP)
   ❑   d. Security (SEC)

Quick Answer: **91**
Detailed Answer: **97**

17. When using IPSec, one of your goals is to ensure data confidentiality. Which of the following components of IPSec will meet your goal?

   ❑   a. Internet Protocol (IP)
   ❑   b. Authentication Header (AH)
   ❑   c. Encapsulation Security Payload (ESP)
   ❑   d. Security (SEC)

Quick Answer: **91**
Detailed Answer: **97**

18. You want to establish a VPN secure tunnel using IPSec. You also desire to have secure authentication and VPN encapsulation. Which of the following components of IPSec will meet your goals?

   ❑   a. RADIUS
   ❑   b. AH
   ❑   c. ESP
   ❑   d. SSH

Quick Answer: **91**
Detailed Answer: **97**

Objective 2.1.8: Vulnerabilities (of Remote Access)

1. Which of the following would most likely pose a dial-up threat?

   ❑   a. Netscape Navigator
   ❑   b. Net use
   ❑   c. L0pht Netcat
   ❑   d. Net send

Quick Answer: **91**
Detailed Answer: **98**

2. Some crackers have taken advantage of modern communication technology. Which of the following remote access methods is likely to be compromised by call forwarding?

   ❑   a. Redial
   ❑   b. Dial out
   ❑   c. Callback
   ❑   d. Call again

Quick Answer: **91**
Detailed Answer: **98**

3. Remote access users may need to communicate with either TCP or UDP. Which of the following are true about these protocols?

- ❑   a.   UDP is connection-oriented and designed for longer messages
- ❑   b.   TCP is connection-oriented and corrects errors
- ❑   c.   TCP does not guarantee delivery, while UDP does
- ❑   d.   UDP guarantees delivery of data

Quick Answer: **91**
Detailed Answer: **98**

4. Rlogin is a remote access tool that uses which one of the following protocols?

- ❑   a.   ICMP
- ❑   b.   TCP
- ❑   c.   UDP
- ❑   d.   SNMP

Quick Answer: **91**
Detailed Answer: **98**

5. Telnet is a remote access tool that uses which one of the following protocols?

- ❑   a.   UDP
- ❑   b.   SNMP
- ❑   c.   TCP
- ❑   d.   ICMP

Quick Answer: **91**
Detailed Answer: **98**

Objective 2.2: Email

1. Which of the following standards applies to email as a message handling protocol?

- ❑   a.   X.800
- ❑   b.   X.509
- ❑   c.   X.500
- ❑   d.   X.400

Quick Answer: **91**
Detailed Answer: **98**

2. When a sender encrypts an email message, what security feature does the message provide?

- ❑   a.   Authenticity
- ❑   b.   Authentication
- ❑   c.   Confidentiality
- ❑   d.   Substantial data

Quick Answer: **91**
Detailed Answer: **98**

3. What does a sender of an email message use to encrypt a message to someone else?

- ❑ a. His private key
- ❑ b. His public key
- ❑ c. The receiver's private key
- ❑ d. The receiver's public key

Objective 2.2.1: S/MIME

1. S/MIME uses which of the following for authentication? (Select all that apply.)

- ❑ a. Username
- ❑ b. Password
- ❑ c. Private key
- ❑ d. Public key

2. Which of the following are appropriate uses for S/MIME? (Select all that apply.)

- ❑ a. Encryption
- ❑ b. Network-Based Intrusion Detection
- ❑ c. Host-Based Intrusion Detection
- ❑ d. Secure email

3. Which of the following is most likely used to digitally sign and encrypt email messages?

- ❑ a. SSL
- ❑ b. S/MIME
- ❑ c. AES
- ❑ d. PGP

4. What does S/MIME stand for?

- ❑ a. Secure Multipurpose Internet Mail Expansion
- ❑ b. Separate Messages in My Email
- ❑ c. Secure Multi Interface Message Extensions
- ❑ d. Separate Mail Internet Extensions

5. Which of the following provides the greatest email security?

- ❑ a. PGP
- ❑ b. S/MIME
- ❑ c. SSL/TLS
- ❑ d. HTTP/S

6. Bill and Mary have been sending encrypted messages for some time. Which of the following methods of encryption have they been using for their email?

Quick Answer: **92**
Detailed Answer: **98**

❏   a. AES
❏   b. SSL
❏   c. DES
❏   d. S/MIME

7. You want to encrypt and digitally sign your email messages. Which of the following meets these requirements?

Quick Answer: **92**
Detailed Answer: **98**

❏   a. SSH
❏   b. S/MIME
❏   c. SSL/TLS
❏   d. IPSec

Objective 2.2.2: PGP

1. Which of the following statements about Pretty Good Privacy (PGP) is *not* correct?

Quick Answer: **92**
Detailed Answer: **98**

❏   a. PGP uses a variation of the public key system
❏   b. PGP is the most widely used program to ensure privacy
❏   c. PGP uses Rivest-Shamir-Adleman (RSA) and Diffie-Hellman
❏   d. PGP works on the physical layer

2. What is the program that gives your email some privacy?

Quick Answer: **92**
Detailed Answer: **98**

❏   a. AGP
❏   b. PGP
❏   c. AH
❏   d. ESP

3. Which of the following is *not* a major encryption method of Pretty Good Privacy (PGP)?

Quick Answer: **92**
Detailed Answer: **98**

❏   a. Carlisle Adams and Stafford Tavares (CAST)
❏   b. International Data Encryption Algorithm (IDEA)
❏   c. Triple Data Encryption Standard (3DES)
❏   d. Secure Hash Algorithm (SHA-1)

4. Pretty Good Privacy (PGP) is available on which of the following platforms? (Select all that apply.)

Quick Answer: **92**
Detailed Answer: **98**

❏   a. DOS
❏   b. Macintosh
❏   c. VMS
❏   d. Unix

5. What kind of encryption does Pretty Good Privacy (PGP) use?

❑ a. Public key encryption

❑ b. XML encryption

❑ c. Session encryption

❑ d. Private key encryption

Quick Answer: **92**
Detailed Answer: **98**

6. Which of the following is an email encryption technology?

❑ a. Wireless

❑ b. ISDN

❑ c. Frame Relay

❑ d. PGP

Quick Answer: **92**
Detailed Answer: **99**

7. What is the standard program for secure email and file encryption on the Internet as created by Philip Zimmerman?

❑ a. CGI

❑ b. Packet sniffing

❑ c. Signed applets

❑ d. PGP

Quick Answer: **92**
Detailed Answer: **99**

8. Which of the following uses passphrases rather than passwords for secure email?

❑ a. SSH

❑ b. SSL

❑ c. PGP

❑ d. IPSec

Quick Answer: **92**
Detailed Answer: **99**

9. Pretty Good Privacy (PGP) products use strong and trusted encryption. How many bits do they use?

❑ a. 32 bits

❑ b. 40 bits

❑ c. 64 bits

❑ d. 128 bits or more

Quick Answer: **92**
Detailed Answer: **99**

10. How large should the Pretty Good Privacy (PGP) public key be to be considered completely secure from direct attacks on the encryption?

❑ a. 512 bits

❑ b. 1,024 bits

❑ c. 2,048 bits

❑ d. 15,554 bits

Quick Answer: **92**
Detailed Answer: **99**

11. Which of the following are related to sending encrypted
email? (Select all that apply.)

Quick Answer: **92**
Detailed Answer: **99**

- ❑ a. Session key
- ❑ b. Public key
- ❑ c. Recipient's private key
- ❑ d. Secret key

Objective 2.2.3: Vulnerabilities (of Email)

1. Which of the following protocols transfers email messages in
clear text and is a concern or vulnerability?

Quick Answer: **92**
Detailed Answer: **99**

- ❑ a. SMTP
- ❑ b. ICMP
- ❑ c. SNMP
- ❑ d. TCP/IP

2. You are the network administrator. What happens when you
restart your email, after deleting a ".*" entry in a relay
domains file?

Quick Answer: **92**
Detailed Answer: **99**

- ❑ a. Your email shuts down
- ❑ b. Your computer shuts down
- ❑ c. You stop forwarding all email
- ❑ d. You prevent relaying of non-explicitly named domains

Objective 2.2.3.1: Spam

1. Your workers are complaining that they are receiving numerous amounts of unsolicited email. What is this called?

Quick Answer: **92**
Detailed Answer: **99**

- ❑ a. Spoofing
- ❑ b. Spam
- ❑ c. Hoax
- ❑ d. Denial of Service

2. Which of the following pay most of the cost for spam activity?
(Select all that apply.)

Quick Answer: **92**
Detailed Answer: **99**

- ❑ a. The recipient
- ❑ b. The carrier
- ❑ c. The sender
- ❑ d. The service provider

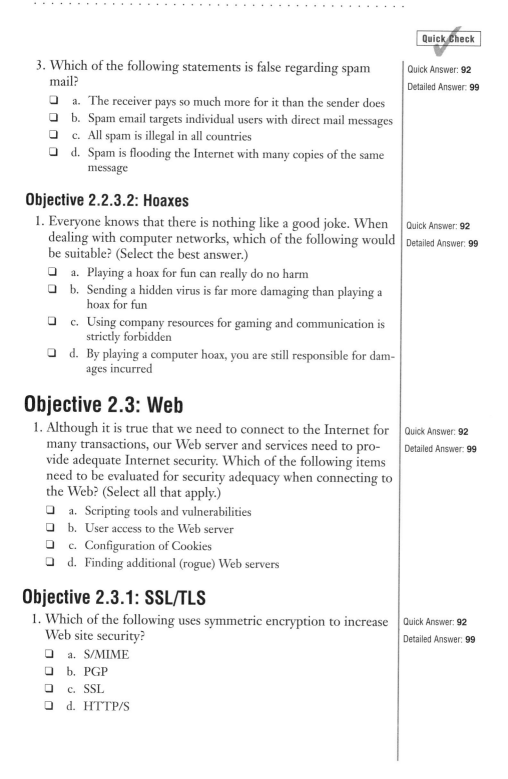

3. Which of the following statements is false regarding spam mail?

Quick Answer: **92**
Detailed Answer: **99**

❑ a. The receiver pays so much more for it than the sender does

❑ b. Spam email targets individual users with direct mail messages

❑ c. All spam is illegal in all countries

❑ d. Spam is flooding the Internet with many copies of the same message

Objective 2.2.3.2: Hoaxes

1. Everyone knows that there is nothing like a good joke. When dealing with computer networks, which of the following would be suitable? (Select the best answer.)

Quick Answer: **92**
Detailed Answer: **99**

❑ a. Playing a hoax for fun can really do no harm

❑ b. Sending a hidden virus is far more damaging than playing a hoax for fun

❑ c. Using company resources for gaming and communication is strictly forbidden

❑ d. By playing a computer hoax, you are still responsible for damages incurred

Objective 2.3: Web

1. Although it is true that we need to connect to the Internet for many transactions, our Web server and services need to provide adequate Internet security. Which of the following items need to be evaluated for security adequacy when connecting to the Web? (Select all that apply.)

Quick Answer: **92**
Detailed Answer: **99**

❑ a. Scripting tools and vulnerabilities

❑ b. User access to the Web server

❑ c. Configuration of Cookies

❑ d. Finding additional (rogue) Web servers

Objective 2.3.1: SSL/TLS

1. Which of the following uses symmetric encryption to increase Web site security?

Quick Answer: **92**
Detailed Answer: **99**

❑ a. S/MIME

❑ b. PGP

❑ c. SSL

❑ d. HTTP/S

2. Your boss wants to establish growth through the use of secure Web commerce. You create a great Web site with all kinds of pictures and special links to equipment that your company sells. Which of the following should you use for security?

- ❑   a. Secure Sockets Layer (SSL)
- ❑   b. Secure Shell (SSH)
- ❑   c. Layer Two Tunneling Protocol (L2TP)
- ❑   d. IP Security (IPSec)

Quick Answer: 92
Detailed Answer: 99

3. Your company hosts a secure Web site and uses Secure Sockets Layer for increased security. When a client attempts to gain access to a secure page on the Web site, which of the following uses a digital certificate to establish an identity to the browser?

- ❑   a. No one, because SSL doesn't use digital certificates
- ❑   b. The server will first use its digital certificate
- ❑   c. The client will first use its digital certificate
- ❑   d. The server and client will perform mutual authentication

Quick Answer: 92
Detailed Answer: 100

4. Many operating systems and Web sites now support Secure Sockets Layer (SSL) for increased security. Which type of encryption does SSL use?

- ❑   a. No encryption
- ❑   b. Public key
- ❑   c. Asymmetric
- ❑   d. Symmetric

Quick Answer: 92
Detailed Answer: 100

5. Which of the following protocols is perfect for secure business commerce on the WWW?

- ❑   a. IP Security (IPSec)
- ❑   b. Secure Sockets Layer (SSL)
- ❑   c. Layer Two Tunneling Protocol (L2TP)
- ❑   d. Secure Shell (SSH)

Quick Answer: 92
Detailed Answer: 100

6. A server that uses Secure Sockets Layer to allow clients to browse secure sites must make a connection to the browser first. What tool does the server use to make the SSL connection?

- ❑   a. A Session Layer Protocol
- ❑   b. A digital certificate
- ❑   c. A challenge and response
- ❑   d. A TCP ACK

Quick Answer: 92
Detailed Answer: 100

7. Which of the following requires six steps to be used between the client and server handshaking process?

   ❑ a. PAP

   ❑ b. CHAP

   ❑ c. MS-CHAP

   ❑ d. SSL

Quick Answer: **92**
Detailed Answer: **100**

8. Which of the following uses six handshaking steps between client and server to increase Web site security?

   ❑ a. S/MIME

   ❑ b. PGP

   ❑ c. SSL

   ❑ d. HTTP/S

Quick Answer: **92**
Detailed Answer: **100**

Objective 2.3.2: HTTP/S

1. Your company is growing. Many departments are grouped with several different types of computers and software, including different browser services. Clients can connect to the Internet and make a secure connection to a Web site, because you have the following protocol installed and running:

   ❑ a. HTTP

   ❑ b. HTTP/S

   ❑ c. SSH

   ❑ d. SSH2

Quick Answer: **92**
Detailed Answer: **100**

2. Which of the following protocols uses port 443 to encrypt traffic from a client's browser to a Web server?

   ❑ a. HTTP/S

   ❑ b. SSH

   ❑ c. LDAP

   ❑ d. IPSec

Quick Answer: **92**
Detailed Answer: **100**

Objective 2.3.3: Instant Messaging

1. Your company does *not* want its users to use Instant Messaging Access Protocol Version 4. Which of the following ports should be closed?

   ❑ a. 23

   ❑ b. 80

   ❑ c. 143

   ❑ d. 3869

Quick Answer: **92**
Detailed Answer: **100**

Objective 2.3.3.1: Vulnerabilities (of Instant Messaging)

1. Because your company is very small and really doesn't have any trade secrets, your boss isn't worried about employees using the Web. However, recently you have been receiving an increase in client complaints: They are receiving files with malicious code attached. Which of the following has these characteristics as a primary vulnerability?

   ❑   a.   HTTP/S
   ❑   b.   IMAP
   ❑   c.   FTP/S
   ❑   d.   TLS

Quick Answer: **92**
Detailed Answer: **100**

2. In today's quest for immediate access to information and communication, Instant Messaging has become very popular at some places of work. Which of the following is a realistic vulnerability of IM?

   ❑   a.   Programmed applications being offered in pop-up screens
   ❑   b.   Advertisements being offered in pop-up screens
   ❑   c.   Spam mail being delivered without request
   ❑   d.   Malicious code being delivered during file transfers

Quick Answer: **92**
Detailed Answer: **100**

3. Which of the following cause the greatest security concern when using Instant Messaging? (Select all that apply.)

   ❑   a.   File transfers
   ❑   b.   Application sharing
   ❑   c.   Network bandwidth
   ❑   d.   Installation time

Quick Answer: **92**
Detailed Answer: **100**

4. Which of the following are causes of concern when using Instant Messaging (IM)? (Select all that apply.)

   ❑   a.   Bandwidth
   ❑   b.   Speed
   ❑   c.   File transfers
   ❑   d.   Application sharing

Quick Answer: **92**
Detailed Answer: **100**

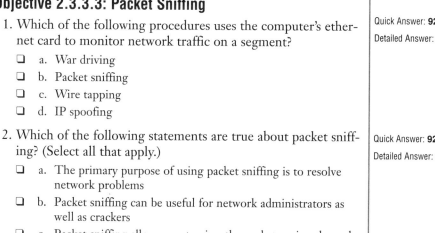

Objective 2.3.3.2: 8.3. Naming Conventions

1. Many older operating systems still use 16-bit applications rather than 32-bit applications. Which naming convention is ideal for 16-bit applications, but degrades the performance of NTFS?

   ❏ a. 3.8 naming convention
   ❏ b. 8.3 naming convention
   ❏ c. 15.3 naming convention
   ❏ d. 16.3 naming convention

Quick Answer: **92**
Detailed Answer: **100**

Objective 2.3.3.3: Packet Sniffing

1. Which of the following procedures uses the computer's ethernet card to monitor network traffic on a segment?

   ❏ a. War driving
   ❏ b. Packet sniffing
   ❏ c. Wire tapping
   ❏ d. IP spoofing

Quick Answer: **92**
Detailed Answer: **101**

2. Which of the following statements are true about packet sniffing? (Select all that apply.)

   ❏ a. The primary purpose of using packet sniffing is to resolve network problems
   ❏ b. Packet sniffing can be useful for network administrators as well as crackers
   ❏ c. Packet sniffing allows you to view the packets going through the network
   ❏ d. A switch is better than a hub in preventing computer data from being sniffed

Quick Answer: **92**
Detailed Answer: **101**

3. Which of the following techniques uses computer ethernet cards to monitor all network traffic on a segment?

   ❏ a. War dialing
   ❏ b. NIC mania
   ❏ c. Packet sniffing
   ❏ d. Wire tapping

Quick Answer: **92**
Detailed Answer: **101**

4. Which of the following statements are true about packet sniffing? (Select all that apply.)

Quick Answer: **92**
Detailed Answer: **101**

- ❑ a. A switch is the best device to prevent data from being sniffed
- ❑ b. The primary use of packet sniffing is to resolve network problems
- ❑ c. Packet sniffing allows visibility of information entering or leaving your computer
- ❑ d. Network Monitor is a packet sniffing hardware device

Objective 2.3.3.4: Privacy

1. One of the greatest concerns for individuals and organizations alike is the right to privacy. With the open use of the Internet, Web site data and exchange of personal information must be protected. Some companies have installed firewalls and audit employee Internet activities, including visited Web sites. Which of the following statements are true regarding such business practices? (Select all that apply.)

Quick Answer: **92**
Detailed Answer: **101**

- ❑ a. This practice is a clear violation of privacy
- ❑ b. This practice should be made public
- ❑ c. This practice should be kept private
- ❑ d. This practice should be made into a policy that is supported by upper management

Objective 2.3.4: Vulnerabilities (of the Web)

1. Your boss wants to host a new secure Web site for the company. What are some of the potential vulnerabilities that you as a network administrator should be concerned about? (Select all that apply.)

Quick Answer: **92**
Detailed Answer: **101**

- ❑ a. Malicious scripting
- ❑ b. Rogue Web servers
- ❑ c. Browser exploits
- ❑ d. Web spoofing

Objective 2.3.4.1: JavaScript

1. One of the vulnerabilities with a Web site is JavaScript, which can potentially inactivate a Web site. Which of the following allows JavaScript to function?

Quick Answer: **92**
Detailed Answer: **101**

- ❑ a. HTML
- ❑ b. ActiveX
- ❑ c. COM+
- ❑ d. HTTP/S

Objective 2.3.4.2: ActiveX

1. When clients want to view embedded objects in HTML documents on a Web site, what control or applet may be used?

   ❑ a. DCOM
   ❑ b. COM+
   ❑ c. SQL
   ❑ d. ActiveX

Quick Answer: **92**
Detailed Answer: **101**

2. You desire to keep your clients informed about your Web site security features. Which of the following can you configure within the security zone parameters?

   ❑ a. ActiveX
   ❑ b. Java
   ❑ c. JavaScript
   ❑ d. Cookies

Quick Answer: **92**
Detailed Answer: **101**

Objective 2.3.4.3: Buffer Overflows

1. You have Netscape clients that are receiving email attack messages containing 256 filename characters. What kind of attack is this?

   ❑ a. A Microsoft mail attack
   ❑ b. A SYN attack
   ❑ c. A teardrop attack
   ❑ d. A buffer overflow attack

Quick Answer: **93**
Detailed Answer: **101**

2. What does the acronym NOP stand for in relation to buffer overflows?

   ❑ a. A decimal value of 90 repeated
   ❑ b. A hexadecimal value of 90 repeated
   ❑ c. An octal value of 90 repeated
   ❑ d. A fractional value of 90 repeated

Quick Answer: **93**
Detailed Answer: **101**

3. What does the term NOP stand for in relation to buffer overflows?

   ❑ a. No Processing
   ❑ b. No Propagation
   ❑ c. Non Operation
   ❑ d. Negative Out Put

Quick Answer: **93**
Detailed Answer: **101**

4. Which of the following could be characteristics of buffer over-flows? (Select the best answer.)

   ❏ a. A packet with a short string of NOPs

   ❏ b. A packet with a short string of NOPs followed by a non-executable command

   ❏ c. A packet with a long string of NOPs

   ❏ d. A packet with a long string of NOPs followed by an executable command

Quick Answer: **93**
Detailed Answer: **101**

Objective 2.3.4.4: Cookies

1. Which of the following statements is *not* true about network cookies?

   ❏ a. Cookies are stored on the users' hard drive

   ❏ b. Cookies can store user logons and passwords

   ❏ c. A user's Web browser can access his or her cookies

   ❏ d. Cookies are too complex to be exploited by hackers

Quick Answer: **93**
Detailed Answer: **101**

2. Which of the following security services do Secure Cookies provide? (Select all that apply.)

   ❏ a. Authentication

   ❏ b. Determination

   ❏ c. Integrity

   ❏ d. Confidentiality

Quick Answer: **93**
Detailed Answer: **101**

3. Which of the following statements describes integrity as provided by Secure Cookies?

   ❏ a. Secure Cookies verifies the cookies' owner

   ❏ b. Secure Cookies store the user's historical visited Web sites

   ❏ c. Secure Cookies protects against the cookie's values being revealed to an unauthorized entity

   ❏ d. Secure Cookies supports dynamic IP addresses or proxy servers and avoids IP spoofing

Quick Answer: **93**
Detailed Answer: **102**

4. Which of following statements refers to cookies? (Select all that apply.)

   ❏ a. A custom Web page sees the users' cookies

   ❏ b. Users can reject cookies

   ❏ c. Cookies are safe from observation

   ❏ d. Cookies show user's unique preferences

Quick Answer: **93**
Detailed Answer: **102**

Objective 2.3.4.5: Signed Applets

1. Which of the following are Web-based vulnerabilities due to Signed Applets? (Select all that apply.)

   ❑   a.   ActiveX
   ❑   b.   Java
   ❑   c.   Java-Man
   ❑   d.   JavaScript

   Quick Answer: **93**
   Detailed Answer: **102**

2. A user uses Internet Explorer or Netscape Navigator to load a Web HTLM document into memory. What is the problem with Signed Applets that execute in this instance?

   ❑   a.   The Java security code is executed first
   ❑   b.   The Java security code is executed last
   ❑   c.   The Java Virtual Machine checks the security code last
   ❑   d.   The Java Virtual Machine does not check all the code

   Quick Answer: **93**
   Detailed Answer: **102**

Objective 2.3.4.6: CGI

1. Poorly written scripts offer crackers an easy access to multiple network components on a Web site. Which of the following scripts would be most vulnerable to a company that has clients accessing distributed files on a server?

   ❑   a.   Programming
   ❑   b.   CGI
   ❑   c.   Server
   ❑   d.   Client

   Quick Answer: **93**
   Detailed Answer: **102**

2. Which of the following uses various scripts that are executed on a distribution server for client access?

   ❑   a.   ActiveS
   ❑   b.   Java
   ❑   c.   CGI
   ❑   d.   Scripting Java

   Quick Answer: **93**
   Detailed Answer: **102**

Objective 2.3.4.7: SMTP Relay

1. Spam is considered unsolicited email. Which of the following allows forwarding of spam through multiple mail servers to multiple clients?

   ❑   a.   SMTP Relay
   ❑   b.   SMTP Forwarding
   ❑   c.   Email Relay
   ❑   d.   Email Forwarding

   Quick Answer: **93**
   Detailed Answer: **102**

Objective 2.4: Directory—Recognition Not Administration

1. Which of the following standards applies to directory services?

    ❏   a.   X.800

    ❏   b.   X.509

    ❏   c.   X.505

    ❏   d.   X.500

Quick Answer: **93**
Detailed Answer: **102**

Objective 2.4.1: SSL/TLS

1. What does SSL stand for?

    ❏   a.   Secure Symmetric Layer

    ❏   b.   Symmetric Single Layer

    ❏   c.   Security Sockets Layer

    ❏   d.   Secure Sockets Layer

Quick Answer: **93**
Detailed Answer: **102**

2. Which of the following protocols was in use before the development of the Transport Layer Security (TLS) protocol, which is now considered the upgrade?

    ❏   a.   Secure Shell (SSH)

    ❏   b.   Secure Sockets Layer (SSL)

    ❏   c.   Point-to-Point Tunneling Protocol (PPTP)

    ❏   d.   Layer Two Firewall (L2F)

Quick Answer: **93**
Detailed Answer: **102**

3. Which of the following protocols functions above the Transport Layer of the OSI model?

    ❏   a.   SSL

    ❏   b.   TCP/IP

    ❏   c.   UPD

    ❏   d.   IPX/SPX

Quick Answer: **93**
Detailed Answer: **102**

4. Which of the following uses symmetric encryption for Web site security?

    ❏   a.   SSL

    ❏   b.   FTP

    ❏   c.   HTTP

    ❏   d.   WWW

Quick Answer: **93**
Detailed Answer: **102**

Objective 2.4.2: LDAP

1. When configuring a network using the Lightweight Directory
   Access Protocol (LDAP) what is the first network computer
   known as?
   - ❑ a. The forest trunk
   - ❑ b. The first tree
   - ❑ c. The primary domain controller
   - ❑ d. The root

Quick Answer: **93**
Detailed Answer: **102**

2. What port must be open for LDAP to work?
   - ❑ a. 139
   - ❑ b. 389
   - ❑ c. 698
   - ❑ d. 1024

Quick Answer: **93**
Detailed Answer: **102**

3. When dealing with an enterprise network, there are several
   security apprehensions. Which of the following items are security concerns when servers are configured to use LDAP?
   (Select all that apply.)
   - ❑ a. Availability
   - ❑ b. Accountability
   - ❑ c. Integrity
   - ❑ d. Confidentiality

Quick Answer: **93**
Detailed Answer: **103**

4. Your company is growing and has many different operating
   systems. You want to encrypt authentication traffic and use
   LDAP. Which of the following is the best choice for this situation?
   - ❑ a. SSL
   - ❑ b. SSH
   - ❑ c. HTTP/S
   - ❑ d. LDAP/S

Quick Answer: **93**
Detailed Answer: **103**

Objective 2.5: File Transfer

1. Which of the following is strictly an Application Layer protocol that offers no security when transferring data?
   - ❑ a. FTP
   - ❑ b. S/FTP
   - ❑ c. FTP/S
   - ❑ d. HTTP

Quick Answer: **93**
Detailed Answer: **103**

2. Which of the following is a component of the TCP/IP suite that uses ports 20 and 21?

  ❏ a. HTTP
  ❏ b. SSH
  ❏ c. SSL
  ❏ d. FTP

Quick Answer: **93**
Detailed Answer: **103**

Objective 2.5.1: S/FTP

1. Which of the following is a valid way to offer security when transferring files or data?

  ❏ a. FTP
  ❏ b. FTP/S
  ❏ c. S/FTP
  ❏ d. Blind FTP

Quick Answer: **93**
Detailed Answer: **103**

Objective 2.5.2: Blind FTP/Anonymous

1. Internet access allows users to download important drivers and other files. How can a user download files from an FTP server without a valid user account on that server?

  ❏ a. Call the server's administrator to set up an account
  ❏ b. Call your network administrator to set up an account
  ❏ c. Call your ISP administrator or use a DNS query to set up an account
  ❏ d. Use the server's anonymous account without setting up a new account

Quick Answer: **93**
Detailed Answer: **103**

2. Which of the following applies to anonymous accounts on FTP servers?

  ❏ a. Crackers can use these accounts to overwrite files
  ❏ b. Anonymous FTP accounts are still very popular
  ❏ c. To increase security, anonymous FTP logins should be allowed
  ❏ d. There is no serious security concern when using anonymous FTP accounts

Quick Answer: **93**
Detailed Answer: **103**

Objective 2.5.3: File Sharing

1. You host an FTP server that clients log on to. To process files quickly, this server is designed to transfer files to other computers for the clients that log on. What is this process also known as?

   ❏   a.   File transferring
   ❏   b.   Proxy server
   ❏   c.   File sharing
   ❏   d.   Exchange server

Quick Answer: **93**
Detailed Answer: **103**

Objective 2.5.4: Vulnerabilities (of File Transfer)

1. Which of the following protocols are concerns because they use clear text passwords? (Select all that apply.)

   ❏   a.   FTP
   ❏   b.   HTTP
   ❏   c.   SSH
   ❏   d.   Telnet

Quick Answer: **93**
Detailed Answer: **103**

2. When transferring data, one of the vulnerabilities is the use of clear text passwords. Which of the following works at the application layer and provides passwords in clear text?

   ❏   a.   FTP
   ❏   b.   HTTP
   ❏   c.   SSH
   ❏   d.   Telnet

Quick Answer: **93**
Detailed Answer: **103**

Objective 2.5.4.1: Packet Sniffing

1. Which of the following is very vulnerable to packet sniffing attacks? (Select all that apply.)

   ❏   a.   Usernames when using FTP
   ❏   b.   Usernames when using SSH
   ❏   c.   Passwords when using HTTPS
   ❏   d.   Passwords when using FTP

Quick Answer: **93**
Detailed Answer: **103**

Objective 2.6: Wireless

1. In a wireless environment, which of the following is designed to identify clients that are attempting to connect to the network?

   ❑ a. WAP
   ❑ b. WEP
   ❑ c. AP
   ❑ d. WLAN

   Quick Answer: **93**
   Detailed Answer: **103**

2. Which of the following items are valid wireless protocols? (Select all that apply.)

   ❑ a. Wireless Transmission Link Protocol (WTLP)
   ❑ b. Wireless Application Protocol (WAP)
   ❑ c. Wireless Equivalent Privacy (WEP)
   ❑ d. Wireless Transport Layer Security (WTLS)

   Quick Answer: **93**
   Detailed Answer: **104**

3. You are considering employing a Wireless Local Area Network (WLAN). When is this a reasonable option? (Select the best answer.)

   ❑ a. After your management has implemented a WLAN security policy
   ❑ b. After you have isolated and secured the WLAN access points
   ❑ c. After you are sure that there are no secrets on the network for others to take
   ❑ d. After you have permission from your supervisor

   Quick Answer: **93**
   Detailed Answer: **104**

Objective 2.6.1: WTLS

1. There are several protocols that support Wireless Application Protocol (WAP). Which of the following provides security support for WAP and behaves like SSL?

   ❑ a. WEP
   ❑ b. WTLS
   ❑ c. WSP
   ❑ d. WTP

   Quick Answer: **93**
   Detailed Answer: **104**

2. What does the acronym WTLS stand for?

   ❑ a. Wireless Transport Layer Security
   ❑ b. Wireless Tunnel Layer Security
   ❑ c. Wired Transport Layer Security
   ❑ d. Wired Tunnel Layer Security

   Quick Answer: **93**
   Detailed Answer: **104**

3. Which of the following uses 35-bit DES encryption and is the security layer of the WAP?

❑ a. AP
❑ b. WEP
❑ c. WAP
❑ d. WTLS

Quick Answer: **93**
Detailed Answer: **104**

Objective 2.6.2: 802.11x

1. The wireless 802.11a standard offers much higher rates of transmission than the 802.11b standard. What is the maximum rate of transmission for the 802.11b wireless connection?

❑ a. 5 Mbps
❑ b. 11 Mbps
❑ c. 16 Mbps
❑ d. 24 Mbps

Quick Answer: **93**
Detailed Answer: **104**

2. Which of the following relates to Frequency Hopping Spread Spectrum (FHSS) and is similar to the 802.11 wireless standard, but uses a greater variety of frequencies within a radio band?

❑ a. WEP
❑ b. Bluetooth
❑ c. WTLS
❑ d. Broadband

Quick Answer: **93**
Detailed Answer: **104**

3. The 802.11b standard uses a frequency range of 2.4 to 2.4835 GHz. What kind of spectrum is this?

❑ a. Direct Sequence Spread Spectrum
❑ b. Indirect Sequence Spread Spectrum
❑ c. Frequency Hopping Spread Spectrum
❑ d. Infrequent Hopping Spread Spectrum

Quick Answer: **93**
Detailed Answer: **104**

4. Which of the following items are *not* required when employing 802.11b wireless networks?

❑ a. A modem
❑ b. A wireless NIC
❑ c. A station
❑ d. An access point

Quick Answer: **93**
Detailed Answer: **104**

5. Which of the following is still the most common standard for wireless networks today?

   ❑ a. 802.3

   ❑ b. 802.11a

   ❑ c. 802.11b

   ❑ d. 802.11g

Quick Answer: **93**
Detailed Answer: **104**

Objective 2.6.3: WEP/WAP

1. What does WEP stand for?

   ❑ a. Web Encryption Protocol

   ❑ b. Wireless Encryption Protocol

   ❑ c. Wired Equivalent Privacy

   ❑ d. Wireless Equivalent Privacy

Quick Answer: **94**
Detailed Answer: **104**

2. Your network administrator has chosen to use a WLAN but wants to prevent eavesdropping and guard against unauthorized access to the network. Which protocol should he use?

   ❑ a. WEP

   ❑ b. WTLS

   ❑ c. WAP

   ❑ d. SSL

Quick Answer: **94**
Detailed Answer: **104**

3. When users log on to an 802.11 standard WLAN where WEP is employed for encryption, what is used for authentication?

   ❑ a. Private keys on the TACACS+ server

   ❑ b. Shared keys on the RRAS server

   ❑ c. Public keys on the RADIUS server

   ❑ d. Shared keys on the access point

Quick Answer: **94**
Detailed Answer: **104**

4. Which of the following protocols is used to provide the same level of security to a Wireless Local Area Network (WLAN) as you would expect of a wired Local Area Network (LAN)?

   ❑ a. WAP

   ❑ b. WEP

   ❑ c. WTLS

   ❑ d. HTTPS

Quick Answer: **94**
Detailed Answer: **104**

5. Which of the following wireless tools makes use of the RC4 algorithm?

   ❑ a. WEP

   ❑ b. WAP

   ❑ c. SSL

   ❑ d. SSH

Quick Answer: **94**
Detailed Answer: **104**

Objective 2.6.3: WAP

1. Which of the following terms and standards relates to WAP?

   ❑ a. Wired Access Point; 802.11
   ❑ b. Wireless Access Point; 802.11b
   ❑ c. Wired Application Protocol; 802.11b
   ❑ d. Wireless Application Protocol; 802.11

Quick Answer: **94**
Detailed Answer: **105**

2. Which of the following devices could make use of WAP?

   ❑ a. Dynamic brouter
   ❑ b. Local bridge
   ❑ c. Mobile phone
   ❑ d. Static router

Quick Answer: **94**
Detailed Answer: **105**

3. Which of the following protocols do clients that possess hand-held digital wireless devices use?

   ❑ a. WEP
   ❑ b. WAP
   ❑ c. WTLS
   ❑ d. IPX/SPX

Quick Answer: **94**
Detailed Answer: **105**

Objective 2.6.4: Vulnerabilities (of Wireless)

1. Wireless networks are vulnerable to home radio frequency (HomeRF) interference and frequency hopping. Which of the following is most vulnerable to such interference?

   ❑ a. 802.3u
   ❑ b. 802.11b
   ❑ c. 802.11g
   ❑ d. 802.11z

Quick Answer: **94**
Detailed Answer: **105**

2. One of your employees reported that a strange fellow in a '98 Chevy was using a laptop computer in the employee parking lot. Apparently, the man was in the same spot when the employee arrived at work and when he went to lunch. What kind of vulnerability could this represent to your wireless network?

   ❑ a. None, because the parking lot is not connected to the network
   ❑ b. PC eavesdropping
   ❑ c. War driving
   ❑ d. AP testing

Quick Answer: **94**
Detailed Answer: **105**

3. Because the WEP RC4 algorithm demonstrates some weaknesses, WLANs are insecure even when using WEP encryption. Which of the following are realistic sources of vulnerability? (Select all that apply.)

- ❏ a. Crackers may use unauthorized mobile stations to gain access to the WLAN
- ❏ b. Crackers may use mathematical or statistical analysis to decrypt wireless traffic
- ❏ c. Crackers may watch users log in to AP from their car windows
- ❏ d. Crackers may fool the access point and obtain valuable data that can be decrypted

Quick Answer: **94**
Detailed Answer: **105**

4. The Initialization Vector (IV) is a weakness that relates to which of the following protocols?

- ❏ a. TCP
- ❏ b. UDP
- ❏ c. WAP
- ❏ d. WEP

Quick Answer: **94**
Detailed Answer: **105**

Objective 2.6.4.1: Site Surveys

1. How can site surveys apply to WLAN technology?

- ❏ a. Site surveys are customer equipment satisfaction surveys at a LAN
- ❏ b. Site surveys are user satisfaction surveys at a local site (WLAN)
- ❏ c. Site surveys may include actions used to identify rogue access points
- ❏ d. Site surveys may include actions used to identify wireless frequencies

Quick Answer: **94**
Detailed Answer: **105**

2. Which of the following would be reasonable tasks used to identify rogue wireless access points? (Select all that apply.)

- ❏ a. Conduct a site survey using NetStumbler
- ❏ b. Conduct a site survey using War dialing
- ❏ c. Conduct a site survey using AiroPeek
- ❏ d. Conduct a site survey using AirSnort

Quick Answer: **94**
Detailed Answer: **105**

Quick Check Answer Key

Objective 2.1: Remote Access

1. a, b, and c.

2. d.

3. b.

Objective 2.1.1: 802.1x

1. a, b, c, and d.

2. d.

Objective 2.1.2: VPN

1. c.

2. c and d.

3. c.

4. d.

5. a, b, and c.

6. a and b.

Objective 2.1.3: RADIUS

1. c.

2. a.

Objective 2.1.4: TACACS/+

1. a.

2. b.

3. b.

Objective 2.1.5: L2TP/PPTP

1. b and c.

2. a and c.

3. c.

4. b.

Objective 2.1.6: SSH

1. b.

2. b.

3. a and c.

4. b.

5. c.

6. d.

7. a.

Objective 2.1.7: IPSec

1. c and d.

2. a and c.

3. a.

4. b.

5. a and c.

6. a.

7. b.

8. a, c, and d.

9. c and d.

10. b.

11. a.

12. c.

13. c.

14. a.

15. c.

16. b.

17. c.

18. c.

Objective 2.1.8: Vulnerabilities (of Remote Access)

1. c.

2. c.

3. b.

4. b.

5. c.

Objective 2.2: Email

1. d.

2. c.

3. d.

Objective 2.2.1: S/MIME

1. c and d.

2. a and d.

3. b.

Quick Check Answer Key

4. a.

5. b.

6. d.

7. b.

Objective 2.2.2. PGP

1. d.

2. b.

3. d.

4. a, b, c, and d.

5. a.

6. d.

7. d.

8. c.

9. d.

10. c.

11. a, b, and c.

Objective 2.2.3. Vulnerabilities (of Email)

1. a.

2. d.

Objective 2.2.3.1: Spam

1. b.

2. a and b.

3. c.

Objective 2.2.3.2: Hoaxes

1. d.

Objective 2.3: Web

1. a, b, c, and d.

Objective 2.3.1: SSL/TLS

1. c.

2. b.

3. b.

4. d.

5. b.

6. b.

7. d.

8. c.

Objective 2.3.2: HTTP/S

1. b.

2. a.

Objective 2.3.3: Instant Messaging

1. c.

Objective 2.3.3.1: Vulnerabilities (of Instant Messaging)

1. b.

2. d.

3. a and b.

4. c and d.

Objective 2.3.3.2: 8.3. Naming Conventions

1. b.

Objective 2.3.3.3: Packet Sniffing

1. b.

2. a, b, c, and d.

3. c.

4. a, b, and c.

Objective 2.3.3.4: Privacy

1. b and d.

Objective 2.3.4: Vulnerabilities (of the Web)

1. a, b, c, and d.

Objective 2.3.4.1: JavaScript

1. a.

Objective 2.3.4.2: ActiveX

1. d.

2. a.

Quick Check Answer Key

Objective 2.3.4.3: Buffer Overflows

1. d.
2. b.
3. c.
4. d.

Objective 2.3.4.4: Cookies

1. d.
2. a, c, and d
3. c.
4. a, b, and d.

Objective 2.3.4.5: Signed Applets

1. a, b, and d.
2. d.

Objective 2.3.4.6: CGI

1. b.
2. c.

Objective 2.3.4.7: SMTP Relay

1. a.

Objective 2.4: Directory— Recognition Not Administration

1. d.

Objective 2.4.1: SSL/TLS

1. d.
2. b.
3. a.
4. a.

Objective 2.4.2: LDAP

1. d.
2. b.
3. a and d.
4. a.

Objective 2.5: File Transfer

1. a.
2. d.

Objective 2.5.1: S/FTP

1. c.

Objective 2.5.2: Blind FTP/Anonymous

1. d.
2. a and b.

Objective 2.5.3: File Sharing

1. c.

Objective 2.5.4: Vulnerabilities (of File Transfer)

1. a, b, and d.
2. a.

Objective 2.5.4.1: Packet Sniffing

1. a and d.

Objective 2.6: Wireless

1. c.
2. b and d.
3. c.

Objective 2.6.1: WTLS

1. b.
2. a.
3. d.

Objective 2.6.2: 802.11x

1. b.
2. b.
3. a.
4. a.
5. c.

Quick Check Answer Key

Objective 2.6.3: WEP/WAP

1. c.

2. a.

3. d.

4. b.

5. a.

Objective 2.6.3: WAP

1. d.

2. c.

3. b.

Objective 2.6.4: Vulnerabilities (of Wireless)

1. b.

2. c.

3. a, b, and d.

4. d.

Objective 2.6.4.1: Site Surveys

1. c.

2. a and c.

Answers and Explanations

Objective 2.1: Remote Access

1. **a, b, and c.** Restricted Address, Callback, and Caller ID are some valid methods to apply security when using remote access.

2. **d.** Callback is a method to provide access protection by calling back the number of a previously authorized location.

3. **b.** Callback is a centralized access control method for remote users.

Objective 2.1.1: 802.1x

1. **a, b, c, and d.** The IEEE 802.1x standard for remote access is concerned with Authentication for remote access to a centralized LAN, including RADIUS server connection, SNMP, and encapsulation of EAP.

2. **d.** The IEEE 802.1x standard for remote access EAP.

Objective 2.1.2: VPN

1. **c.** IPSec is also used in conjunction with VPN.

2. **c and d.** IPSec and L2TP protocols offer a secure solution for Virtual Private Network (VPN).

3. **c.** IPSec, combined with L2TP, offers a secure solution for VPN.

4. **d.** L2TP, combined with IPSec, offers a secure solution for VPN.

5. **a, b, and c.** PPTP, L2F, and L2FP are tunneling protocols used for VPN remote computing. TCP stands for Transmission Control Protocol, a connection-oriented protocol used on the Internet.

6. **a and b.** PPTP, L2F, and L2FP are tunneling protocols used for VPN remote computing. UDP and TCP are other protocols.

Objective 2.1.3: RADIUS

1. **c.** Remote Access Dial-In User Service (RADIUS) is a remote authentication method that provides a central server for all remote network access. Be aware that TACACS/+ uses TCP and RADIUS uses UDP.

2. **a.** Remote Access Dial-In User Service (RADIUS) is a remote authentication method that provides a central server for all remote network access, but provides less security than TACACS.

Objective 2.1.4: TACACS/+

1. **a.** CISCO improved on TACACS to make TACACS+, which is better than RADIUS.

2. **b.** Cisco's Terminal Access Controller Access Control System (TACACS+) enables a user to change passwords, enables two-factor authentication, and uses and resynchronizes security tokens.

3. **b.** The Terminal Access Controller Access Control System (TACACS) uses a user ID and static password for remote access.

Objective 2.1.5. L2TP/PPTP

1. **b and c.** L2TP and PPTP directly support VPN.

2. **a and c.** L2TP and IPSec protocols are used frequently together to offer authentication and encryption.

3. **c.** PPTP uses Transmission Control Protocol (TCP) port 1723. Notice that there are three "Ps" in PPTP.

4. **b.** L2TP uses Transmission Control Protocol (TCP) port 1721. Notice that there is only one "P" in L2TP.

Objective 2.1.6. SSH

1. **b.** Secure Shell (SSH) uses Transmission Control Protocol (TCP) on port 22.

2. **b.** Secure Shell (SSH) uses Transmission Control Protocol (TCP) on port 22.

3. **a and c.** SSH listens on port 22. It encapsulates FTP authentication sessions and Telnet sessions.

4. **b.** SSH is the specific protocol used to secure data transmissions between two sites, even if the network is not secure.

5. **c.** SSH is the protocol used to secure data transmissions between two sites, even if the network is not secure.

6. **d.** RSA offers a digital certificate exchange for clients using SSH for authentication.

7. **a.** SSH is the protocol that should be used to provide secure remote login when communicating over an insecure network.

Objective 2.1.7. IPSec

1. **c and d.** The routers at both locations need IPSec tunnel configuration if secure connections are needed over a public network.

2. **a and c.** IPSec offers data integrity and data confidentiality.

3. **a.** IPSec achieves data integrity by use of an Authentication Header (AH).

4. **b.** IPSec achieves data confidentiality by use of an Encapsulation Security Payload (ESP).

5. **a and c.** L2TP and IPSec protocols are used frequently together to offer authentication and encryption.

6. **a.** IPSec uses a 40-bit DES algorithm.

7. **b.** IPSec is used to authenticate and encrypt. IPSec grants Diffie-Hellman authentication and 40-bit DES encryption.

8. **a, c, and d.** IPSec has the following benefits: Authentication, Non-Repudiation, and Privacy.

9. **c and d.** IPSec uses Authentication Header (AH) for IP source authentication and Encrypted Security Payload (ESP) for confidentiality.

10. **b.** IPSec is a standard that is used to encrypt private data so that it can move securely through the public Internet.

11. **a.** Only the data is encrypted when IPSec is in Transport mode.

12. **c.** Both the data and IP headers are encrypted when IPSec is in Tunnel mode.

13. **c.** Transport mode is used to establish a VPN connection from one computer to another using IPSec.

14. **a.** Tunnel mode is used to establish a VPN connection from one computer to a router, or router to router, or router to groups when using IPSec.

15. **c.** A router at each location should be configured to use IPSec in Tunnel mode.

16. **b.** The Authentication Header (AH) is a component of IPSec that ensures data integrity.

17. **c.** The Encapsulation Security Payload (ESP) is a component of IPSec that ensures data confidentiality.

18. **c.** The Encapsulation Security Payload (ESP) is a component of IPSec that ensures data confidentiality through secure tunneling, VPN encapsulation, and secure authentication.

Objective 2.1.8: Vulnerabilities (of Remote Access)

1. **c.** L0pht Netcat, which is used for penetration, could pose a dial-up threat to remote access.

2. **c.** Callback is likely to be compromised by call forwarding. This is a known weakness of callback systems.

3. **b.** TCP is a connection-oriented transport for guaranteed delivery of data. UDP (nicknamed: Unreliable Datagram Protocol) does not offer error correction, but is useful for shorter messages.

4. **b.** Rlogin uses TCP.

5. **c.** Telnet uses TCP.

Objective 2.2: Email

1. **d.** The X.400 standard applies to email as a message handling protocol.

2. **c.** The encrypted message provides confidentiality.

3. **d.** The receiver's public key is used to encrypt an email message.

Objective 2.2.1: S/MIME

1. **c and d.** S/MIME uses a Private key and a Public key for authentication.

2. **a and d.** Encryption and secure email are appropriate uses for S/MIME.

3. **b.** S/MIME is used to digitally sign and encrypt email messages.

4. **a.** S/MIME stands for Secure Multipurpose Internet Mail Expansion.

5. **b.** S/MIME provides the greatest email security.

6. **d.** S/MIME provides email security using encryption.

7. **b.** A major benefit of S/MIME is the ability to encrypt and digitally sign email messages.

Objective 2.2.2: PGP

1. **d.** Pretty Good Privacy (PGP) works at the Application Layer.

2. **b.** Pretty Good Privacy (PGP) is the program that gives your electronic mail some privacy.

3. **d.** Secure Hash Algorithm is *not* a major encryption method of PGP.

4. **a, b, c, and d.** All listed platforms have been ported to PGP.

5. **a.** PGP uses "public key" encryption.

6. **d.** Pretty Good Privacy is an email encryption technology.

7. **d.** Pretty Good Privacy (PGP) is the standard program for secure email and file encryption on the Internet.

8. **c.** Pretty Good Privacy (PGP) uses passphrases rather than passwords for secure email.

9. **d.** PGP uses 128 bits or more with a symmetrical crypto key.

10. **c.** The Pretty Good Privacy (PGP) public key should be 2,048 bits to be considered completely secure from direct attacks on the encryption.

11. **a, b, and c.** First we encrypt plaintext with the session key; then, the session key is encrypted with a public key. We then decrypt an encrypted message using a recipient's private key.

Objective 2.2.3: Vulnerabilities (of Email)

1. **a.** Simple Mail Transport Protocol transfers or relays email messages in clear text.

2. **d.** After deleting a ".*" entry in a relay domains file, you prevent relaying of nonexplicitly named domains.

Objective 2.2.3.1: Spam

1. **b.** Spam is the term for unsolicited email.

2. **a and b.** Spam costs the sender very little to transmit. Most of the costs are paid for by the recipient or the carriers rather than by the sender.

3. **c.** Spam is *not* illegal in all countries.

Objective 2.2.3.2: Hoaxes

1. **d.** By playing a computer hoax, you are still responsible for damages incurred. A hoax can be as lethal as a virus.

Objective 2.3: Web

1. **a, b, c, and d.** All of these items and more need to be evaluated for security adequacy when connecting to the Web.

Objective 2.3.1: SSL/TLS

1. **c.** SSL stands for Secure Sockets Layer, used to increase Web site security by symmetric encryption.

2. **b.** SSL is ideal for secure business commerce on the WWW.

3. **b.** The server will first use its digital certificate. SSL stands for Secure Sockets Layer, used to increase Web site security by symmetric encryption.

4. **d.** Secure Sockets Layer (SSL) supports symmetric encryption. Note that SSL and symmetric both start with "S".

5. **b.** SSL is the perfect choice for secure business commerce on the WWW.

6. **b.** The server uses a digital certificate to make the SSL connection.

7. **d.** SSL requires six steps to be used between the client and server handshaking process.

8. **c.** SSL stands for Secure Sockets Layer, used to increase Web site security by symmetric encryption and uses six handshaking steps.

Objective 2.3.2: HTTP/S

1. **b.** HTTP/S is used to make a secure connection to a Website, regardless of the type of browser the user is running.

2. **a.** HTTP/S uses port 443 to encrypt traffic from a client's browser to a Web server.

Objective 2.3.3: Instant Messaging

1. **c.** Port 143 deals with IMAP4.

Objective 2.3.3.1: Vulnerabilities (of Instant Messaging)

1. **b.** Instant Messaging is very vulnerable to files with malicious code attached.

2. **d.** Delivery of malicious code through file transfers is a realistic vulnerability of IM.

3. **a and b.** File transfers and application sharing cause the greatest security concern when using Instant Messaging.

4. **c and d.** File transfers and application sharing are causes of concern when using Instant Messaging (IM).

Objective 2.3.3.2: 8.3 Naming Conventions

1. **b.** The 8.3 naming convention is ideal for 16-bit applications, but degrades the performance of NTFS.

Objective 2.3.3.3: Packet Sniffing

1. **b.** Packet sniffing uses the computer's Ethernet card to monitor network traffic on a segment.

2. **a, b, c, and d.** All the listed statements are true for packet sniffing.

3. **c.** Packet sniffing uses computer ethernet cards to monitor all network traffic on a segment.

4. **a, b, and c.** Network Monitor is a packet sniffing software device. All other statements are true.

Objective 2.3.3.4: Privacy

1. **b and d.** Before auditing employee Internet activities, employees have the right to be informed and a policy needs to have the written support of upper management.

Objective 2.3.4: Vulnerabilities (of the Web)

1. **a, b, c, and d.** All the items listed should be considered when hosting a secure Web site.

Objective 2.3.4.1: JavaScript

1. **a.** JavaScript usually is part of an HTML document.

Objective 2.3.4.2: ActiveX

1. **d.** ActiveX allows clients to view embedded objects in HTML documents on a Web site.

2. **a.** You can configure ActiveX parameters to keep clients informed.

Objective 2.3.4.3: Buffer Overflows

1. **d.** A buffer attack could be the cause of this situation.

2. **b.** A repeated hexadecimal value of 90 creates a "non operation" (NOP).

3. **c.** A repeated hexadecimal value of 90 creates a "non operation" (NOP).

4. **d.** A packet with a long string of NOPs followed by an executable command is an example of a buffer overflow.

Objective 2.3.4.4: Cookies

1. **d.** Cookies are easily exploited by hackers.

2. **a, c, and d.** Secure Cookies provide authentication, integrity, and confidentiality.

3. **c.** Secure Cookies protects against the cookie's values being revealed to an unauthorized entity.

4. **a, b, and d.** A custom Web page sees the users' cookies, which show user's unique preferences. Users can reject cookies.

Objective 2.3.4.5: Signed Applets

1. **a, b, and d.** ActiveX, Java, and JavaScript are Web-based vulnerabilities due to signed applets.

2. **d.** The Java Virtual Machine does not check all the code.

Objective 2.3.4.6: CGI

1. **b.** Poorly written CGI scripts are a serious vulnerability to Web sites.

2. **c.** CGI uses various scripts that are executed on a distribution server for client access.

Objective 2.3.4.7: SMTP Relay

1. **a.** SMTP Relay allows forwarding of spam through multiple mail servers to multiple clients.

Objective 2.4: Directory—Recognition Not Administration

1. **d.** X.500 applies to directory services.

Objective 2.4.1: SSL/TLS

1. **d.** SSL stands for Secure Sockets Layer, used to increase Web site security by symmetric encryption.

2. **b.** Transport Layer Security (TLS) protocol is an upgrade of SSL. However, TLS and SSL are not compatible with each other.

3. **a.** SSL functions above the Transport Layer of the OSI model.

4. **a.** Secure Sockets Layer (SSL) uses symmetric encryption for Web site security.

Objective 2.4.2: LDAP

1. **d.** When configuring a network using the Lightweight Directory Access Protocol (LDAP) the first network computer stores the root.

2. **b.** Port 389 must be open for LDAP to work.

3. **a and d.** Availability and confidentiality are security concerns when servers use LDAP.

4. **a.** SSL can be used to encrypt authentication traffic and can be used with LDAP.

Objective 2.5: File Transfer

1. **a.** FTP is an Application Layer protocol that offers no security when transferring data.

2. **d.** FTP is a component of the TCP/IP suite that uses ports 20 and 21.

Objective 2.5.1: S/FTP

1. **c.** S/FTP is a valid way to offer security when transferring files or data, because it is very similar to SSH.

Objective 2.5.2: Blind FTP/Anonymous

1. **d.** Many FTP servers still use blind FTP or anonymous accounts to allow unknown users access.

2. **a and b.** Although anonymous FTP accounts are still very popular, crackers can use these accounts to overwrite files.

Objective 2.5.3: File Sharing

1. **c.** File sharing is a security concern and feature of the FTP server.

Objective 2.5.4: Vulnerabilities (of File Transfer)

1. **a, b, and d.** FTP, HTTP, and Telnet are security concerns because they use clear text passwords.

2. **a.** FTP works at the application layer and provides passwords in clear text.

Objective 2.5.4.1 Packet Sniffing

1. **a and d.** Usernames and passwords are very vulnerable to packet sniffing attacks when using FTP.

Objective 2.6: Wireless

1. **c.** In a wireless network, AP stands for access point; WAP stands for Wireless Application Protocol; WEP stands for Wired Equivalent Privacy; and WLAN stands for Wireless Local Area Network.

2. **b and d**. Wireless Application Protocol (WAP), note "Wired" Equivalent Privacy (WEP), and Wireless Transport Layer Security (WTLS) are valid wireless protocols.

3. **c**. You only want to consider using a wireless network after you are sure that there are no secrets on the network for others to take.

Objective 2.6.1: WTLS

1. **b**. Wireless Transport Layer Security Protocol provides security support for WAP and behaves like SSL.

2. **a**. Wireless Transport Layer Security is the meaning of WTLS.

3. **d**. Wireless Transport Layer Security (WTLS) uses 35-bit DES encryption and is the security layer of the WAP.

Objective 2.6.2: 802.11x

1. **b**. The 802.11b wireless connection transmits at a maximum of 11 Mbps.

2. **b**. Bluetooth is similar to the 802.11 wireless standard, but has less bandwidth and less range.

3. **a**. The 802.11b standard uses Direct Sequence Spread Spectrum (DSSS) at a frequency range of 2.4 to 2.4835 GHz.

4. **a**. A modem is not required for a WLAN or 802.11b Wireless network.

5. **c**. The 802.11b standard is still the most common standard for wireless networks today.

Objective 2.6.3: WEP/WAP

1. **c**. WEP stands for Wired Equivalent Privacy, which is used in wireless LANs (WLANs) for encryption and authentication.

2. **a**. The Wired Equivalent Privacy (WEP) protocol prevents eavesdropping and guards against unauthorized access through shared-key authentication.

3. **d**. WEP uses shared keys on the access point or on clients to provide authentication in a WLAN.

4. **b**. The Wired Equivalent Privacy (WEP) protocol provides security for a WLAN.

5. **a**. Wired Equivalent Privacy (WEP) protocol makes use of the RC4 algorithm.

Objective 2.6.3: WAP

1. **d.** WAP stands for Wireless Application Protocol and relates to the 802.11 standard.

2. **c.** The Wireless Application Protocol (WAP) is used for wireless devices like a Mobile Phone.

3. **b.** Clients that possess handheld digital wireless devices use Wireless Application Protocol (WAP).

Objective 2.6.4: Vulnerabilities (of Wireless)

1. **b.** 802.11b is most vulnerable to such interference.

2. **c.** This is an example of war driving.

3. **a, b, and d.** Crackers may use unauthorized mobile stations to gain access to the WLAN, use mathematical or statistical analysis to decrypt wireless traffic or may fool the access point and obtain valuable data that can be decrypted.

4. **d.** The Initialization Vector (IV) is a weakness that relates to WEP.

Objective 2.6.4.1: Site Surveys

1. **c.** Site surveys may include actions taken to identify rogue access points on a WLAN.

2. **a and c.** Conduct a site survey using AiroPeek and NetStumbler.

Infrastructure Security

Objective 3.1: Devices

1. Your company has a large internal network that you would like to subnet into smaller parts. Which of the following devices can you use to separate your LAN and still protect critical resources? (Select all that apply.)

   ❏ a. An internal firewall
   ❏ b. A router between subnets
   ❏ c. A modem between computers
   ❏ d. A switch between departments

Quick Answer: **136**
Detailed Answer: **140**

2. Which of the following are considered to be possible components of an ethernet LAN? (Select all that apply.)

   ❏ a. Access Point (AP)
   ❏ b. Coax
   ❏ c. Fiber
   ❏ d. STP

Quick Answer: **136**
Detailed Answer: **140**

3. Which of the following devices is specially designed to forward packets to specific ports based on the packet's address?

   ❏ a. Specialty hub
   ❏ b. Switching hub
   ❏ c. Port hub
   ❏ d. Filtering hub

Quick Answer: **136**
Detailed Answer: **140**

Objective 3.1.1: Firewalls

1. Your company receives Internet access through a network or gateway server. Which of the following devices is best suited to protect resources and subnet your LAN directly on the network server?

   ❏ a. DSL modem
   ❏ b. A multi-homed firewall
   ❏ c. VLAN
   ❏ d. A brouter that acts both as a bridge and a router

Quick Answer: **136**
Detailed Answer: **140**

2. What are some of the benefits of using a firewall for your LAN? (Select all that apply.)

Quick Answer: **136**
Detailed Answer: **140**

- ❑   a.   Increased access to Instant Messaging
- ❑   b.   Stricter access control to critical resources
- ❑   c.   Greater security to your LAN
- ❑   d.   Less expensive than NAT servers

3. Which of the following are true about firewalls? (Select all that apply.)

Quick Answer: **136**
Detailed Answer: **140**

- ❑   a.   Filters network traffic
- ❑   b.   Can be either a hardware or software device
- ❑   c.   Follows a set of rules
- ❑   d.   Can be configured to drop packets

4. Which of the following are true about firewall protection when using static packet filtering on the router? (Select all that apply.)

Quick Answer: **136**
Detailed Answer: **140**

- ❑   a.   Static packet filtering is less secure than stateful filtering
- ❑   b.   Static packet filtering is less secure than proxy filtering
- ❑   c.   Static packet filtering is more secure than dynamic packet filtering
- ❑   d.   Static packet filtering is more secure than stateful filtering

5. A packet filtering firewall operates at which of the following OSI layers? (Select all that apply.)

Quick Answer: **136**
Detailed Answer: **140**

- ❑   a.   At the Application layer
- ❑   b.   At the Transport layer
- ❑   c.   At the Network layer
- ❑   d.   At the Gateway layer

6. Firewalls are designed to perform all the following except:

Quick Answer: **136**
Detailed Answer: **140**

- ❑   a.   Limiting security exposures
- ❑   b.   Logging Internet activity
- ❑   c.   Enforcing the organization's security policy
- ❑   d.   Protecting against viruses

7. Stateful firewalls may filter connection-oriented packets that are potential intrusions to the LAN. Which of the following types of packets can a stateful packet filter deny?

Quick Answer: **136**
Detailed Answer: **140**

- ❑   a.   UDP
- ❑   b.   TCP
- ❑   c.   IP
- ❑   d.   ICMP

8. Which of the following systems run an application layer firewall using Proxy software?

❑ a. Proxy NAT

❑ b. Proxy client

❑ c. Client 32

❑ d. Proxy server

9. Which of the following use routers with packet filtering rules to allow or deny access based on source address, destination address, or port number?

❑ a. Application layer firewall

❑ b. Packet filtering firewall

❑ c. Router enhanced firewall

❑ d. IP enabled firewall

10. Which of the following firewalls keeps track of the connection state?

❑ a. Application layer firewall

❑ b. Packet filtering firewall

❑ c. Router enhanced firewall

❑ d. Stateful packet filtering firewall

Objective 3.1.2: Routers

1. Which of following devices discriminates between multicast and unicast packets?

❑ a. Multicast switch

❑ b. Bicast switch

❑ c. Bicast router

❑ d. Multicast router

2. Your primary concern is LAN security. You want to subnet your internal network with a device that provides security and stability. Which of the following devices do you choose to meet these needs?

❑ a. Static router

❑ b. Dynamic router

❑ c. Static switch

❑ d. Dynamic switch

3. Which of the following will help you to improve your LAN security? (Select all that apply.)

□ a. Change user passwords frequently

□ b. Install a firewall program

□ c. Use a dynamic rather than static router

□ d. Use a proxy

Quick Answer: **136**
Detailed Answer: **140**

4. Which of the following is the most difficult to configure, but safest device to use on a LAN?

□ a. Static router

□ b. IP enabled router

□ c. Dynamic router

□ d. RIP enabled router

Quick Answer: **136**
Detailed Answer: **140**

5. Which of the following statements are true about routers and bridges? (Select all that apply.)

□ a. Bridges connect two networks at the Data Link Layer

□ b. Bridges are types of inexpensive routers

□ c. Routers are improved bridges

□ d. Routers connect two networks at the Network Layer

Quick Answer: **136**
Detailed Answer: **141**

6. Remember, routers work at the Network Layer of the International Standards Organization/Open Systems Interconnection (ISO/OSI) established sequence of OSI Layers. What is the correct and complete OSI sequence in order from user interface (Layer 7) to the delivery of binary bits (Layer 1)?

□ a. Physical Layer, Network Layer, Data Link Layer, Transport Layer, Session Layer, Presentation Layer, Application Layer

□ b. Application Layer, Presentation Layer, Session Layer, Transport Layer, Network Layer, Data Link Layer, Physical Layer

□ c. Application Layer, Physical Layer, Session Layer, Transport Layer, Network Layer, Data Link Layer, Presentation Layer

□ d. Physical Layer, Data Link Layer, Network Layer, Session Layer, Transport Layer, Presentation Layer, Application Layer

Quick Answer: **136**
Detailed Answer: **141**

7. Most networks employ devices for routing services. Routers work at which of the following OSI layers?

□ a. Transport

□ b. Network

□ c. Presentation

□ d. Session

Quick Answer: **136**
Detailed Answer: **141**

Objective 3.1.3: Switches

1. You manage a company network and the network budget. You want to minimize costs, but desire to prevent crackers from sniffing your local network (LAN). Which of the following devices would you recommend to meet your goals?

   - ❏ a. Hub
   - ❏ b. Switch
   - ❏ c. Router
   - ❏ d. Firewall

   Quick Answer: **136**
   Detailed Answer: **141**

2. Which of the following statements apply to security concerns when using a switch in the LAN? (Select all that apply.)

   - ❏ a. Switches use SSH to manage interfaces by default
   - ❏ b. Switches use Telnet or HTTP to manage interfaces
   - ❏ c. Switches are more secure than routers since they are internal to the LAN
   - ❏ d. Switches should be placed behind a dedicated firewall

   Quick Answer: **136**
   Detailed Answer: **141**

3. Which of following is a type of hub that forwards packets to an appropriate port based on the packet's address?

   - ❏ a. Smart hub
   - ❏ b. Switching hub
   - ❏ c. Routing hub
   - ❏ d. Porting hub

   Quick Answer: **136**
   Detailed Answer: **141**

Objective 3.1.4: Wireless

1. Which of the following is actually considered a critical wireless device?

   - ❏ a. AP
   - ❏ b. WAP
   - ❏ c. WEP
   - ❏ d. WLAN

   Quick Answer: **136**
   Detailed Answer: **141**

Objective 3.1.5: Modems

1. Which of the following are true statements about modems? (Select all that apply.)

   - ❏ a. Modems use the telephone lines
   - ❏ b. Modem stands for modulator and demodulator
   - ❏ c. Modems are no longer used in secure networks
   - ❏ d. A modem's fastest transfer rate is 56 Kbps

   Quick Answer: **136**
   Detailed Answer: **141**

2. Modems can be configured to automatically answer any incoming call. Many user computers have modems installed from the manufacturer. What is the greatest security risk when dealing with modems in this situation?

    ❑ a. Remote access without network administrator knowledge

    ❑ b. Local access without network administrator knowledge

    ❑ c. Client access without network administrator knowledge

    ❑ d. Server access without network administrator knowledge

Quick Answer: **136**
Detailed Answer: **141**

Objective 3.1.6: RAS

1. Which of the following terms defines RAS?

    ❑ a. Random Access Security

    ❑ b. Remote Access Security

    ❑ c. Random Access Service

    ❑ d. Remote Access Service

Quick Answer: **136**
Detailed Answer: **141**

2. Usually, a RAS connection is a dial-up connection. What network connections also apply to RAS? (Select all that apply.)

    ❑ a. Client–Server

    ❑ b. ISDN

    ❑ c. VPN

    ❑ d. DSL

Quick Answer: **136**
Detailed Answer: **141**

Objective 3.1.7: Telecom/PBX

1. Your company has gone through several phone company changes to reduce costs. Last week, two new phone company employees indicated that they needed remote access to your company network and wanted to establish a permanent guest account on your RAS server for continued maintenance support. Which of the following actions are your best recommendations for this situation? (Select all that apply.)

    ❑ a. Agree with their requests so that maintenance costs are reduced

    ❑ b. Recommend that user accounts be verified with strong authentication

    ❑ c. Remove the guest account and create verifiable remote accounts

    ❑ d. Create a phone company group account and place that inside the guest account

Quick Answer: **136**
Detailed Answer: **141**

2. Which of the following applies to PBX? (Select all that apply.)
- ❑ a. PBX stands for Private Branch Exchange
- ❑ b. PBX allows for analog, digital, and data to transfer over a high-speed phone system
- ❑ c. PBX stands for Public Broadcasting Exchange
- ❑ d. PBX is used to carry analog messages and modem communication originating at the phone company

Quick Answer: **136**
Detailed Answer: **141**

Objective 3.1.8: VPN

1. You want to have a private communication between two sites that also allows for encryption and authorization. Which of the following is the best choice in this instance?
- ❑ a. Modem
- ❑ b. Firewall
- ❑ c. VPN
- ❑ d. Bastion Host

Quick Answer: **136**
Detailed Answer: **142**

2. VPN tunnels have end points. Which of the following methods is used to offer Strong Authentication at each end point?
- ❑ a. DES
- ❑ b. Block cipher
- ❑ c. Stream cipher
- ❑ d. Diffie-Hellman

Quick Answer: **136**
Detailed Answer: **142**

3. VPNs transfer encrypted data through tunneling technology. Which of the following performs fast data encryption and may be used with VPNs?
- ❑ a. Stream cipher
- ❑ b. RSA
- ❑ c. DES
- ❑ d. IPSec

Quick Answer: **136**
Detailed Answer: **142**

4. You desire to secure a VPN connection. Which protocols should you use? (Select all that apply.)
- ❑ a. TLS
- ❑ b. IPSec
- ❑ c. SSL
- ❑ d. L2TP

Quick Answer: **136**
Detailed Answer: **142**

Objective 3.1.9: IDS

1. What does the acronym IDS stand for?

   ❑   a. Intrusion Detection System

   ❑   b. Internet Detection Standard

   ❑   c. Internet Detection System

   ❑   d. Intrusion Detection Standard

Quick Answer: **136**
Detailed Answer: **142**

2. Which of the following devices is used to monitor network traffic, including DoS attacks in real time?

   ❑   a. A host-based Intrusion Detection System

   ❑   b. A network-based Intrusion Detection System

   ❑   c. A router-based Intrusion Detection System

   ❑   d. A server-based Intrusion Detection System

Quick Answer: **136**
Detailed Answer: **142**

3. Which of the following security devices acts more like a detective rather than a preventative measure?

   ❑   a. IDS

   ❑   b. DMZ

   ❑   c. NAT

   ❑   d. Proxy

Quick Answer: **136**
Detailed Answer: **142**

Objective 3.1.10: Network Monitoring/Diagnostic

1. Which of the following protocols is used to monitor network devices such as hubs, switches, and routers?

   ❑   a. SMTP

   ❑   b. SNMP

   ❑   c. RIP

   ❑   d. OSPF

Quick Answer: **136**
Detailed Answer: **142**

2. You have been using a network monitor or protocol analyzer to monitor ethernet packets. One of the messages sent has an IP header protocol field value of "1". What does this value classify?

   ❑   a. UDP

   ❑   b. ICMP

   ❑   c. IGMP

   ❑   d. TCP

Quick Answer: **136**
Detailed Answer: **142**

3. You have been using a network monitor or protocol analyzer to monitor ethernet packets. One of the messages sent has an IP header protocol field value of "6". What does this value classify?

❑   a. UDP
❑   b. ICMP
❑   c. IGMP
❑   d. TCP

Objective 3.1.11: Workstations

1. Which of the following LAN devices is frequently a source of security concern because of its ability to process applications, share files, and perform network services in a peer-to-peer network?

❑   a. SQL Servers
❑   b. Routers
❑   c. Switches
❑   d. Workstations

2. You want to prevent users from downloading software on company workstations. What is this called?

❑   a. Desktop lookup
❑   b. Desktop lockup
❑   c. Desktop lockdown
❑   d. Desktop lookdown

Objective 3.1.12: Servers

1. Which of the following is a group of independent servers that are grouped together to appear like one server?

❑   a. Proxy Server
❑   b. SQL Server
❑   c. Server Array
❑   d. Server Cluster

2. Which of the following devices have similar security concerns because they provide file sharing, network connection, and application services? (Select all that apply.)

❑   a. Switches
❑   b. Routers
❑   c. Workstations
❑   d. Servers

3.1.13. Mobile Devices

1. Many mobile devices use wireless technology and may lack security. Which of the following devices are considered mobile devices used to connect to a network? (Select all the apply.)

   ❏ a. PDR

   ❏ b. PDA

   ❏ c. Pager

   ❏ d. PPP

Quick Answer: **136**
Detailed Answer: **143**

2. Which one of the following is a small network device that is a security concern for network administrators because the device is easily misplaced?

   ❏ a. Workstation

   ❏ b. Server

   ❏ c. Mobile device

   ❏ d. VPN

Quick Answer: **136**
Detailed Answer: **143**

Objective 3.2: Media

1. Which of the following are types of network cabling? (Select all that apply.)

   ❏ a. Twisted pair

   ❏ b. Token ring

   ❏ c. Fiber optic

   ❏ d. Coaxial

Quick Answer: **137**
Detailed Answer: **143**

2. For which one of the following situations would a crossover cable be effective?

   ❏ a. Between a modem and a computer

   ❏ b. Between a hub and a computer

   ❏ c. Between two computers

   ❏ d. Between a switch and a router

Quick Answer: **137**
Detailed Answer: **143**

3. What does CSMA represent?

   ❏ a. Carrier Sensing Minimal Access

   ❏ b. Carrier Sensing Multiple Access

   ❏ c. Carrier Sense Minimal Access

   ❏ d. Carrier Sense Multiple Access

Quick Answer: **137**
Detailed Answer: **143**

. . . .

Objective 3.2.1: Coax

1. Which of the following is a type of coax cabling transmission method? (Select all that apply.)

   ❑   a. Baseband
   ❑   b. Broadband
   ❑   c. CSMA/CD
   ❑   d. CSMA/CA

Quick Answer: **137**
Detailed Answer: **143**

2. Which of the following is the greatest advantage of coax cabling?

   ❑   a. High security
   ❑   b. Physical dimensions
   ❑   c. Long distances
   ❑   d. Easily tapped

Quick Answer: **137**
Detailed Answer: **143**

3. Which one of the following types of coax cabling has two outer conductors, or shields, and offers greater resistance and decreased attenuation?

   ❑   a. STP coax
   ❑   b. Dual-shielded coax
   ❑   c. Multi-shielded coax
   ❑   d. Bi-coax

Quick Answer: **137**
Detailed Answer: **143**

Objective 3.2.2: UTP/STP

1. Which of the following can transmit data at speeds of up to 16 Mbps?

   ❑   a. Category 1 UTP
   ❑   b. Category 2 UTP
   ❑   c. Category 3 UTP
   ❑   d. Category 4 UTP

Quick Answer: **137**
Detailed Answer: **143**

2. Which of the following is *not* a property of twisted-pair cabling?

   ❑   a. Twisted-pair cabling is a relatively low-speed transmission
   ❑   b. The wires can be shielded
   ❑   c. The wires can be unshielded
   ❑   d. Twisted-pair cable carries signals as light waves

Quick Answer: **137**
Detailed Answer: **143**

. . . .

3. What is the media standard for most local network installations?

Quick Answer: **137**
Detailed Answer: **143**

- ❑   a. Fiber
- ❑   b. CAT 3
- ❑   c. CAT 5
- ❑   d. Thinnet

Objective 3.2.3: Fiber

1. Which of the following is *not* a property of fiber optic cabling?

Quick Answer: **137**
Detailed Answer: **143**

- ❑   a. Transmits at faster speeds than copper cabling
- ❑   b. Easier to capture a signal from than copper cabling
- ❑   c. Very resistant to interference
- ❑   d. Carries signals as light waves

2. What does fiber use to transmit data?

Quick Answer: **137**
Detailed Answer: **143**

- ❑   a. Vibrations
- ❑   b. Sound
- ❑   c. Electrical current
- ❑   d. Light

3. Which of the following network cabling would you choose to
install around a noisy room where machines were constantly
running?

Quick Answer: **137**
Detailed Answer: **143**

- ❑   a. Fiber
- ❑   b. STP
- ❑   c. Coax
- ❑   d. UTP

4. You've been told about radio frequency eavesdropping and
want to protect your network from this threat. Which of the
following media types would you choose in this situation?

Quick Answer: **137**
Detailed Answer: **143**

- ❑   a. UTP
- ❑   b. STP
- ❑   c. Coax
- ❑   d. Fiber

5. Which of the following is most resistant to electrical and noise
interference?

Quick Answer: **137**
Detailed Answer: **144**

- ❑   a. STP
- ❑   b. UDP
- ❑   c. Coax
- ❑   d. Fiber

6. Which of the following is capable of conducting modulated light transmissions?

   ❏   a. Category 3 UTP
   ❏   b. Category 5 UTP
   ❏   c. Fiber
   ❏   d. Coax

7. Which of the following is the most expensive to install and terminate?

   ❏   a. Fiber optic
   ❏   b. Coaxial cable
   ❏   c. Category 4 UTP
   ❏   d. Category 5 UTP

Objective 3.2.4: Removable Media

1. What is the best way to avoid a catastrophic loss of computer data?

   ❏   a. Make backup copies of data
   ❏   b. Save all data to floppy disks
   ❏   c. Encrypt the data and backup to CD-R
   ❏   d. Check for viruses and worms

2. Which of the following are examples of magnetic storage media? (Select all that apply.)

   ❏   a. Zip disk
   ❏   b. CD-ROM
   ❏   c. Floppy disk
   ❏   d. DVD

3. Which of the following has the largest storage capacity for removable media?

   ❏   a. Floppy disk
   ❏   b. CD-ROM
   ❏   c. DVD
   ❏   d. Partitioned space

Objective 3.2.4.1: Tape

1. Which of the following are concerns when using tape as a backup method? (Select all that apply.)

   ❏ a. You are unable to reuse the data
   ❏ b. It is extremely difficult to restore the data
   ❏ c. If a crash occurs, you may have to reenter data
   ❏ d. Data transfers during restores may be slow

Quick Answer: **137**
Detailed Answer: **144**

2. Which of the following media is one of the oldest media designed to store data, but should be carefully checked with antivirus software before restoration?

   ❏ a. Magnetic tape
   ❏ b. Laptops
   ❏ c. Hard drives
   ❏ d. CDR

Quick Answer: **137**
Detailed Answer: **144**

Objective 3.2.4.2: CDR

1. Which of the following media is a relatively new media designed to store data, but should be carefully checked with antivirus software before restoration?

   ❏ a. Magnetic tape
   ❏ b. Laptops
   ❏ c. Hard drives
   ❏ d. CDR

Quick Answer: **137**
Detailed Answer: **144**

Objective 3.2.4.3: Hard Drives

1. Your company has decided to dispose of a few of the older computers that once stored critical data. What should you do first?

   ❏ a. Use Western Digital Clear (wdclear) to low-level format the hard disk
   ❏ b. Use FIPS to overwrite all data on the hard disk with zeroes
   ❏ c. Use a demagnetizer to demagnetize the hard disk
   ❏ d. Remove all the files and folders on the hard disk

Quick Answer: **137**
Detailed Answer: **144**

2. Which of the following media is used for fault tolerant RAID arrays?

   ❏ a. Magnetic tape
   ❏ b. Laptops
   ❏ c. Hard drives
   ❏ d. CDR

Quick Answer: **137**
Detailed Answer: **144**

Objective 3.2.4.4: Diskettes

1. Which of the following are one of the greatest sources of viruses, which are also a small type of media that are frequently carried from one computer to another?

 ❑ a. Hard drives
 ❑ b. Smartcards
 ❑ c. Flashcards
 ❑ d. Diskettes

Quick Answer: **137**
Detailed Answer: **144**

Objective 3.2.4.5: Flashcards

1. Which of the following devices are also known as memory sticks?

 ❑ a. Flashcards
 ❑ b. Hard drives
 ❑ c. CDR
 ❑ d. Diskettes

Quick Answer: **137**
Detailed Answer: **144**

Objective 3.2.4.6: Smartcards

1. Which of the following devices provides secure, mobile storage of users' Private keys in a PKI?

 ❑ a. Flashcard
 ❑ b. Smartcard
 ❑ c. Public key
 ❑ d. Session key

Quick Answer: **137**
Detailed Answer: **145**

2. Which one of the following is the most dependable authentication tool?

 ❑ a. Flashcards
 ❑ b. Smartcards
 ❑ c. Memory cards
 ❑ d. Authentication cards

Quick Answer: **137**
Detailed Answer: **145**

Objective 3.3: Security Topologies

1. Which of the following are known as the registered ports, according to the IANA?

 ❑ a. Ports 1 to 255
 ❑ b. Ports 255 to 1024
 ❑ c. Ports 1024 to 49151
 ❑ d. Ports 1025 to 65535

Quick Answer: **137**
Detailed Answer: **145**

Objective 3.3.1: Security Zones

1. Which of the following terms could be considered security zones? (Select all that apply.)

   ❑   a.   Intranet

   ❑   b.   Internet

   ❑   c.   DMZ

   ❑   d.   Extranet

Quick Answer: **137**
Detailed Answer: **145**

Objective 3.3.1.1: DMZ

1. You have decided to create a DMZ to allow public access to your business assets. Which of the following should you place within the DMZ? (Select all that apply.)

   ❑   a.   Web server

   ❑   b.   Proxy server

   ❑   c.   Email server

   ❑   d.   FTP server

Quick Answer: **137**
Detailed Answer: **145**

Objective 3.3.1.2: Intranet

1. Which of the following security zones is considered to be a private company network?

   ❑   a.   Forward lookup zone

   ❑   b.   Internal lookup zone

   ❑   c.   Intranet

   ❑   d.   Internet

Quick Answer: **137**
Detailed Answer: **145**

2. Which of the following characteristics of an intranet are true? (Select all that apply.)

   ❑   a.   An intranet can be a part of a Local Area Network (LAN)

   ❑   b.   An intranet is designed to be publicly available

   ❑   c.   An intranet can work with Wide Area Networks (WAN)

   ❑   d.   An intranet may be restricted to a community of users

Quick Answer: **137**
Detailed Answer: **145**

Objective 3.3.1.3: Extranet

1. Which of the following security zones is designed to allow one company to connect to another company through trust relationships and possible tunneling technology?

   ❑   a.   Intranet

   ❑   b.   DMZ

   ❑   c.   Extranet

   ❑   d.   Internet

Quick Answer: **137**
Detailed Answer: **145**

Objective 3.3.2: VLANs

1. When you think of Virtual Local Area Networks (VLANs), how are workstations connected? (Select all that apply.)

   ❏ a. Same functional department
   ❏ b. Same LAN geographic location
   ❏ c. Same group of users
   ❏ d. Same application

2. Which one of the following is software used to logically connect workgroups, thereby improving network performance for group members in different physical locations?

   ❏ a. Virtual Private Network (VPN)
   ❏ b. Virtual Local Area Network (VLAN)
   ❏ c. Remote Authentication Dial-in User Service (RADIUS)
   ❏ d. Network Address Translation (NAT)

3. You are in charge of a large network and have been using many devices. You finally want to subnet your network and allow users from the sales department in one office to communicate with sales representatives in another city. Which device should you use to improve connectivity?

   ❏ a. Router
   ❏ b. VLAN
   ❏ c. Brouter
   ❏ d. Bridge

Objective 3.3.3: NAT

1. A company desires to use a private addressing scheme for their LAN users. What solution should they implement?

   ❏ a. NAT
   ❏ b. Honey pot
   ❏ c. IDS
   ❏ d. Proxy server

2. Which of the following is relatively more secure than proxy, because it assigns private IP addresses to the clients on your LAN, acting as a firewall?

   ❏ a. RADIUS
   ❏ b. Internet Control Message Protocol (ICMP)
   ❏ c. Network Address Translation (NAT)
   ❏ d. ICMP Router Discovery Protocol (IRDP)

3. What is the primary purpose for Network Address Translation (NAT)?

Quick Answer: **138**
Detailed Answer: **146**

- ❑ a. Multiple users sharing one IP address for Instant Messenger (IM)
- ❑ b. Hiding the IP addresses of the internal network from those outside of the network
- ❑ c. Showing the IP addresses of the external network to clients on the internal network
- ❑ d. Single users gaining access to multiple email accounts

4. Which of the following are true statements about Network Address Translation (NAT)? (Select all that apply.)

Quick Answer: **138**
Detailed Answer: **146**

- ❑ a. Provides for private addressing ranges for internal network
- ❑ b. Hides the true IP addresses of internal computer systems
- ❑ c. Ensures that private addresses can be globally routable
- ❑ d. Translates private IP addresses into registered Internet IP addresses

5. Which of the following is an example of a private IP address, which is *not* to be used on the Internet?

Quick Answer: **138**
Detailed Answer: **146**

- ❑ a. 10.13.40.15
- ❑ b. 131.10.42.5
- ❑ c. 129.101.22.15
- ❑ d. 193.10.143.105

6. Which of the following is an example of a private IP address, which is *not* to be used on the Internet?

Quick Answer: **138**
Detailed Answer: **146**

- ❑ a. 171.15.40.32
- ❑ b. 172.46.32.2
- ❑ c. 171.90.22.1
- ❑ d. 172.16.12.5

7. Which of the following is an example of a private IP address, which is not to be used on the Internet?

Quick Answer: **138**
Detailed Answer: **146**

- ❑ a. 172.111.12.15
- ❑ b. 192.168.141.15
- ❑ c. 192.165.142.15
- ❑ d. 19.176.134.15

Objective 3.3.4: Tunneling

1. Which of the following applies to the networking concept of tunneling? (Select all that apply.)
   - ❑ a. Private network data is encapsulated or encrypted
   - ❑ b. Public network data is encapsulated or encrypted
   - ❑ c. Private data is transmitted over a public network
   - ❑ d. Private network data is lost in a black hole

Quick Answer: **138**
Detailed Answer: **146**

2. There are several tunneling protocols. Which of the following are types of VPN remote computing tunneling protocols? (Select all that apply.)
   - ❑ a. LP
   - ❑ b. L2F
   - ❑ c. L2TP
   - ❑ d. PPTP

Quick Answer: **138**
Detailed Answer: **146**

Objective 3.4: Intrusion Detection

1. IDS may be configured to report attack occurrences. You just received a notification that an attack occurred, but after checking, you find that it really wasn't an attack at all. What is the term for this type of alarm?
   - ❑ a. True positive
   - ❑ b. False positive
   - ❑ c. True negative
   - ❑ d. False negative

Quick Answer: **138**
Detailed Answer: **146**

2. You are looking for a security tool to exam or audit system configurations and find areas that pose security risks in conjunction with your Intrusion Detection plan. What tool should you use?
   - ❑ a. DES
   - ❑ b. KSA
   - ❑ c. RSA
   - ❑ d. NAT

Quick Answer: **138**
Detailed Answer: **146**

3. Which of the following terms relates to sending an ICMP request to each IP address on a subnet and waiting for replies?
   - ❑ a. Port scanning
   - ❑ b. Echo scanning
   - ❑ c. Ping scanning
   - ❑ d. Node scanning

Quick Answer: **138**
Detailed Answer: **146**

4. Which of the following terms relates to sending an initial SYN packet, receiving an ACK packet, and then immediately sending an RST packet?

- ❏ a. Port scanning
- ❏ b. TCP full scanning
- ❏ c. Ping scanning
- ❏ d. TCP half scanning

Quick Answer: **138**
Detailed Answer: **146**

5. Which of the following is most useful when detecting network intrusions?

- ❏ a. Audit policies
- ❏ b. Audit trails
- ❏ c. Access control policies
- ❏ d. Audit practices

Quick Answer: **138**
Detailed Answer: **146**

Objective 3.4.1: Network Based

1. Which of the following describes how a network-based IDS acquires data?

- ❏ a. Passive
- ❏ b. Active
- ❏ c. Very quiet
- ❏ d. Very noisy

Quick Answer: **138**
Detailed Answer: **147**

2. Which of the following apply to network-based IDS? (Select all that apply.)

- ❏ a. Provides reliable, real-time intrusion data
- ❏ b. Remains passive and transparent on the network
- ❏ c. Uses many network or host resources
- ❏ d. Becomes active when identifying intrusions

Quick Answer: **138**
Detailed Answer: **147**

3. Which of the following intrusion detection systems functions in current or real time to monitor network traffic?

- ❏ a. Network based
- ❏ b. Host based
- ❏ c. Gateway based
- ❏ d. Router based

Quick Answer: **138**
Detailed Answer: **147**

Objective 3.4.2: Host Based

1. What tool would you use to monitor for intrusions by review-ing computer system and event logs on a client computer?

Quick Answer: **138**
Detailed Answer: **147**

- ❏ a. Honey pot
- ❏ b. Client IDS
- ❏ c. Network-based IDS
- ❏ d. Host-based IDS

Objective 3.4.2.2: Active Detection

1. What does active detection refer to when using an intrusion detection system (IDS)? (Select all that apply.)

Quick Answer: **138**
Detailed Answer: **147**

- ❏ a. An IDS that is constantly running 24 hours a day
- ❏ b. An IDS that responds to the suspicious activity by logging off a user
- ❏ c. An IDS that reprograms the firewall to block the suspected source
- ❏ d. An IDS that shuts down the Internet after a suspected attack

Objective 3.4.2.2: Passive Detection

1. What does Passive Detection refer to when using an IDS? (Select all that apply.)

Quick Answer: **138**
Detailed Answer: **147**

- ❏ a. A host-based IDS that responds to a potential security breach
- ❏ b. A network-based IDS that logs a security breach and raises an alert
- ❏ c. Any IDS that simply detects the potential security breach
- ❏ d. An IDS that is turned to passive mode

Objective 3.4.3: Honey Pots

1. Which type of network device is characterized by the follow-ing description: Used to fool crackers, allowing them to con-tinue an attack on a sacrificial computer that contains fictitious information?

Quick Answer: **138**
Detailed Answer: **147**

- ❏ a. Fake firewall
- ❏ b. Rogue router
- ❏ c. IDS
- ❏ d. Honey pot

. . . .

Objective 3.4.4: Incident Response

1. Your network administrator has installed a network-based IDS
   and a honey pot on the network. What is the written plan
   called that indicates who will monitor these tools and how
   users should react once a malicious attack has occurred?

   ❏ a. Active response
   ❏ b. Incident response
   ❏ c. Monitoring and response
   ❏ d. Security alert and response

Quick Answer: **138**
Detailed Answer: **147**

Objective 3.5: Security Baselines

1. Which of the following items relates to the fundamental principal of implementing security measures on computer equipment to ensure that minimum standards are being met?

   ❏ a. Security baselines
   ❏ b. Security policies
   ❏ c. Security standards
   ❏ d. Security countermeasures

Quick Answer: **138**
Detailed Answer: **147**

Objectives 3.5.1: OS/NOS Hardening (Concepts and Processes)

1. You have just installed a Network Operating System (NOS)
   and want to establish a security baseline. Which of the following tasks should you perform to harden your new NOS?
   (Select all that apply.)

   ❏ a. Check the installation CD for a valid expiration date
   ❏ b. Check the manufacture's Web site for any additional service
       patches for the NOS
   ❏ c. Lock the back of the computer with a padlock
   ❏ d. Disable any unused services

Quick Answer: **138**
Detailed Answer: **148**

3.5.1.1. File System

1. Which of the following file systems allows for both file and
   folder level permissions?

   ❏ a. FAT
   ❏ b. FAT16
   ❏ c. FAT32
   ❏ d. NTFS

Quick Answer: **138**
Detailed Answer: **148**

2. You want to harden your Linux file system by modifying folder permissions. Which command allows you to change folder permissions on a Linux system?

- ❏ a. chmod
- ❏ b. ls
- ❏ c. ls –l
- ❏ d. top

3. When would you consider restoring a clean version of a file from a backup?

- ❏ a. When you are in a financial position to do so
- ❏ b. When you have time to do so
- ❏ c. When things are quiet at night
- ❏ d. When a system file has become infected

Objective 3.5.1.2: Updates (Hotfixes, Service Packs, and Patches)

1. You frequently browse the Internet for new products and updates. You notice that one of your computer manufacturers has distributed a new security patch. When should you install this update?

- ❏ a. As soon as possible to prevent catastrophic security threats
- ❏ b. After you have tested the security patch on a nonproduction server
- ❏ c. After you have called the manufacturer to verify the source
- ❏ d. After you have verified that patch for safety on a production server

Objective 3.5.2: Network Hardening

1. Even in a large, mixed environment, TCP/IP is the protocol of choice for most networks. Which of the following protocols would you want to *deny* passage over your Firewall?

- ❏ a. TCP
- ❏ b. IP
- ❏ c. IPX/SPX
- ❏ d. NetBEUI

. . . .

Objective 3.5.2.1: Updates (Firmware)

1. Which of the following terms refers to actions taken by a programmer to fix logic errors in a program under development
before actual production?

Quick Answer: **138**
Detailed Answer: **148**

- ❑   a.   Compiling
- ❑   b.   Compressing
- ❑   c.   Debugging
- ❑   d.   Degaussing

Objective 3.5.2.2: Configuration

1. Which of the following steps might be appropriate to harden
your network system? (Select all that apply.)

Quick Answer: **138**
Detailed Answer: **148**

- ❑   a.   Configure ACL settings on select servers
- ❑   b.   Configure your servers to have unused services disabled
- ❑   c.   Configure your servers to all run NAT
- ❑   d.   Configure your servers to all run in promiscuous mode

Objective 3.5.2.2.1: Enabling and Disabling Services and Protocols

1. Which of the following is the best method to disable services?

Quick Answer: **138**
Detailed Answer: **148**

- ❑   a.   Verify the dependencies of all unused services before
removing
- ❑   b.   Verify the dependencies of all active services before removing
- ❑   c.   Verify the dependencies of all unused services after removing
- ❑   d.   Verify the dependencies of all active services after removing

2. There are several common TCP and UDP ports, some of
which you may wish to disable. List the matching service provided by ports 20, 21, 23, 25, 42, 53, 67, 70, 80, 110, 119, 135,
139, 161, and 443. How many common ports do you recog-
nize?

Quick Answer: **138**
Detailed Answer: **148**

- ❑   a.   At least 13 of the 15 ports
- ❑   b.   At least 10 of the 15 ports
- ❑   c.   At least 5 of the 15 ports
- ❑   d.   At least 2 of the 15 ports

3. Your network administrator has found one of your unused server services enabled. What should you do?

Quick Answer: **138**
Detailed Answer: **148**

- ❏ a. Disable the unused service for security reasons after verifying dependencies
- ❏ b. Monitor the unused service for security reasons before verifying dependencies
- ❏ c. Troubleshoot the unused service for security reasons and functionality
- ❏ d. Maintain the enabled unused service for security reasons and functionality

Objective 3.5.2.2.2: Access Control Lists

1. Which of the following hardening methods gives you the capability to deny access to one individual computer by IP address or computer name?

Quick Answer: **138**
Detailed Answer: **149**

- ❏ a. NTFS permissions
- ❏ b. Authentication keys
- ❏ c. PKI
- ❏ d. Access control lists

Objective 3.5.3: Application Hardening

1. Which of the following relates best to application hardening?

Quick Answer: **138**
Detailed Answer: **149**

- ❏ a. Buying the most recent application version available
- ❏ b. Buying the most recent software package available
- ❏ c. Configuring network applications with the most recent updates and service packs
- ❏ d. Testing the most recent hotfixes, service packs, and patches after purchasing

Objective 3.5.3.1: Updates (Hotfixes, Service Packs, and Patches)

1. You are responsible for your network security. Where would you go to ensure that you have the most current network updates, including hotfixes, service packs, and patches?

Quick Answer: **139**
Detailed Answer: **149**

- ❏ a. Your purchasing manager
- ❏ b. Your CEO
- ❏ c. The manufacturer's Web site
- ❏ d. Your network administrator

Objective 3.5.3.2: Web Servers

1. You have added a new Web server to your network. Which of the following are sound practices when checking a Web server for security features? (Select all that apply.)

   ❏ a. Check with the vendor for the latest security patches for the Web software

   ❏ b. Check the Web Server for any additional unused services

   ❏ c. Check the Web Server for date of software distribution

   ❏ d. Check the Internet for any reports of software vulnerabilities

Quick Answer: **139**
Detailed Answer: **149**

Objective 3.5.3.3: Email Servers

1. Your small company is growing and has decided to host a Web page and dedicate a server for email. What protocol is used to support email traffic?

   ❏ a. ARP

   ❏ b. DNS

   ❏ c. SMTP

   ❏ d. IM

Quick Answer: **139**
Detailed Answer: **149**

2. Which of the following functions has an email message relay agent?

   ❏ a. SMTP

   ❏ b. SNMP

   ❏ c. S/MIME

   ❏ d. LDAP

Quick Answer: **139**
Detailed Answer: **149**

3. You desire to protect your email server. What should you configure to protect your email server? (Select all that apply.)

   ❏ a. SMTP relay settings

   ❏ b. SNMP relay settings

   ❏ c. Antivirus software

   ❏ d. Access control permissions

Quick Answer: **139**
Detailed Answer: **149**

Objective 3.5.3.4: FTP Servers

1. What is the primary purpose of an FTP server?

   ❏ a. Simplify storage of files

   ❏ b. Allow for backup storage of files

   ❏ c. Report security violations of files

   ❏ d. Facilitate transfer of files

Quick Answer: **139**
Detailed Answer: **149**

2. Which of the following is frequently used to send and receive text-based files and messages, including router configurations and ACL information?

- ❑ a. File Transport Protocol (FTP)
- ❑ b. Trivial File Transfer Protocol (TFTP)
- ❑ c. Fast File Transfer Protocol (FFTP)
- ❑ d. Trivial Transport Protocol (TTP)

Objective 3.5.3.5: DNS Servers

1. What is the primary function of a DNS server?

- ❑ a. Resolve 32-bit addresses in IPv4
- ❑ b. Find other DNS servers
- ❑ c. Resolve Fully Qualified Domain Names to IP addresses
- ❑ d. Find MAC, 48-bit hardware addresses

2. Which of the following is one of the most important tasks to perform when hardening a DNS server?

- ❑ a. Check the forward lookup zone for proper connections
- ❑ b. Perform a DNS recursive query
- ❑ c. Check the reverse lookup zone for proper connections
- ❑ d. Restrict zone transfers to authorized computers

Objective 3.5.3.6: NNTP Servers

1. Which of the following servers allows for a high volume of group network traffic and is a potential source for malicious code or DoS?

- ❑ a. FTP server
- ❑ b. NNTP server
- ❑ c. DNS server
- ❑ d. File and Print server

2. Which one of the following is an easy way to protect an NNTP server from malicious attacks?

- ❑ a. Implement a firewall protection plan on the NNTP server
- ❑ b. Use a bastion host on the NNTP server
- ❑ c. Implement virus scanning on the NNTP server
- ❑ d. Turn off the NNTP server, because there is no way to protect a NNTP server from malicious attacks

Objective 3.5.3.7: File/Print Servers

1. Because networks were created to share resources, file and print servers announce network shares by default. Which of the following provides the best hardening technique for file and print servers?

   ❑ a. Limit access to less than ten users at a time

   ❑ b. Configure network shares to the default settings

   ❑ c. Evaluate and set each folder share for the appropriate file and folder permissions

   ❑ d. Audit all folders for successful access

Quick Answer: **139**
Detailed Answer: **150**

Objective 3.5.3.8: DHCP Servers

1. What is the primary network security concern with DHCP servers?

   ❑ a. Statically configured clients have the same address as DHCP clients

   ❑ b. A cracker pretending to be the DHCP server, maliciously spoofs DHCP clients

   ❑ c. The DNS server can be vulnerable to DHCP changes, causing clients to disconnect

   ❑ d. The router is no longer available to DHCP clients

Quick Answer: **139**
Detailed Answer: **150**

2. Which of the following could pose a conflict of IP addressing for clients on your network, thereby removing them from your zone?

   ❑ a. A primary DHCP server

   ❑ b. A secondary DHCP server

   ❑ c. A rogue DHCP server

   ❑ d. An Active Directory DHCP server

Quick Answer: **139**
Detailed Answer: **150**

Objective 3.5.3.9: Data Repositories

1. Which of the following are used as large Data Repositories? (Select all that apply.)

   ❑ a. SAN

   ❑ b. WAN

   ❑ c. NAS

   ❑ d. DEN

Quick Answer: **139**
Detailed Answer: **150**

Objective 3.5.3.9.1: Directory Services

1. Which of the following is considered a Directory Service?

   ❑   a. Lightweight Directory Access Protocol (LDAP)

   ❑   b. Heavyweight Directory Access Protocol (HDAP)

   ❑   c. Hierarchical Directory Access Protocol (HDAP)

   ❑   d. Local Directory Access Protocol (LDAP)

Quick Answer: **139**
Detailed Answer: **150**

Objective 3.5.3.9.2: Databases

1. Which of the following databases have this default security vulnerability: The "sa" account is established with a blank password?

   ❑   a. LDAP

   ❑   b. SQL

   ❑   c. Proxy

   ❑   d. Exchange

Quick Answer: **139**
Detailed Answer: **150**

2. Which of the following is the best definition for the term polyinstantiation?

   ❑   a. Many instances or copies of a file

   ❑   b. Keeping database information hidden

   ❑   c. Many instances or copies of a database

   ❑   d. Lower-level databases have access to many upper-level databases

Quick Answer: **139**
Detailed Answer: **150**

Quick Check Answer Key

Objective 3.1: Devices

1. a, b, and d.
2. b, c, and d.
3. b.

Objective 3.1.1: Firewalls

1. b.
2. b and c.
3. a, b, c, and d
4. a and b.
5. b and c.
6. d.
7. b.
8. d.
9. b.
10. d.

Objective 3.1.2: Routers

1. d.
2. a.
3. a, b, and d.
4. a.
5. a and d.
6. b.
7. b.

Objective 3.1.3: Switches

1. b.
2. b and d.
3. b.

Objective 3.1.4: Wireless

1. a.

Objective 3.1.5: Modems

1. a and b.
2. a.

Objective 3.1.6: RAS

1. d.
2. b, c, and d.

Objective 3.1.7: Telecom/PBX

1. b and c.
2. a and b.

Objective 3.1.8: VPN

1. c.
2. d.
3. c.
4. b and d.

Objective 3.1.9: IDS

1. a.
2. b.
3. a.

Objective 3.1.10: Network Monitoring/ Diagnostic

1. b.
2. b.
3. d.

Objective 3.1.11: Workstations

1. d.
2. c.

Objective 3.1.12: Servers

1. d.
2. c and d.

Objective 3.1.13: Mobile Devices

1. b and c.
2. c.

Quick Check Answer Key

Objective 3.2: Media

1. a, c, and d.
2. c.
3. d.

Objective 3.2.1: Coax

1. a and b.
2. c.
3. b.

Objective 3.2.2: UTP/STP

1. d.
2. d.
3. c.

Objective 3.2.3: Fiber

1. b.
2. d.
3. a.
4. d.
5. d.
6. c.
7. a.

Objective 3.2.4: Removable Media

1. a.
2. a and c.
3. c.

Objective 3.2.4.1: Tape

1. c and d.
2. a.

Objective 3.2.4.2: CDR

1. d.

Objective 3.2.4.3: Hard Drives

1. c.
2. c.

Objective 3.2.4.4: Diskettes

1. d.

Objective 3.2.4.5: Flashcards

1. a.

Objective 3.2.4.6: Smartcards

1. b.
2. b.

Objective 3.3: Security Topologies

1. c.

Objective 3.3.1: Security Zones

1. a, b, c, and d.

Objective 3.3.1.1: DMZ

1. a, c, and d.

Objective 3.3.1.2: Intranet

1. c.
2. a, c, and d.

Objective 3.3.1.3: Extranet

1. c.

Objective 3.3.2: VLANs

1. a, c, and d.
2. b.
3. b.

Objective 3.3.3: NAT

1. a.
2. c.

Quick Check Answer Key

3. b.

4. a, b, and d

5. a.

6. d.

7. b.

Objective 3.3.4: Tunneling

1. a and c.

2. b, c, and d.

Objective 3.4: Intrusion Detection

1. b.

2. b.

3. c.

4. d.

5. b.

Objective 3.4.1: Network Based

1. a.

2. a and b.

3. a.

Objective 3.4.2: Host Based

1. d.

Objective 3.4.2.2: Active Detection

1. b and c.

Objective 3.4.2.2: Passive Detection

1. b and c.

Objective 3.4.3: Honey Pots

1. d.

Objective 3.4.4: Incident Response

1. b.

Objective 3.5: Security Baselines

1. a.

Objective 3.5.1: OS/NOS Hardening (Concepts and Processes)

1. b and d.

Objective 3.5.1.1: File System

1. d.

2. a.

3. d.

Objective 3.5.1.2: Updates (Hotfixes, Service Packs, and Patches)

1. b.

Objective 3.5.2: Network Hardening

1. d.

Objective 3.5.2.1: Updates (Firmware)

1. c.

Objective 3.5.2.2: Configuration

1. a and b.

Objective 3.5.2.2.1: Enabling and Disabling Services and Protocols

1. a.

2. a.

3. a.

Objective 3.5.2.2.2: Access Control Lists

1. d.

Objective 3.5.3: Application Hardening

1. c.

Quick Check Answer Key

**Objective 3.5.3.1:
Updates (Hotfixes,
Service Packs, and
Patches)**

1. c.

**Objective 3.5.3.2:
Web Servers**

1. a, b, and d.

**Objective 3.5.3.3:
Email Servers**

1. c.

2. a.

3. a, c, and d.

**Objective 3.5.3.4: FTP
Servers**

1. d.

2. b.

**Objective 3.5.3.5:
DNS Servers**

1. c.

2. d.

**Objective 3.5.3.6:
NNTP Servers**

1. b.

2. c.

**Objective 3.5.3.7:
File/Print Servers**

1. c.

**Objective 3.5.3.8:
DHCP Servers**

1. b.

2. c.

**Objective 3.5.3.9:
Data Repositories**

1. a, c, and d.

**Objective 3.5.3.9.1:
Directory Services**

1. a.

**Objective 3.5.3.9.2:
Databases**

1. b.

2. b.

Answers and Explanations

Objective 3.1: Devices

1. **a, b, and d.** Firewalls, routers, and switches will help you protect critical resources and separate your LAN.

2. **b, c, and d.** Access Point (AP) is a component of a wireless LAN.

3. **b.** A switching hub is specially designed to forward packets to a specific port based on the packet's address.

Objective 3.1.1: Firewalls

1. **b.** A firewall is best suited to protect resources and subnet your LAN directly on the network or gateway server.

2. **b and c.** A firewall protects LAN resources from other networks.

3. **a, b, c, and d.** All items listed are true about firewalls.

4. **a and b.** Static packet filtering is less secure than stateful filtering, proxy filtering, or dynamic packet filtering.

5. **b and c.** A packet filtering firewall operates at the Network or Transport layers.

6. **d.** Firewalls are designed to perform all the functions listed except protect against viruses.

7. **b.** Stateful firewalls may filter connection-oriented packets such as TCP.

8. **d.** Proxy server runs an Application layer firewall using proxy software.

9. **b.** A packet filtering firewall uses routers with packet filtering rules to allow or deny access based on source address, destination address, or port number.

10. **d.** A stateful packet filtering firewall keeps track of the connection state.

Objective 3.1.2: Routers

1. **d.** A multicast router discriminates between multicast and unicast packets and informs switching devices what to do with the multicast packet.

2. **a.** The static router offers a stable table that you, as the network administrator, generate.

3. **a, b, and d.** A dynamic router offers less security than a static router.

4. **a.** Of the items listed, a static router is the most difficult to configure, but safest device to use on a LAN.

5. **a and d.** Bridges connect two networks at the Data Link layer and routers connect two networks at the Network layer. Network spelled backward (kRowten) is similar to router with a silent k.

6. **b.** My useful mnemonic for this is "A Priest Says To Never Delay Praying."

7. **b.** Routers work at the Network layer. Network spelled backward (kRowten) is similar to Router with a silent k.

Objective 3.1.3: Switches

1. **b.** A switch will meet your goals for this situation.

2. **b and d.** Switches generally use Telnet or HTTP to manage interfaces and should be placed behind a dedicated firewall.

3. **b.** A switching hub forwards packets to an appropriate port based on the packet's address.

Objective 3.1.4: Wireless

1. **a.** Access point is a critical wireless device.

Objective 3.1.5: Modems

1. **a and b.** The term modem stands for modulator and demodulator. Modems use telephone lines. DSL and cable modems are faster than 56 Kbps.

2. **a.** Remote access without network administrator knowledge is the greatest security risk when dealing with modems.

Objective 3.1.6: RAS

1. **d.** RAS stands for Remote Access Service.

2. **b, c, and d.** A Remote Access Service (RAS) connection can be a dial-up connection or network connection using ISDN, DSL, VPN, or cable modem.

Objective 3.1.7: Telecom/PBX

1. **b and c.** Recommend that user accounts be verified with strong authentication, remove the guest account, and create verifiable remote accounts.

2. **a and b.** PBX stands for Private Branch Exchange, which allows for analog, digital, and data to transfer over a high-speed phone system.

Objective 3.1.8: VPN

1. **c.** A Virtual Private Network (VPN) provides for a private communication between two sites that also permits encryption and authorization.

2. **d.** Diffie-Hellman provides Strong Authentication used to verify the VPN tunnel end points.

3. **c.** DES performs fast data encryption and may be used with VPNs.

4. **b and d.** IPSec and L2TP are protocols that work together to create a secure VPN connection.

Objective 3.1.9: IDS

1. **a.** IDS stands for Intrusion Detection System.

2. **b.** A network-based Intrusion Detection System monitors network traffic in real time.

3. **a.** IDS is a security device that acts more like a detective rather than a preventative measure.

Objective 3.1.10: Network Monitoring/Diagnostic

1. **b.** Simple Network Management Protocol (SNMP) is used to monitor network devices such as hubs, switches, and routers.

2. **b.** The IP header protocol field value of 1 = ICMP; 2 = IGMP; 6 = TCP; and 17 = UDP.

3. **d.** The IP header protocol field value of 6 = TCP; 1 = ICMP; 2 = IGMP; and 17 = UDP.

Objective 3.1.11: Workstations

1. **d.** Workstations are a source of security concern in a LAN.

2. **c.** Desktop lockdown is the term used to prevent users from downloading software on company workstations.

Objective 3.1.12: Servers

1. **d.** A server cluster is a group of independent servers that are grouped together to appear like one server.

2. **c and d.** Workstations and servers have similar security concerns because they provide file sharing, network connection, and application services.

Objective 3.1.13: Mobile Devices

1. **b and c.** A Personal Digital Assistant (PDA) and pagers are examples of mobile devices.

2. **c.** Mobile devices are smaller network devices, which are a security concern for network administrators because they are easily misplaced.

Objective 3.2: Media

1. **a, c, and d.** Twisted pair, fiber optic, and coaxial are types of network cabling. Token ring is a type of physical topology.

2. **c.** You use a crossover cable directly between two like components, like between two computers.

3. **d.** CSMA represents Carrier Sense Multiple Access.

Objective 3.2.1: Coax

1. **a and b.** Baseband and broadband are the two common types of coax cabling transmission methods.

2. **c.** Of the choices listed for coax cabling, long distance is the best answer.

3. **b.** Dual-shielded coax has two outer conductors, or shields, and offers greater resistance and decreased attenuation.

Objective 3.2.2: UTP/STP

1. **d.** Category 4 UTP is used in token ring networks and can transmit data at speeds of up to 16 Mbps.

2. **d.** Fiber optic cable carries signals as light waves.

3. **c.** CAT 5 twisted-pair cabling is the media standard for most local network installations.

Objective 3.2.3: Fiber

1. **b.** Fiber optic cabling transmits at faster speeds than copper cabling, is very resistant to interference, and carries signals as light waves.

2. **d.** Fiber uses light to transmit data.

3. **a.** Fiber is the best choice in this situation.

4. **d.** Fiber protects against RF eavesdropping.

5. **d.** Fiber is most resistant to electrical and noise interference.

6. **c.** Fiber optic cable is a physical medium that is capable of conducting modulated light transmission.

7. **a.** Fiber optic cable is the most reliable cable type, but it is also the most expensive to install and terminate.

Objective 3.2.4: Removable Media

1. **a.** Making backup copies of data is the best way to avoid a catastrophic loss of computer data.

2. **a and c.** Zip disks and floppy disks are magnetic storage media.

3. **c.** DVD has the largest storage capacity for removable media.

Objective 3.2.4.1: Tape

1. **c and d.** When using tape backup data re-entry may need to be performed after a crash and slow data transfer may occur during backups and restores.

2. **a.** Magnetic tape is one of the oldest media designed to store data but should be carefully checked with antivirus software before restoration.

Objective 3.2.4.2: CDR

1. **d.** CDR is one of the newest media designed to store data but should be carefully checked with antivirus software before restoration.

Objective 3.2.4.3: Hard Drives

1. **c.** You should use a demagnetizer to demagnetize the hard disk.

2. **c.** Multiple hard drives are used for fault tolerant RAID arrays.

Objective 3.2.4.4: Diskettes

1. **d.** Diskettes are one of the greatest sources of viruses, which are also a small type of media that has traditionally been carried from one computer to another.

Objective 3.2.4.5: Flashcards

1. **a.** Flashcards are also known as memory sticks.

Objective 3.2.4.6: Smartcards

1. **b.** Smartcards provide secure, mobile storage of users' Private keys in a PKI.

2. **b.** Smartcards are the most dependable authentication tool.

Objective 3.3: Security Topologies

1. **c.** Ports 1024 to 49151. There are three accepted ranges for port numbers: the Well Known Ports, the Registered Ports, which are registered by the Internet Assigned Numbers Authority (IANA), and the Dynamic (Private) Ports.

Objective 3.3.1: Security Zones

1. **a, b, c, and d.** All of the items listed are examples of security zones

Objective 3.3.1.1: DMZ

1. **a, c, and d.** You should place your Web servers, FTP servers, and email servers within the DMZ. Web servers, FTP servers, and email servers are typically hosted within the DMZ.

Objective 3.3.1.2: Intranet

1. **c.** An intranet is a security zone that is considered to be a private company network.

2. **a, c, and d.** The Internet, *not* intranet, is designed to be publicly available.

Objective 3.3.1.3: Extranet

1. **c.** Extranet is a security zone designed to allow one company to connect to another company through trust relationships and possible tunneling technology.

Objective 3.3.2: VLANs

1. **a, c, and d.** A Virtual Local Area Network (VLAN) ties workstations together by functional department, same type of user, or primary application.

2. **b.** A Virtual Local Area Network (VLAN) improves network performance by decreasing broadcast traffic and additionally reducing the chances that sniffing devices will compromise information.

3. **b.** A VLAN will improve connectivity in this situation.

Objective 3.3.3: NAT

1. **a.** Network Address Translation (NAT) offers a private addressing scheme for LAN users, hiding their IP addresses from the Internet.

2. **c.** Network Address Translation (NAT) is relatively more secure than proxy, because it assigns private IP addresses to the client on your LAN, acting as a firewall.

3. **b.** Network Address Translation (NAT) has the primary purpose to shield the IP addresses of the internal network from those outside of the network.

4. **a, b, and d.** NAT translates private IP addresses into registered Internet IP addresses, allows for private addressing ranges for internal networks, and is designed to hide the true IP addresses of internal computer systems.

5. **a.** The internal IP of 10.13.40.15 is an example of a private IP address reserved for internal networks, and not a valid address to use on the Internet. The Class A reserved addresses are 10.0.0.0–10.255.255.255.

6. **d.** The internal IP of 172.16.12.5 is an example of a private IP address reserved for internal networks, and not a valid address to use on the Internet. The Class B reserved addresses are 172.16.0.0–172.31.255.255.

7. **b.** The internal IP of 192.168.141.15 is an example of a private IP address reserved for internal networks, and not a valid address to use on the Internet. The Class C reserved addresses are 192.168.0.0–192.168.255.255.

Objective 3.3.4: Tunneling

1. **a and c.** With tunneling, private network data, which is encapsulated or encrypted, is transmitted over a public network.

2. **b, c, and d.** L2F, L2FP, and PPTP are used for VPN remote computing.

Objective 3.4: Intrusion Detection

1. **b.** This is an example of a false positive result.

2. **b.** The Kane Security Analyst (KSA) is a system security analyzer and assessment tool.

3. **c.** Ping scanning sends an ICMP request to each IP address on a subnet and waits for replies.

4. **d.** TCP half scanning relates to sending an initial SYN packet, receiving an ACK packet, and then immediately sending an RST packet.

5. **b.** Audit trails are most useful when detecting intrusions to your network.

Objective 3.4.1: Network Based

1. **a.** A network-based IDS is passive when it acquires data.

2. **a and b.** A network-based IDS provides reliable, real-time intrusion data, remains passive and transparent on the network, and uses few network or host resources.

3. **a.** The network-based IDS monitors network traffic in real time.

Objective 3.4.2: Host Based

1. **d.** A host-based IDS can review computer system and event logs to detect a successful attack on a client computer.

Objective 3.4.2.2: Active Detection

1. **b and c.** Active detection refers to an IDS that responds to the suspicious activity by logging off a user or one that reprograms the firewall to block the suspected source.

Objective 3.4.2.2: Passive Detection

1. **b and c.** Passive detection refers to an IDS system that simply detects the potential security breach, logs a security breach, and raises an alert.

Objective 3.4.3: Honey Pots

1. **d.** A honey pot is a computer configured as a sacrificial lamb so that administrators are aware when malicious attacks are in progress.

Objective 3.4.4: Incident Response

1. **b.** An Incident Response is a written plan that indicates who will monitor these tools and how users should react once a malicious attack has occurred.

Objective 3.5: Security Baselines

1. **a.** Security baselines relate to the fundamental principal of implementing security measures on computer equipment to ensure that minimum standards are being met.

. . . .

Objective 3.5.1: OS/NOS Hardening (Concepts and Processes)

1. **b and d.** To harden your NOS, check the manufacturer's Web site for any additional service patches for the NOS and disable any unused services.

Objective 3.5.1.1: File System

1. **d.** New Technology File System (NTFS) allows for both file and folder level permissions.

2. **a.** The command, chmod, allows you to change folder permissions on a Linux system.

3. **d.** When a system file has become infected, you should consider restoring a clean version of a file from a backup.

Objective 3.5.1.2: Updates (Hotfixes, Service Packs, and Patches)

1. **b.** You should install this update after you have tested the security patch to be safe on a nonproduction server.

Objective 3.5.2: Network Hardening

1. **d.** NetBEUI should be denied passage over your firewall for security reasons.

Objective 3.5.2.1: Updates (Firmware)

1. **c.** Debugging refers to actions taken by a programmer to fix logic errors in a program under development before actual production.

Objective 3.5.2.2: Configuration

1. **a and b.** Configure ACL settings on select servers and disable unused services are appropriate steps to harden your network system.

Objective 3.5.2.2.1: Enabling and Disabling Services and Protocols

1. **a.** When disabling services, verify the dependencies of all unused services before removing.

2. **a.** FTP = ports 20 (data) and 21 (session), Telnet = port 23, SMTP = port 25, Wins replication = port 42, DNS = 53, bootp = 67, IIS Gopher = 70, HTTP = 80, pop3 = 110, NNTP = 119, RPC = port 135, NetBIOS over IP = 139, SNMP =161, and SSL = 44   3.

3. **a.** Verify that the unused service has no dependencies, then disable the service for security reasons.

Objective 3.5.2.2.2: Access Control Lists

1. **d.** Access control lists let you deny access to one individual computer by IP address or computer name.

Objective 3.5.3: Application Hardening

1. **c.** Of the items listed, configuring network applications with the most recent updates and service packs relates best to Application Hardening.

Objective 3.5.3.1: Updates (Hotfixes, Service Packs, and Patches)

1. **c.** The manufacturer's Web site should have the most current network updates, including hotfixes, service packs, and patches.

Objective 3.5.3.2: Web Servers

1. **a, b, and d.** The sound security practices include checking with the vendor for the latest security patches for Web software, checking for any additional unused services, and checking the Internet for any reports of software vulnerabilities.

Objective 3.5.3.3: Email Servers

1. **c.** Simple Mail Transfer Protocol (SMTP) is used to support email traffic.

2. **a.** Simple Mail Transfer Protocol (SMTP) works as a message relay agent.

3. **a, c, and d.** To protect your email server you should configure your Simple Mail Transfer Protocol (SMTP) relay settings, antivirus software, and access control permissions.

Objective 3.5.3.4: FTP Servers

1. **d.** The primary purpose of an FTP server is to facilitate file transfers.

2. **b.** Trivial File Transfer Protocol (TFTP) is frequently used to send and receive text-based files and messages, including router configurations and ACL information.

Objective 3.5.3.5: DNS Servers

1. **c.** The primary function of a DNS server is to resolve Fully Qualified Domain Names to IP addresses.

2. **d.** One of the most important tasks to perform when hardening a DNS server is to restrict zone transfers to authorized computer.

Objective 3.5.3.6: NNTP Servers

1. **b.** A Network News Transfer Protocol (NNTP) server, which runs on port 119, allows for a high volume of group network traffic and is a potential source for malicious code or Denial of Service (DoS) attacks.

2. **c.** One of the best ways to protect a NNTP server from malicious attack is to implement virus scanning on the NNTP server and use antivirus software.

Objective 3.5.3.7: File/Print Servers

1. **c.** Of the items listed, the best hardening technique for File and Print servers is to evaluate and set each folder share for the appropriate file and folder permissions.

Objective 3.5.3.8: DHCP Servers

1. **b.** Of the items listed, the primary network security concern with DHCP servers is that a cracker could pretend to be the DHCP server and maliciously spoof DHCP clients.

2. **c.** A rogue DHCP server could pose a conflict of IP addressing for clients on your network, thereby taking them away from your zone.

Objective 3.5.3.9: Data Repositories

1. **a, c, and d.** Large Data Repositories may include Storage Area Network (SAN), Network Attached Storage (NAS), and Directory Enabled Networks (DEN).

Objective 3.5.3.9.1: Directory Services

1. **a.** Lightweight Directory Access Protocol (LDAP) is considered a Directory Service.

Objective 3.5.3.9.2: Databases

1. **b.** SQL has this default security vulnerability, because the "sa" account is established with a blank password.

2. **b.** Polyinstantiation refers to keeping database information hidden in different sections.

Basics of Cryptography

Objective 4.1: Algorithms

1. What is an algorithm?

Quick Answer: **173**
Detailed Answer: **176**

    ❏ a. A series of steps used to guarantee a result

    ❏ b. A group of mathematical additions

    ❏ c. A process of using calculus

    ❏ d. A solution to an equation

Objective 4.1.1: Hashing

1. You have decided to digitally sign a message using a hash function. What is true of the message digest?

Quick Answer: **173**
Detailed Answer: **176**

    ❏ a. The sender's Public key encrypts the message digest

    ❏ b. The sender's Private key encrypts the message digest

    ❏ c. The sender's Public key encrypts the message contents

    ❏ d. The sender's Private key encrypts the message contents

2. Which of the following consistently uses 128-bit encryption?

Quick Answer: **173**
Detailed Answer: **176**

    ❏ a. CAST

    ❏ b. 3DES

    ❏ c. DES

    ❏ d. Hash

3. What is it called when you use mathematics to create a message digest?

Quick Answer: **173**
Detailed Answer: **176**

    ❏ a. PKI

    ❏ b. Hashing algorithm

    ❏ c. Symmetric algorithm

    ❏ d. Asymmetric algorithm

4. You use mathematics to create a message digest, which is called a hashing algorithm. What do you use to encrypt this message digest before transmission?

- ❏ a. A Private key
- ❏ b. A Public key
- ❏ c. Kerberos
- ❏ d. PKI

5. Hashing algorithms use message digests to send encrypted files. The receiver of the file uses which key to verify his identity before comparing the results of the message digest?

- ❏ a. The Public key of the signer of the encrypted message
- ❏ b. The Private key of the signer of the encrypted message
- ❏ c. The Public key of the receiver of the encrypted message
- ❏ d. The Private key of the receiver of the encrypted message

6. Which of the following message digest sizes does Secure Hash Algorithm (SHA-1) use with Data Encryption Standard (DES) to create digital signatures?

- ❏ a. 56-bit
- ❏ b. 128-bit
- ❏ c. 160-bit
- ❏ d. 256-bit

7. Which of the following algorithms offers mathematical hashing? (Select all that apply.)

- ❏ a. SHA-1
- ❏ b. MD2
- ❏ c. MD5
- ❏ d. RC4

Objective 4.1.2: Symmetric

1. Which of the following algorithms use symmetric keys?

- ❏ a. RSA
- ❏ b. Ring
- ❏ c. Rijndael
- ❏ d. Star

2. Which of the following algorithms use symmetric keys? (Select all that apply.)

Quick Answer: **173**
Detailed Answer: **176**

- ❑ a. RSA
- ❑ b. AES
- ❑ c. IDEA
- ❑ d. DES

3. Which of the following symmetric algorithms is a 128-bit block cipher that accepts a variable-length key up to 256 bits and behaves like a Rubik's cube?

Quick Answer: **173**
Detailed Answer: **176**

- ❑ a. RC
- ❑ b. AES
- ❑ c. Twofish
- ❑ d. CAST

4. Which of the following applies to symmetric algorithms?

Quick Answer: **173**
Detailed Answer: **176**

- ❑ a. Client and server keys are similar or shared
- ❑ b. Client and server keys are dissimilar (private and public)
- ❑ c. Even if a key is confiscated, symmetric algorithms are secure
- ❑ d. Confidentiality is *not* an issue with symmetric algorithms

5. Which of the following uses symmetric encryption when securing a Web site?

Quick Answer: **173**
Detailed Answer: **173**

- ❑ a. RSA
- ❑ b. SSL
- ❑ c. ECC
- ❑ d. El Gamal

6. Which of the following relates to stream cipher? (Select all that apply.)

Quick Answer: **173**
Detailed Answer: **176**

- ❑ a. Symmetric key
- ❑ b. Used for encryption
- ❑ c. Asymmetric key
- ❑ d. Private key

7. Which of the following relates to block cipher? (Select all that apply.)

Quick Answer: **173**
Detailed Answer: **176**

- ❑ a. Symmetric key
- ❑ b. Used for encryption
- ❑ c. Asymmetric key
- ❑ d. Private key

8. Rijndael is the basis for which of the following symmetric encryption algorithms?

❑   a. CAST

❑   b. ECC

❑   c. AES

❑   d. RC

Quick Answer: **173**
Detailed Answer: **176**

9. Which of the following are known weaknesses of symmetric cryptography? (Select all that apply.)

❑   a. Speed

❑   b. Limited security

❑   c. Scalability

❑   d. Key distribution

Quick Answer: **173**
Detailed Answer: **176**

10. Which of the following statements about block ciphers are true? (Select all that apply.)

❑   a. Block ciphers use a fixed-size block of plain text

❑   b. Block ciphers use a fixed-size block of encrypted text

❑   c. Text is encrypted with a Public key and decrypted with a Private key

❑   d. Text is encrypted with a Private key and decrypted with a Public key

Quick Answer: **173**
Detailed Answer: **176**

11. You want to send a Data Encryption Standard (DES) encrypted message to a company in Europe. Which of the following bit key sizes is used for encrypting data?

❑   a. 24-bit

❑   b. 40-bit

❑   c. 56-bit

❑   d. 128-bit

Quick Answer: **173**
Detailed Answer: **177**

12. Data Encryption Standard (DES) uses block cipher encryption. What is the standard block size for DES encrypted data?

❑   a. 24-bit

❑   b. 56-bit

❑   c. 64-bit

❑   d. 128-bit

Quick Answer: **173**
Detailed Answer: **177**

13. Data Encryption Standard (DES) uses block cipher encryption. What is the standard key size for DES encrypted data?

❑   a. 24-bit

❑   b. 56-bit

❑   c. 64-bit

❑   d. 128-bit

Quick Answer: **173**
Detailed Answer: **177**

14. When using AES, or the Rijndael encryption algorithm, which of the following is the maximum allowable key size?

  ❏ a. 64 bits

  ❏ b. 128 bits

  ❏ c. 256 bits

  ❏ d. 512 bits

Quick Answer: **173**
Detailed Answer: **177**

15. Which of the following have key sizes of 128-bits, 192-bits, or 256-bits?

  ❏ a. DES

  ❏ b. 3DES

  ❏ c. MD5

  ❏ d. AES

Quick Answer: **173**
Detailed Answer: **177**

16. Because Data Encryption Standard (DES) protected sensitive, rather than classified data, a replacement was found, called Advanced Encryption Standard (AES). Which algorithm does AES use?

  ❏ a. Double DES

  ❏ b. DES version 2

  ❏ c. Triple DES

  ❏ d. Rijndael

Quick Answer: **173**
Detailed Answer: **177**

17. Triple Data Encryption Standard (DES) (three keys) is a method of encryption. What is the key size for triple DES encrypted data?

  ❏ a. 64-bits

  ❏ b. 128-bits

  ❏ c. 160-bits

  ❏ d. 168-bits

Quick Answer: **173**
Detailed Answer: **177**

18. Which of the following apply to the term CAST? (Select all that apply.)

  ❏ a. One type of symmetric algorithm

  ❏ b. One type of asymmetric algorithm

  ❏ c. CAST may use 128-bit encryption

  ❏ d. CAST may use 256-bit encryption

Quick Answer: **173**
Detailed Answer: **177**

19. One of the symmetric algorithms is RC5. What is the maximum key size for the RC5 algorithm?

  ❏ a. 56-bits

  ❏ b. 256-bits

  ❏ c. 1024-bits

  ❏ d. 2040-bits

Quick Answer: **173**
Detailed Answer: **177**

20. Which of the following meets this description: A symmetric block cipher with variable-length key that was designed to be a free replacement for DES or IDEA.

Quick Answer: **173**
Detailed Answer: **177**

- ❏ a. DES3
- ❏ b. RC5
- ❏ c. Blowfish
- ❏ d. El Gamal

Objective 4.1.3: Asymmetric

1. Which of the following algorithms use asymmetric keys? (Select all that apply.)

Quick Answer: **173**
Detailed Answer: **177**

- ❏ a. RSA
- ❏ b. ECC
- ❏ c. El Gamal
- ❏ d. Twofish

2. Which one of the following algorithms does not use asymmetric keys?

Quick Answer: **173**
Detailed Answer: **177**

- ❏ a. Diffie-Hellman
- ❏ b. ECC
- ❏ c. El Gamal
- ❏ d. Blowfish

3. Which of the following asymmetric algorithms uses variable length encryption?

Quick Answer: **173**
Detailed Answer: **177**

- ❏ a. AES
- ❏ b. 3DES
- ❏ c. CAST
- ❏ d. RSA

4. Which of the following statements is true about asymmetric encryption?

Quick Answer: **173**
Detailed Answer: **177**

- ❏ a. Slower than symmetric encryption, because of its client-server configuration requirements
- ❏ b. Faster than symmetric encryption, because it doesn't require client-server configuration
- ❏ c. Slower than symmetric encryption, because of its variable key length
- ❏ d. Faster than symmetric encryption, because of its variable key length

5. What does RSA represent?

   ❏   a. Rivest Shamir Adelman (RSA)

   ❏   b. Rivest Secure Application (RSA)

   ❏   c. Rivest Shell Adelman (RSA)

   ❏   d. Rivest Shell Application (RSA)

Quick Answer: **173**
Detailed Answer: **177**

6. Your company wants to make use of a Public key algorithm that provides both encryption and is used as a digital signature. Which of the following meet these requirements?

   ❏   a. DES3

   ❏   b. RSA

   ❏   c. DES

   ❏   d. IDEA

Quick Answer: **173**
Detailed Answer: **177**

7. Which of the following encryption algorithms is best suited for communication with handheld wireless devices?

   ❏   a. RSA

   ❏   b. ECC

   ❏   c. SHA

   ❏   d. RC5

Quick Answer: **173**
Detailed Answer: **177**

Objective 4.2: Concepts of Using Cryptography

1. Cryptography, which is Greek for hidden writings, uses two secret key algorithms to encrypt clear text into cipher text. What are these two methods?

   ❏   a. Block cipher encrypts data in chunks of a specified size

   ❏   b. Block cipher uses a fixed-length block or variable block key

   ❏   c. Stream cipher uses a fixed-length or variable key

   ❏   d. Stream cipher encrypts data in chunks of a specified size

Quick Answer: **173**
Detailed Answer: **178**

2. Which of the following is the best term for this definition: A type of symmetric-key encryption algorithm that changes a fixed-size block of clear text data into a block of ciphertext data of the same length?

   ❏   a. Block plaintext

   ❏   b. Block ciphertext

   ❏   c. Block text

   ❏   d. Block cipher

Quick Answer: **173**
Detailed Answer: **178**

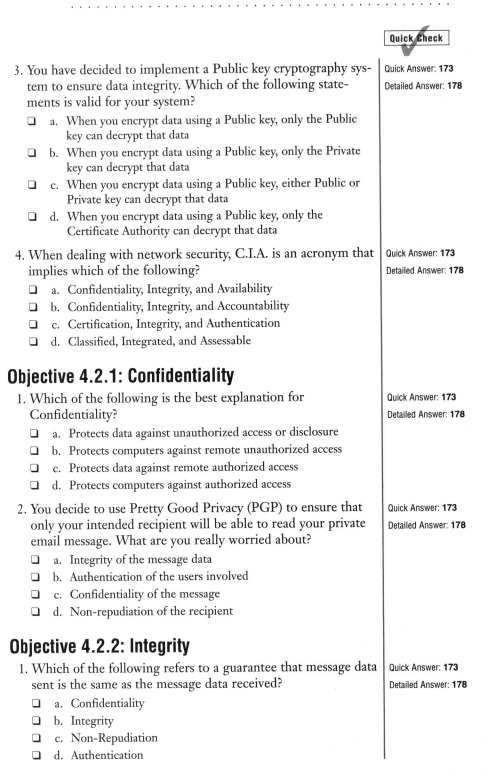

Quick Answer: **173**
Detailed Answer: **178**

3. You have decided to implement a Public key cryptography system to ensure data integrity. Which of the following statements is valid for your system?

   ❏ a. When you encrypt data using a Public key, only the Public key can decrypt that data

   ❏ b. When you encrypt data using a Public key, only the Private key can decrypt that data

   ❏ c. When you encrypt data using a Public key, either Public or Private key can decrypt that data

   ❏ d. When you encrypt data using a Public key, only the Certificate Authority can decrypt that data

Quick Answer: **173**
Detailed Answer: **178**

4. When dealing with network security, C.I.A. is an acronym that implies which of the following?

   ❏ a. Confidentiality, Integrity, and Availability

   ❏ b. Confidentiality, Integrity, and Accountability

   ❏ c. Certification, Integrity, and Authentication

   ❏ d. Classified, Integrated, and Assessable

Objective 4.2.1: Confidentiality

Quick Answer: **173**
Detailed Answer: **178**

1. Which of the following is the best explanation for Confidentiality?

   ❏ a. Protects data against unauthorized access or disclosure

   ❏ b. Protects computers against remote unauthorized access

   ❏ c. Protects data against remote authorized access

   ❏ d. Protects computers against authorized access

Quick Answer: **173**
Detailed Answer: **178**

2. You decide to use Pretty Good Privacy (PGP) to ensure that only your intended recipient will be able to read your private email message. What are you really worried about?

   ❏ a. Integrity of the message data

   ❏ b. Authentication of the users involved

   ❏ c. Confidentiality of the message

   ❏ d. Non-repudiation of the recipient

Objective 4.2.2: Integrity

Quick Answer: **173**
Detailed Answer: **178**

1. Which of the following refers to a guarantee that message data sent is the same as the message data received?

   ❏ a. Confidentiality

   ❏ b. Integrity

   ❏ c. Non-Repudiation

   ❏ d. Authentication

Quick Check

2. A message digest provides for which of the following?

Quick Answer: **173**
Detailed Answer: **178**

- ❑ a. Data Integrity
- ❑ b. Message Non-Repudiation
- ❑ c. Sender Confidentiality
- ❑ d. Recipient Authentication

3. Which of the following security terms refers to a method that ensures all data is sequenced, and numbered?

Quick Answer: **173**
Detailed Answer: **178**

- ❑ a. PKI
- ❑ b. Algorithms
- ❑ c. Data Integrity
- ❑ d. Encryption

Objective 4.2.2.1: Digital Signatures

1. Which of the following is one of the primary reasons to use digital signatures in network operations?

Quick Answer: **173**
Detailed Answer: **178**

- ❑ a. Digital signatures offer subjectivity
- ❑ b. Digital signatures maintain integrity
- ❑ c. Digital signatures provide a code of ethics
- ❑ d. Digital signatures support risk assessment

2. Which of the following apply to digital signatures? (Select all that apply.)

Quick Answer: **173**
Detailed Answer: **178**

- ❑ a. The recipient uses the signature to verify the data's origin
- ❑ b. The recipient uses the signature to verify the data's integrity
- ❑ c. A value created with an algorithm and appended to data
- ❑ d. A value created with an algorithm and encrypted within the data

3. Which of the following is used to create a unique digital signature?

Quick Answer: **173**
Detailed Answer: **178**

- ❑ a. Public key
- ❑ b. Private key
- ❑ c. Session Key
- ❑ d. Kerberos Key

4. Which of the following threats can you *not* prevent even if you implement token technologies and use digital signatures?

Quick Answer: **173**
Detailed Answer: **178**

- ❑ a. Replay
- ❑ b. Spoofing
- ❑ c. Sniffing
- ❑ d. Denial of Service

Objective 4.2.3: Authentication

1. Which of the following refers to Strong Authentication?

    ☐ a. Use of a Public key to verify a digital signature for authenticity

    ☐ b. Use of a private key to verify a digital signature for authenticity

    ☐ c. Use of a PGP to verify a digital signature for authenticity

    ☐ d. Use of a RADIUS to verify a digital signature for authenticity

Quick Answer: **173**
Detailed Answer: **179**

2. What kind of certificate is used to authenticate users?

    ☐ a. Private key certificate

    ☐ b. Public key certificate

    ☐ c. Session key certificate

    ☐ d. Keys are not used for authentication

Quick Answer: **173**
Detailed Answer: **179**

3. Which of the following provides for Authentication, Key Distribution Services, and Single Sign-On (SSO)?

    ☐ a. PKI

    ☐ b. CA

    ☐ c. VPN

    ☐ d. Honey pot

Quick Answer: **173**
Detailed Answer: **179**

Objective 4.2.4: Non-Repudiation

1. Which of the following offer non-repudiation and integrity?

    ☐ a. Digital signatures

    ☐ b. Message digest

    ☐ c. Hashing algorithms

    ☐ d. Symmetric algorithms

Quick Answer: **173**
Detailed Answer: **179**

2. Which of the following OSI layers offers non-repudiation?

    ☐ a. Application layer 7

    ☐ b. Presentation layer 6

    ☐ c. Session layer 5

    ☐ d. Transport layer 4

Quick Answer: **173**
Detailed Answer: **179**

3. Which of the following applies to non-repudiation? (Select all that apply.)

    ☐ a. Authentication of transactions

    ☐ b. Record of all transactions

    ☐ c. Record made during a certificate services session

    ☐ d. Record made after completion of a transaction

Quick Answer: **173**
Detailed Answer: **179**

Quick Check

Objective 4.2.4.1: Digital Signatures

1. Which of the following is one of the primary reasons to use digital signatures in network operations?
   - ❑ a. Digital signatures offer non-repudiation
   - ❑ b. Digital signatures maintain convenience
   - ❑ c. Digital signatures provide a code of ethics
   - ❑ d. Digital signatures support risk assessment

Quick Answer: **174**
Detailed Answer: **179**

Objective 4.2.5: Access Control

1. What is the primary security action to ensure data integrity, network availability, and confidentiality?
   - ❑ a. Control access to routers and firewalls
   - ❑ b. Control access to information systems and associated networks
   - ❑ c. Control access to entrances and server rooms
   - ❑ d. Control access to email and Web servers

Quick Answer: **174**
Detailed Answer: **179**

Objective 4.3: PKI

1. What does PKI stand for?
   - ❑ a. Private Krypto Intelligence
   - ❑ b. Public Krypto Intelligence
   - ❑ c. Private Key Infrastructure
   - ❑ d. Public Key Infrastructure

Quick Answer: **174**
Detailed Answer: **179**

2. Which of the following refer to Public Key Infrastructure (PKI)? (Select all that apply.)
   - ❑ a. The ability to issue a new certificate for a Public key
   - ❑ b. The ability to revoke a certificate for a Private key
   - ❑ c. The ability to cancel a previously issued certificate
   - ❑ d. The ability to determine if a certificate is valid

Quick Answer: **174**
Detailed Answer: **179**

3. Which of the following apply to PKI? (Select all that apply.)
   - ❑ a. Responsible for locating and issuing certificates
   - ❑ b. Responsible for trusting and renewing certificates
   - ❑ c. Responsible for revoking certificates
   - ❑ d. Stands for Private key infrastructure

Quick Answer: **174**
Detailed Answer: **179**

4. Which of the following capabilities does the Public Key Infrastructure (PKI) offer when used with certificate services? (Select all that apply.)

- ❏ a. Privacy
- ❏ b. Authentication
- ❏ c. Decentralized security
- ❏ d. Non-repudiation

Quick Answer: **174**
Detailed Answer: **179**

5. What does the Public Key Infrastructure (PKI) provide? (Select all that apply.)

- ❏ a. Integrity
- ❏ b. Authentication
- ❏ c. Access Control
- ❏ d. Confidentiality

Quick Answer: **174**
Detailed Answer: **179**

Objective 4.3.1: Certificates—Distinguish Which Certificates Are Used for What Purpose. Basics Only

1. Certificate services use Public keys. What do Public keys provide? (Select all that apply.)

- ❏ a. Nonrepudiation
- ❏ b. Privacy
- ❏ c. Authentication
- ❏ d. Integrity

Quick Answer: **174**
Detailed Answer: **180**

2. In Public Key Infrastructure, who is responsible for certificates and digitally signing them using a Private key?

- ❏ a. Certificate Authority (CA)
- ❏ b. Digital Certificate (DC)
- ❏ c. TKIP
- ❏ d. OCSP

Quick Answer: **174**
Detailed Answer: **180**

3. Which of the following is *not* a component of digital certificates?

- ❏ a. Public key
- ❏ b. Certificate information
- ❏ c. Private key
- ❏ d. Digital signature

Quick Answer: **174**
Detailed Answer: **180**

4. Which of following instant access methods is used to check the status of certificates?

- ❏ a. CA
- ❏ b. DN
- ❏ c. OCSP
- ❏ d. CRL

Quick Answer: **174**
Detailed Answer: **180**

5. You have a Certificate Authority (CA) that uses a Public key Infrastructure. How does the CA maintain network access? (Select all that apply.)

- ❏ a. Through CRL
- ❏ b. Through ACL
- ❏ c. Through OCSP
- ❏ d. Through PKI

Quick Answer: **174**
Detailed Answer: **180**

6. Which of the following is responsible for issuing certificates to authorized users?

- ❏ a. PDC
- ❏ b. CA
- ❏ c. PKI
- ❏ d. OCSP

Quick Answer: **174**
Detailed Answer: **180**

7. Which of the following is an industry standard for digital certificates?

- ❏ a. X.405
- ❏ b. X.509
- ❏ c. X.905
- ❏ d. X.911

Quick Answer: **174**
Detailed Answer: **180**

8. What is the top-level Certificate Authority also known as?

- ❏ a. Key Note
- ❏ b. Top Dog
- ❏ c. Root
- ❏ d. Enterprise

Quick Answer: **174**
Detailed Answer: **180**

9. You want to obtain a new certificate from a trusted Certificate Authority. What must you have available? (Select all that apply.)

- ❏ a. DNA sample
- ❏ b. Some form of proven identity
- ❏ c. A Private key
- ❏ d. A Public key

Quick Answer: **174**
Detailed Answer: **180**

Objective 4.3.1.1: Certificate Policies

1. Which of the following best relates to a set of rules for the detailed use of certificates?
   - ❑ a. Certificate Authority
   - ❑ b. Certificate Rule Set
   - ❑ c. Certificate Policy
   - ❑ d. Certificate Practice Statement

Quick Answer: **174**
Detailed Answer: **180**

2. You want to establish a written Certificate Policy. Which of the following would be causes to revoke certificates? (Select all that apply.)
   - ❑ a. The administrator of your certificate server is leaving the company
   - ❑ b. The Private key has been potentially compromised
   - ❑ c. The company is moving to a new city
   - ❑ d. The company is adding a new Web site

Quick Answer: **174**
Detailed Answer: **180**

Objective 4.3.1.2: Certificate Practice Statements

1. Which of the following best explains how to implement the set of rules for the detailed use of certificates?
   - ❑ a. Certificate Authority
   - ❑ b. Certificate Rule Set
   - ❑ c. Certificate Policy
   - ❑ d. Certificate Practice Statement

Quick Answer: **174**
Detailed Answer: **180**

Objective 4.3.2: Revocation

1. Which of the following is a reference list of certificates that have been identified for revocation prior to their original expiration date?
   - ❑ a. Certificate Revocation List (CRL)
   - ❑ b. Expired Certificate Renewals (ECR)
   - ❑ c. Revocation Security System (RSS)
   - ❑ d. Request Revocation Certificate List (RRCL)

Quick Answer: **174**
Detailed Answer: **180**

2. Which of the following is the meaning of "revocation?"
   - ❑ a. Certificates have to be terminated before their expiration date
   - ❑ b. Certificates have to be terminated after their expiration date
   - ❑ c. Certificates are revoked rather than terminated
   - ❑ d. Certificates have been relocated

Quick Answer: **174**
Detailed Answer: **180**

3. What list does the Certificate Authority use when a Private key has become compromised?

   ❑ a. Expiration list
   ❑ b. Revocation list
   ❑ c. Schindler's list
   ❑ d. Outdated list

Objective 4.3.3: Trust Models

1. Which of the following are PKI trust models? (Select all that apply.)

   ❑ a. Asymmetric
   ❑ b. Direct
   ❑ c. Hierarchical
   ❑ d. Web of Trust

2. Which of following is a Trust Model where the user trusts a key because the user knows where it came from?

   ❑ a. Direct Trust
   ❑ b. Hierarchical Trust
   ❑ c. Web of Trust
   ❑ d. Trusted Introducer

3. Which of the following is *not* an example of a PKI Trust Model?

   ❑ a. Direct Trust
   ❑ b. Web of Trust
   ❑ c. Tree Trust
   ❑ d. Hierarchical Trust

4. Which of the following is a Trust Model based on a number of Root Certificates?

   ❑ a. Direct Trust
   ❑ b. Hierarchical Trust
   ❑ c. Web of Trust
   ❑ d. Trusted Root User

5. Which of the following are *not* PKI Trust Models? (Select all that apply.)

   ❑ a. Direct Trust
   ❑ b. Hierarchical Trust
   ❑ c. Key Trust
   ❑ d. Indirect Trust

Objective 4.4: Standards and Protocols

1. Which of the following standards allows Certificate
   Authorities to implement unique passwords that protect
   encrypted network transmissions?
   - ❑ a. X.509
   - ❑ b. PKCS #1
   - ❑ c. ISO17799
   - ❑ d. PKCS #11

Quick Answer: **174**
Detailed Answer: **181**

2. Which of the following is a standard for Information Security
   Management?
   - ❑ a. ISO17799
   - ❑ b. X.509
   - ❑ c. X.400
   - ❑ d. PKS #6

Quick Answer: **174**
Detailed Answer: **181**

3. What does the acronym PKCS stand for?
   - ❑ a. Public key Cryptography Security
   - ❑ b. Public key Cryptography Sanctions
   - ❑ c. Public key Cryptography Standards
   - ❑ d. Public key Cryptography Software

Quick Answer: **174**
Detailed Answer: **181**

4. Which of the following standards is concerned with the handling of email messages?
   - ❑ a. X.900
   - ❑ b. X.509
   - ❑ c. X.500
   - ❑ d. X.400

Quick Answer: **174**
Detailed Answer: **181**

Objective 4.5: Key Management/Certificate Lifecycle

1. What does Key management *not* deal with?
   - ❑ a. Secure generation
   - ❑ b. Distribution of keys
   - ❑ c. Storage of keys
   - ❑ d. Creation of keys

Quick Answer: **174**
Detailed Answer: **181**

2. What do keys in PKI offer?

- ❑ a. Two-key security
- ❑ b. Public encryption
- ❑ c. Private decryption
- ❑ d. Group policy

Quick Answer: **174**
Detailed Answer: **181**

3. Which of the following relates to Certificate Lifecycle? (Select all that apply.)

- ❑ a. Key expiration
- ❑ b. Key revocation
- ❑ c. Key renewal
- ❑ d. Key usage

Quick Answer: **174**
Detailed Answer: **181**

Objective 4.5.1: Centralized Versus Decentralized

1. Which of the following models use centralized key management when implementing PKI?

- ❑ a. Escrow
- ❑ b. Hierarchical
- ❑ c. Pretty Good Privacy
- ❑ d. Subordinate CA

Quick Answer: **174**
Detailed Answer: **181**

2. Which of the following models use decentralized key management when implementing PKI?

- ❑ a. Escrow
- ❑ b. Hierarchical
- ❑ c. Pretty Good Privacy
- ❑ d. Subordinate CA

Quick Answer: **174**
Detailed Answer: **181**

Objective 4.5.2: Storage

1. Which of the following are accepted techniques to store PKI keys? (Select all that apply.)

- ❑ a. Public key protection
- ❑ b. Private key protection
- ❑ c. Hardware key storage
- ❑ d. Software key storage

Quick Answer: **174**
Detailed Answer: **181**

. . . .

Objective 4.5.2.1: Hardware Versus Software

1. Which of the following is a software key storage implementation to protect Private keys?

   ❑　a.　Smart card storage

   ❑　b.　HSM

   ❑　c.　CA key folder on a server

   ❑　d.　PCMCIA storage

Quick Answer: **174**
Detailed Answer: **182**

2. Which of the following are hardware key storage implementations to protect Private keys? (Select all that apply.)

   ❑　a.　Smart card storage

   ❑　b.　HSM

   ❑　c.　Root CA on a server

   ❑　d.　PCMCIA storage

Quick Answer: **174**
Detailed Answer: **182**

Objective 4.5.2.2: Private Key Protection

1. Which of the following are ways to protect Private keys? (Select all that apply.)

   ❑　a.　Off-site storage

   ❑　b.　Escrow

   ❑　c.　Hardware key storage

   ❑　d.　Software key storage

Quick Answer: **175**
Detailed Answer: **182**

Objective 4.5.3: Escrow

1. Which of the following allows for third-party agents to maintain knowledge of portions of a cryptographic key for later recovery?

   ❑　a.　Partitioning key

   ❑　b.　Escrow

   ❑　c.　Limited key access

   ❑　d.　Separation of keys

Quick Answer: **175**
Detailed Answer: **182**

2. Escrow incorporates which tenet of security?

   ❑　a.　Loose Lips Sink Ships

   ❑　b.　Separation of Duties

   ❑　c.　Management by Objectives

   ❑　d.　Tighten the Rope

Quick Answer: **175**
Detailed Answer: **182**

Objective 4.5.4: Expiration

1. Which one of the following applies to the certificate expiration date?

 ❑ a. After the Valid To date is reached, the certificate must be destroyed

 ❑ b. After the Valid To date is reached, the certificate must be renewed

 ❑ c. After the Valid To date is reached, the certificate must be returned or regenerated

 ❑ d. After the Valid To date is reached, the certificate must be destroyed or renewed

Objective 4.5.5: Revocation

1. If a company thinks that a user's Private key has been compromised, what should it do?

 ❑ a. Turn the CA server on and off

 ❑ b. Shut down the CA server

 ❑ c. Revoke the person's key before expiration

 ❑ d. Renew the person's key before expiration

Objective 4.5.5.1: Status Checking

1. Which of the following methods provide for the status of revoked keys? (Select all that apply.)

 ❑ a. PKI admin

 ❑ b. CRL

 ❑ c. CA revocation list

 ❑ d. OCSP

2. Which of the following provides accurate information about revocation lists?

 ❑ a. CRL files are generally smaller than OCSP

 ❑ b. OCSP files are generally smaller than CRL

 ❑ c. Only CRL contains revocation lists

 ❑ d. Only OCSP contains revocation lists

Objective 4.5.6: Suspension

1. One of your university professors is going on a three-month sabbatical in Europe. What is the best course of action for his user's certificate?

❏ a. Suspension
❏ b. Deletion
❏ c. Expiration
❏ d. Extension

Objective 4.5.6.1: Status Checking

1. You are reviewing the status of certificates and notice Mr. Brown has a Certificate Hold. What does this mean?

❏ a. Mr. Brown's key has been revoked
❏ b. Mr. Brown's key has been suspended
❏ c. Mr. Brown's key has expired
❏ d. Mr. Brown's key has been recovered

Objective 4.5.7: Recovery

1. One key recovery technique is to first encrypt a cryptographic key with another key and then to give that key to a third party to hold or decrypt as needed. What is this technique called?

❏ a. Third-party recovery
❏ b. Standard practice for CAs
❏ c. Key encapsulation
❏ d. Root CA recovery

2. Which of the following are needed to recover a CA key? (Select all that apply.)

❏ a. Key creation time
❏ b. Key owner's name
❏ c. Name of issuing CA server
❏ d. Time of recovery

Objective 4.5.7.1: M of N Control

1. Which of the following terms relates to a key recovery technique that splits the responsibility to a group of key recovery agents so that no one single entity can recover the key?

❏ a. Key recovery control
❏ b. Status checking control
❏ c. Split recovery
❏ d. M of N control

Objective 4.5.8: Renewal

1. Which of the following applies to key renewal? (Select all that apply.)

Quick Answer: **175**
Detailed Answer: **183**

   ❑ a. Renewal is required when information changes

   ❑ b. Renewal is *not* required when information changes

   ❑ c. Renewal requires proof of identity

   ❑ d. Renewal does *not* require proof of identity

Objective 4.5.9: Destruction

1. What should be done when it becomes necessary to fully destroy a set of CA keys?

Quick Answer: **175**
Detailed Answer: **183**

   ❑ a. Nothing can be done; the keys remain at the root CA

   ❑ b. Revoke the keys

   ❑ c. Deregister the keys

   ❑ d. Destroy the CA

Objective 4.5.10: Key Usage

1. What kinds of keys are used within PKI when we use the Internet? (Select all that apply.)

Quick Answer: **175**
Detailed Answer: **183**

   ❑ a. Public key

   ❑ b. Private key

   ❑ c. Secret key

   ❑ d. Trusted key

2. Which of the following statements about keys is true?

Quick Answer: **175**
Detailed Answer: **183**

   ❑ a. A Session key is an encrypted key that was mathematically obtained from a Public key

   ❑ b. A Public key is an encrypted key that was mathematically obtained from a Private key

   ❑ c. A Session key is a decrypted key that was mathematically obtained from a Private key

   ❑ d. A Private key is an encrypted key that was mathematically obtained from a Public key

3. Which of the following cryptographic keys is used to encipher application data?

Quick Answer: **175**
Detailed Answer: **183**

   ❑ a. Data encryption key

   ❑ b. Public encryption key

   ❑ c. Secret data key

   ❑ d. Session encryption key

4. When could you use keys to implement PKI? (Select all that apply.)

Quick Answer: **175**
Detailed Answer: **183**

- ❏ a. PGP
- ❏ b. S/MIME
- ❏ c. VPN
- ❏ d. SSH

Objective 4.5.10.1: Multiple Key Pairs (Single, Dual)

1. What should your company do if it fears that digital signatures may be forged?

Quick Answer: **175**
Detailed Answer: **183**

- ❏ a. Destroy the digital signatures
- ❏ b. Remove the Certificate Authority
- ❏ c. Use multiple key pairs
- ❏ d. Use only VPN connections

Quick Check Answer Key

Objective 4.1: Algorithms

1. a.

Objective 4.1.1: Hashing

1. b.
2. d.
3. b.
4. a.
5. a.
6. c.
7. a, b, and c.

Objective 4.1.2: Symmetric

1. c.
2. b, c, and d.
3. c.
4. a.
5. b.
6. a and b.
7. a and b.
8. c.
9. b, c, and d.
10. a and b.
11. b.
12. c.

13. b.
14. c.
15. d.
16. d.
17. d.
18. a, c, and d.
19. d.
20. c.

Objective 4.1.3: Asymmetric

1. a, b, and c.
2. d.
3. d.
4. a.
5. a.
6. b.
7. b.

Objective 4.2: Concepts of Using Cryptography

1. a and c.
2. d.
3. b.
4. d.

Objective 4.2.1: Confidentiality

1. a.
2. c.

Objective 4.2.2: Integrity

1. b.
2. a.
3. c.

Objective 4.2.2.1: Digital Signatures

1. b.
2. a, b, and c.
3. b.
4. d.

Objective 4.2.3: Authentication

1. a.
2. b.
3. b.

Objective 4.2.4: Non-Repudiation

1. a.
2. a.
3. b and c.

Quick Check Answer Key

**Objective 4.2.4.1:
Digital Signatures**

1. a.

**Objective 4.2.5:
Access Control**

1. b.

**Objective 4.3:
PKI**

1. d.

2. a, c, and d.

3. a, b, and c.

4. a, b, and d.

5. a, b, c, and d.

**Objective 4.3.1:
Certificates—
Distinguish Which
Certificates Are
Used for What
Purpose. Basics
Only.**

1. a, b, and c.

2. a.

3. c.

4. c.

5. a and c.

6. b.

7. b.

8. c.

9. b and d.

**Objective 4.3.1.1:
Certificate Policies**

1. c.

2. a, b, and c.

**Objective 4.3.1.2:
Certificate Practice
Statements**

1. d.

**Objective 4.3.2:
Revocation**

1. a.

2. a.

3. b.

**Objective 4.3.3:
Trust Models**

1. b, c, and d.

2. a.

3. c.

4. b.

5. c and d.

**Objective 4.4:
Standards and
Protocols**

1. a.

2. a.

3. c.

4. d.

**Objective 4.5:
Key
Management/
Certificate
Lifecycle**

1. d.

2. a.

3. a, b, c, and d.

**Objective 4.5.1:
Centralized Versus
Decentralized**

1. b.

2. c.

**Objective 4.5.2:
Storage**

1. b, c, and d.

**Objective 4.5.2.1:
Hardware Versus
Software**

1. c.

2. a, b, and d.

Quick Check Answer Key

**Objective 4.5.2.2:
Private Key Protection**

1. a, b, c and d.

**Objective 4.5.3:
Escrow**

1. b.

2. b.

**Objective 4.5.4:
Expiration**

1. d.

**Objective 4.5.5:
Revocation**

1. c.

**Objective 4.5.5.1:
Status Checking**

1. b and d.

2. b.

**Objective 4.5.6:
Suspension**

1. a.

**Objective 4.5.6.1:
Status Checking**

1. b.

**Objective 4.5.7:
Recovery**

1. c.

2. a, b, and c.

**Objective 4.5.7.1:
M of N Control**

1. d.

**Objective 4.5.8:
Renewal**

1. b and d.

**Objective 4.5.9:
Destruction**

1. c.

**Objective 4.5.10:
Key Usage**

1. a and b.

2. b.

3. a.

4. a, b, c, and d.

**Objective 4.5.10.1:
Multiple Key Pairs
(Single, Dual)**

1. c.

Answers and Explanations

Objective 4.1: Algorithms

1. **a.** An algorithm is a series of steps used to obtain a result.

Objective 4.1.1: Hashing

1. **b.** When digitally signing a message using a hash function, the sender's Private key encrypts the message digest.

2. **d.** Hash consistently uses 128-bit encryption.

3. **b.** A hashing algorithm is the name for creating a message digest using mathematics.

4. **a.** A Private key is used to sign or encrypt the message digest.

5. **a.** The receiver of the file uses the Public key of the signer of the encrypted message.

6. **c.** Secure Hash Algorithm (SHA-1) uses 160-bit message digests.

7. **a, b, and c.** SHA-1, MD2, and MD5 offer mathematical hashing.

Objective 4.1.2: Symmetrical

1. **c.** Rijndael is a symmetric algorithm.

2. **b, c, and d.** AES, IDEA, and DES are symmetric algorithms.

3. **c.** Although each one is a symmetrical algorithm, only Twofish meets all of the requirements.

4. **a.** With symmetric algorithms, client and server keys are similar or shared.

5. **b.** Secure Sockets Layer (SSL) uses symmetric encryption when securing a Web site.

6. **a and b.** Stream cipher uses a symmetric key and is used for encryption.

7. **a and b.** Block cipher uses a symmetric key and is also used for encryption.

8. **c.** Rijndael is the basis for the AES encryption algorithm.

9. **b, c, and d.** Limited security, scalability, and key distribution are known weaknesses of symmetric cryptography. Speed is the only advantage.

10. **a and b.** Block ciphers use a fixed-size block of plain text that is encrypted into a fixed-size block of encrypted text.

11. **b.** When exporting data from the United States, DES uses a 40-bit key size to encrypt data.

12. **c.** The standard block size for DES encrypted data should be 64-bit blocks.

13. **b.** The standard key size for DES encrypted data should be 56-bit blocks.

14. **c.** The chosen AES standard that replaces DES is the Rijndael encryption algorithm, which uses a maximum of 256 bits for its key size.

15. **d.** AES uses key sizes of 128-bits, 192-bits, or 256-bits.

16. **d.** Rijndael algorithm is used with Advanced Encryption Standard (AES), at key lengths of 128, 192, and 256 bits.

17. **d.** The key size for triple DES (three keys) encrypted data is 168-bit keys, or three (3) times 56 bits.

18. **a, c, and d.** CAST is one type of symmetric algorithm that may use 128-bit or 256-bit encryption.

19. **d.** The maximum key size for the RC5 algorithm is 2040-bits.

20. **c.** Blowfish is a symmetric block cipher with variable-length key that was designed to be a free replacement for DES or IDEA.

Objective 4.1.3: Asymmetric

1. **a, b, and c.** RSA, ECC, and El Gamal are algorithms that use asymmetric keys.

2. **d.** Diffie-Hellman, ECC, and El Gamal are algorithms that use asymmetric keys. Blowfish uses symmetric keys.

3. **d.** Of those listed, RSA is the only asymmetric algorithm.

4. **a.** Asymmetric encryption is slower than symmetric encryption, because of its client-server configuration requirements.

5. **a.** RSA represents Rivest, Shamir, and Adelman an asymmetric algorithm. RSA ends in the letter "A" for asymmetric, whereas DES, AES, and 3DES end in "S" for symmetric.

6. **b.** RSA is used for encryption, key exchange, and digital signatures.

7. **b.** The Elliptic Curve Cryptosystems (ECC) is best suited for communication with handheld wireless devices.

. . . .

Objective 4.2: Concepts of Using Cryptography

1. **a and c.** The two secret key algorithms are block cipher, which encrypts data in chunks of a specified size and stream cipher, which uses a fixed-length or variable key.

2. **d.** Block cipher is a type of symmetric-key encryption algorithm that changes a fixed-size block of clear text data into a block of ciphertext data of the same length.

3. **b.** When using a Public key cryptography system and after you encrypt data using a Public key, only the Private key can decrypt that data.

4. **d.** When dealing with network security, C.I.A. is an acronym that implies Confidentiality, Integrity, and Availability.

Objective 4.2.1: Confidentiality

1. **a.** Confidentiality is the protection of data against unauthorized access or disclosure.

2. **c.** You are really concerned with confidentiality of the message in this situation.

Objective 4.2.2: Integrity

1. **b.** Integrity guarantees that message data sent is the same as the message data received.

2. **a.** A message digest provides for data integrity.

3. **c.** Data integrity is a security term, referring to a method that ensures all data is sequenced, and numbered.

Objective 4.2.2.1: Digital Signatures

1. **b.** Digital signatures offer non-repudiation and maintain integrity.

2. **a, b, and c.** A digital signature is a value created with an algorithm and appended to data so that a recipient can verify the data's origin and integrity.

3. **b.** A Private key is used to create a unique Digital Signature.

4. **d.** You will still not be able to prevent Denial of Service even if you implement token technologies and use digital signatures.

Objective 4.2.3: Authentication

1. **a.** Strong Authentication uses a Public key to verify a digital signature for authenticity.

2. **b.** A Public key certificate is used to authenticate users.

3. **b.** KryptoKnight provides for authentication, key distribution services, and single sign-on (SSO).

Objective 4.2:4: Non-Repudiation

1. **a.** Digital signatures offer non-repudiation and maintain integrity.

2. **a.** The Application Layer 7 offers non-repudiation.

3. **b and c.** Non-repudiation is a term that relates to a record of all transactions made during a certificate services session.

Objective 4.2.4.1: Digital Signatures

1. **a.** Digital signatures offer non-repudiation and maintain integrity.

Objective 4.2.5: Access Control

1. **b.** Controlling access to information systems and associated networks is the primary security action to ensure data integrity, network availability, and confidentiality.

Objective 4.3: PKI

1. **d.** PKI stands for Public Key Infrastructure.

2. **a, c, and d.** Public Key Infrastructure (PKI) has the ability to issue a new certificate for a Public Key, the ability to cancel a previously issued Certificate, and the ability to determine whether a Certificate is valid.

3. **a, b, and c.** PKI stands for Public Key Infrastructure, which is responsible for locating, issuing, trusting, renewing, and revoking Certificates.

4. **a, b, and d.** Public Key Infrastructure (PKI) offers Privacy, Authentication, and Nonrepudiation when used with Certificate services.

5. **a, b, c, and d.** Public Key Infrastructure (PKI) offers all the items listed.

Objective 4.3.1: Certificates—Distinguish Which Certificates Are Used for What Purpose. Basics Only.

1. **a, b, and c.** Public keys offer Nonrepudiation, Privacy, and Authentication.

2. **a.** The Certificate Authority (CA) is responsible for Certificates and digitally signing them using a Private key.

3. **c.** Digital certificates consist of a Public key, certificate information, and a digital signature.

4. **c.** Online Certificate Status Protocol (OCSP) is an instant access method used to check the status of certificates.

5. **a and c.** A Certificate Revocation List (CRL) is a reference list of certificates that have been identified for revocation prior to their original expiration date and Online Certificate Status Protocol (OCSP) is an instant access method used to check the status of certificates.

6. **b.** The Certificate Authority (CA) is responsible for issuing certificates to authorized users.

7. **b.** X.509 is an industry standard for digital certificates.

8. **c.** The root CA is the top-level Certificate Authority.

9. **b and d.** To obtain a new certificate from a trusted Certificate Authority, you must have some form of proven identity and a Public key.

Objective 4.3.1.1: Certificate Policies

1. **c.** A certificate policy is a set of rules for the detailed use of certificates.

2. **a, b, and c.** You should list these items in your certificate policy.

Objective 4.3.1.2: Certificate Practice Statements

1. **d.** A certificate practice statement explains the implementation methods to a set of rules for the detailed use of certificates.

Objective 4.3.2: Revocation

1. **a.** A Certificate Revocation List (CRL) is a reference list of certificates that have been identified for revocation prior to their original expiration date.

2. **a.** Revocation requires certificates to be terminated before their expiration date.

3. **b.** A Certificate Revocation List (CRL) is a reference list of certificates that have been identified for revocation prior to their original expiration date.

Objective 4.3.3: Trust Models

1. **b, c, and d.** The PKI trust models consist of Direct Trust, Hierarchical Trust, and Web of Trust.

2. **a.** Direct Trust is a trust model where the user trusts a key because the user knows where it came from.

3. **c.** The trust model contains three different models Direct Trust, Web of Trust, and Hierarchical Trust.

4. **b.** Hierarchical Trust is based on a number of root certificates.

5. **c and d.** There are three PKI trust models: Direct Trust, Hierarchical Trust, and Web of Trust.

Objective 4.4: Standards and Protocols

1. **a.** X.509 allows Certificate Authorities to implement unique passwords that protect encrypted network transmissions.

2. **a.** ISO17799 is a standard for Information Security Management.

3. **c.** PKCS stands for Public key Cryptography Standards, which deals with PKI methods to securely exchange data.

4. **d.** The X.400 standard is concerned with the handling of email messages.

Objective 4.5: Key Management/Certificate Lifecycle

1. **d.** Key management doesn't deal with key creation.

2. **a.** PKI keys offer two-key security.

3. **a, b, c, and d.** Certificate Lifecycle deals with all the items listed and more.

Objective 4.5.1: Centralized Versus Decentralized

1. **b.** The Hierarchical Model uses centralized key management when implementing PKI.

2. **c.** Pretty Good Privacy uses decentralized key management when implementing PKI.

Objective 4.5.2: Storage

1. **b, c, and d.** Private key protection, hardware key storage and software key storage are accepted techniques to store PKI keys.

Objective 4.5.2.1: Hardware Versus Software

1. **c.** Establishing a CA key folder on a server is a software key storage implementation to protect Private keys.

2. **a, b, and d.** Hardware Storage Modules (HSM), smart card storage, and PCMCIA storage are hardware key storage implementations to protect Private keys.

Objective 4.5.2.2: Private Key Protection

1. **a, b, c, and d.** All the items listed are ways to protect Private keys.

Objective 4.5.3: Escrow

1. **b.** Escrow allows for third party agents to maintain knowledge of portions of a cryptographic key for later recovery.

2. **b.** Escrow incorporates the security tenant of Separation of Duties.

Objective 4.5.4: Expiration

1. **d.** After the Valid To date is reached, the certificate must be destroyed or renewed.

Objective 4.5.5: Revocation

1. **c.** If a company thinks that a Private key has been compromised, revoke the person's key before expiration.

Objective 4.5.5.1: Status Checking

1. **b and d.** Certificate Revocation Lists (CRL) and Online Certificate Status Protocol (OCSP) provide for the status of revoked keys.

2. **b.** OCSP files are generally smaller than CRL.

Objective 4.5.6: Suspension

1. **a.** Suspension is the best course of action.

Objective 4.5.6.1: Status Checking

1. **b.** Certificate Hold means that Mr. Brown's key has been suspended.

Objective 4.5.7: Recovery

1. **c.** Key encapsulation is a key recovery technique that first encrypts a cryptographic key with another key and then gives that key to a third party to hold or decrypt as needed.

2. **a, b, and c.** The key creation time, key owner's name, and name of issuing CA server are needed to recover a CA key.

Objective 4.5.7.1: M of N Control

1. **d.** M of N control relates to a key recovery technique that splits the responsibility to a group of key recovery agents so that no one single entity can recover the key.

Objective 4.5.8: Renewal

1. **b and d.** Key renewal is *not* required when information changes and does *not* require proof of identity.

Objective 4.5.9: Destruction

1. **c.** Deregister the keys when it becomes necessary to fully destroy a set of CA keys.

Objective 4.5.10: Key Usage

1. **a and b.** We exchange data through the use of a Public and a Private cryptographic key pair that is obtained and shared through a trusted authority.

2. **b.** A Public key is an encrypted key that was mathematically obtained from a Private key.

3. **a.** The data encryption key is used to encipher application data.

4. **a, b, c, and d.** All the items listed offer key usage.

Objective 4.5.10.1: Multiple Key Pairs (Single, Dual)

1. **c.** Use multiple key pairs if you fear that digital signatures may be forged.

Domain 5.0: Operational/Organizational Security

Quick Check

Objective 5.1: Physical Security

1. Which of the following provide some degree of physical security for your network? (Select all that apply.)
   - ❑ a. Use intrusion detection systems
   - ❑ b. Develop and adhere to security procedures
   - ❑ c. Install anti-theft devices
   - ❑ d. Review facilities engineering to protect against fire or water damage

Quick Answer: **217**
Detailed Answer: **222**

2. Which of the following are examples of physical security controls? (Select all that apply.)
   - ❑ a. A double-locked server room
   - ❑ b. Night watchmen
   - ❑ c. Storing backups of critical files
   - ❑ d. Training an emergency response team

Quick Answer: **217**
Detailed Answer: **222**

3. What is the purpose of implementing physical security? (Select all that apply.)
   - ❑ a. Prevent theft
   - ❑ b. Prevent unauthorized disclosure of data
   - ❑ c. Prevent physical damage
   - ❑ d. Prevent system integrity

Quick Answer: **217**
Detailed Answer: **222**

Objective 5.1.1: Access Control

1. One of your known employees gained legal access to a secure building, but another, illegal person snuck in behind him before the door locked. This is an example of what type of situation?

   ❑   a. A physical security risk known as open door
   ❑   b. A physical security risk known as piggybacking
   ❑   c. A logical security risk known as payback, or sucker attack
   ❑   d. A logical security risk known as corporate espionage

Quick Answer: **217**
Detailed Answer: **222**

2. Your employer wants to know why you requested a fail-soft rather than fail-safe door on your server room, especially after he placed such emphasis on security access control in the last meeting. Which of the following provides the best answer?

   ❑   a. The cost of a fail-soft door is less than a fail-safe door
   ❑   b. The fail-soft door provides a safer employer environment
   ❑   c. The weight of a fail-soft door is less than a fail-safe door
   ❑   d. The fail-soft door provides a more secure environment

Quick Answer: **217**
Detailed Answer: **222**

3. You want to implement technical access controls that are detective in nature. Which of the following would apply? (Select all that apply.)

   ❑   a. Honey pot
   ❑   b. Auditing
   ❑   c. Software firewall
   ❑   d. Intrusion detection system

Quick Answer: **217**
Detailed Answer: **222**

4. One method of maintaining access control is the use of security guards. Why is this a potential concern?

   ❑   a. Training time
   ❑   b. High cost
   ❑   c. Possible human error
   ❑   d. Possible theft

Quick Answer: **217**
Detailed Answer: **222**

5. Your building uses a transponder for access control. Which of the following are true about this device?

   ❑   a. It is a proximity identification device
   ❑   b. It requires no user interaction
   ❑   c. It responds with an access code to signals
   ❑   d. It contains a radio receiver and transmitter

Quick Answer: **217**
Detailed Answer: **222**

6. Which of the following are physical access controls? (Select all that apply.)

Quick Answer: **217**
Detailed Answer: **222**

❑ a. Locks

❑ b. Passwords

❑ c. Iris scans

❑ d. Security guards

7. Which of the following statements pertaining to access control is true? (Select all that apply.)

Quick Answer: **217**
Detailed Answer: **222**

❑ a. When access to data is not explicitly denied, it should be implicitly allowed

❑ b. Typically, users only have access to data on a need-to-know basis

❑ c. Users who perform specific group tasks may be assigned group rights

❑ d. No access is a tighter control than partial access with limited permissions

8. Which of the following is true about access control on production programs?

Quick Answer: **217**
Detailed Answer: **222**

❑ a. Unrestricted access should only be given to programmers

❑ b. Unrestricted access should only be given to auditors

❑ c. No one should have unrestricted access

❑ d. Everyone should have unrestricted access

Objective 5.1.1.1: Physical Barriers

1. When a surgeon scrubs his fingers, he must scrub all portions to ensure a physical barrier protects him from germs. Likewise, what is true of a network server room when considering a physical barrier?

Quick Answer: **217**
Detailed Answer: **222**

❑ a. Scrub all walls clean before installing the server for a good physical barrier

❑ b. Lock all doors before leaving the server room

❑ c. Consider securing or hardening the ceiling and floor, as well as the walls

❑ d. Place monitors so that they see all sides of the room

2. Which of the following physical barriers are reasonable alternatives to a separate or centralized server room? (Select all that apply.)

Quick Answer: **217**
Detailed Answer: **222**

❑ a. Use a server cluster

❑ b. Use a locked cabinet

❑ c. Use an off-site storage facility

❑ d. Use a secure rack

Objective 5.1.1.2: Biometrics

1. Which of the following terms relates to control of user access to critical information using a human being's physical characteristics?

Quick Answer: **217**
Detailed Answer: **223**

 ❑   a. Physical control
 ❑   b. Biophysics
 ❑   c. Biometrics
 ❑   d. Physical access

2. One of the most critical errors in biometrics is allowing unauthorized access to an imposter. Which of the following names this situation?

Quick Answer: **217**
Detailed Answer: **223**

 ❑   a. True Acceptance Rate, Type IV error
 ❑   b. True Rejection Rate, Type III error
 ❑   c. False Acceptance Rate, Type II error
 ❑   d. False Rejection Rate, Type I error

3. You want to implement biometrics as an access control for your network. Which of the following order of biometric methods are listed as most accurate to least accurate methods?

Quick Answer: **217**
Detailed Answer: **223**

 ❑   a. Fingerprint, voice verification, iris scan
 ❑   b. Iris scan, voice verification, fingerprint
 ❑   c. Voice verification, iris scan, fingerprint
 ❑   d. Iris scan, fingerprint, voice verification

Objective 5.1.2: Social Engineering

1. Some people are very kind, dynamic, and trustworthy from the very first moment you meet them. You almost want to tell them your life story and even share work-related problems. What has occurred when such people take advantage of this trust to gain access to network passwords, shared files, or other critical resources?

Quick Answer: **217**
Detailed Answer: **223**

 ❑   a. Social intervention
 ❑   b. Social spoofing
 ❑   c. Social engineering
 ❑   d. Socializing

2. Social engineering takes advantage of which organizational weakness?

Quick Answer: **217**
Detailed Answer: **223**

 ❑   a. Network design or topology
 ❑   b. Network hardware or software
 ❑   c. Human work schedules
 ❑   d. Human behavior

Objective 5.1.3: Environment

1. Which of the following is a potential cause for chip creep?

  Quick Answer: **217**
  Detailed Answer: **223**

  ❑ a. Environmental fluctuations in room temperature

  ❑ b. Theft of one or two domain platforms

  ❑ c. Physical destruction of network components

  ❑ d. Termination of a network administrator

2. Your network is spread throughout several rooms. You use forced air heating and ventilation. What would be the ideal environmental humidity range for operating your computers?

  Quick Answer: **217**
  Detailed Answer: **223**

  ❑ a. 10–30% relative humidity

  ❑ b. 15–40% relative humidity

  ❑ c. 40–60% relative humidity

  ❑ d. 55–80% relative humidity

Objective 5.1.3.1: Wireless Cells

1. Your company headquarters works with highly sensitive data and the president now insists on using wireless cell technology for his private office, which happens to overlook the park. Which one of the following security measures would you recommend to increase your network security.

  Quick Answer: **217**
  Detailed Answer: **223**

  ❑ a. Consider placing wireless antennae near windows for greater connectivity

  ❑ b. Consider shielding the outer walls for greater security

  ❑ c. Consider shielding walls and ceilings for greater security

  ❑ d. Consider removing windows for total isolation

Objective 5.1.3.2: Location

1. Your office is moving to a new location downtown. You want to recommend the safest area for the main network department to locate computers and other major networking equipment. The building height is eight floors. What do you recommend?

  Quick Answer: **217**
  Detailed Answer: **223**

  ❑ a. Locate your department on the ground floor

  ❑ b. Locate your department on the first floor near the exit

  ❑ c. Locate your department on the third or fourth floor

  ❑ d. Locate your department on the top floor

2. Facility location is extremely important from a security standpoint. If your company requires greater security and less public interaction, which of the following is a primary goal?

- ❏ a. Increased population
- ❏ b. Decreased visibility
- ❏ c. Increased advertisement
- ❏ d. Decreased costs

Quick Answer: 217
Detailed Answer: 223

Objective 5.1.3.3: Shielding

1. Your company purchased only one Uninterruptible Power Supply (UPS). Which of the following pieces of equipment should have priority for protection?

- ❏ a. Network cabling
- ❏ b. Telephone lines
- ❏ c. Workstations
- ❏ d. Servers

Quick Answer: 217
Detailed Answer: 223

2. One form of shielding is known as a Faraday's cage. What kind of shielding is this?

- ❏ a. A physical stronghold, an impenetrable building
- ❏ b. A building that is free from outside noise
- ❏ c. A building that is free from outside electricity
- ❏ d. A cage to store electrical equipment

Quick Answer: 217
Detailed Answer: 223

Objective 5.1.3.4: Fire Suppression

1. Which type of fire extinguisher is most appropriate for server room?

- ❏ a. Type A
- ❏ b. Type B
- ❏ c. Type A-B combo
- ❏ d. Type C

Quick Answer: 217
Detailed Answer: 223

2. Which of the following are effective fire suppression systems?

- ❏ a. Halon systems
- ❏ b. CO_2 systems
- ❏ c. Soda acid systems
- ❏ d. H_2O systems

Quick Answer: 217
Detailed Answer: 223

3. Within a dry pipe system what does a clapper valve do?

  ❑ a. It stops the fire

  ❑ b. It suppresses the fire

  ❑ c. It stops the flow of water

  ❑ d. It allows for the flow of water

Quick Answer: **217**
Detailed Answer: **224**

4. Which of the following are preferred ways to suppress an electrical fire? (Select all that apply.)

  ❑ a. CO_2

  ❑ b. Soda acid

  ❑ c. Halon, if not banned

  ❑ d. Water

Quick Answer: **217**
Detailed Answer: **224**

Objective 5.2: Disaster Recovery

1. Even though your company suffered a small earthquake and power outage, you were able to continue operations at an alternate location. Now, it's time to return to your main site. Which of the following processes should you start there first?

  ❑ a. The most critical process

  ❑ b. Any functioning process

  ❑ c. The least critical process

  ❑ d. The most expensive process

Quick Answer: **217**
Detailed Answer: **224**

2. Which of the following are critical requirements for disaster recovery? (Select all that apply.)

  ❑ a. Record change levels

  ❑ b. Record any revisions

  ❑ c. Record network traffic

  ❑ d. Record security audits

Quick Answer: **217**
Detailed Answer: **224**

Objective 5.2.1: Backups

1. Which of the following is the *best* way to protect data against disaster, corruption, or loss?

  ❑ a. Cache backup

  ❑ b. Tape backup

  ❑ c. RAID 5

  ❑ d. RAID 1

Quick Answer: **217**
Detailed Answer: **224**

2. Which of the following are current tape backup methods? (Select all that apply.)

Quick Answer: **217**
Detailed Answer: **224**

❑   a. Full backup
❑   b. Partial backup
❑   c. Incremental backup
❑   d. Differential backup

3. When selecting a tape backup method, which of the following is *best* (without regard to time, space, or finances)?

Quick Answer: **217**
Detailed Answer: **224**

❑   a. Partial backup
❑   b. Incremental backup
❑   c. Full backup
❑   d. Differential backup

4. You have decided to use a backup method that does *not* track deletions, thereby increasing your storage requirements. Which method have you chosen?

Quick Answer: **217**
Detailed Answer: **224**

❑   a. Partial backup
❑   b. Incremental backup
❑   c. Full backup
❑   d. Differential backup

5. Which of the following backup methods are used together most often?

Quick Answer: **217**
Detailed Answer: **224**

❑   a. Partial backup and full backup
❑   b. Incremental backup and full backup
❑   c. Incremental backup and differential backup
❑   d. Differential backup and full backup

6. Which of the following should you select when you want to copy only files that were modified since the last full backup?

Quick Answer: **217**
Detailed Answer: **224**

❑   a. Incremental
❑   b. Selected
❑   c. Differential
❑   d. Partial

Objective 5.2.1.1: Off Site Storage

1. Which of the following are required items at a hot site? (Select all that apply.)

Quick Answer: **217**
Detailed Answer: **224**

❑   a. Cables and network peripherals
❑   b. Computers
❑   c. Current data backups
❑   d. Climate control

2. Which of the following are true about a cold site when planning for off site storage? (Select all that apply.)

❏ a. Cold sites are difficult to get to
❏ b. Cold sites are least expensive
❏ c. Cold sites are most expensive
❏ d. Cold sites are most difficult to test

3. Which of the following equipment would you likely see at a
cold site? (Select all that apply.)

❏ a. Electricity
❏ b. Air Conditioning
❏ c. Flooring
❏ d. Networked Computers

Objective 5.2.2: Secure Recovery

1. What should be the goal when planning for a disaster that
affects your network?

❏ a. Total recall
❏ b. Secure recovery
❏ c. Software recall
❏ d. Hardware recovery

Objective 5.2.2.1: Alternate Sites

1. Which of the following are considered alternate sites for
secure recovery in case of a disaster? (Select all that apply.)

❏ a. Hot site
❏ b. Warm site
❏ c. Secondary site
❏ d. Primary site

Objective 5.2.3: Disaster Recovery Plan

1. You are establishing a disaster recovery plan. Which of the
following must be included?

❏ a. A security plan
❏ b. A risk assessment plan
❏ c. A standing operating procedure
❏ d. A fire plan

2. When making and testing a disaster recovery plan, what should be the first step of disaster recovery?

Quick Answer: **218**
Detailed Answer: **225**

    ❏   a. Ensure that critical systems are moved first from the alternate site back to the primary site

    ❏   b. Ensure that noncritical systems are moved first from the alternate site back to the primary site

    ❏   c. Ensure that critical personnel are moved first from the alternate site back to the primary site

    ❏   d. Ensure that noncritical personnel are moved first from the alternate site back to the primary site

3. When you plan for recovery of a networked office after a disaster, what should be of primary concern?

Quick Answer: **218**
Detailed Answer: **225**

    ❏   a. Personnel safety and data security

    ❏   b. Personnel security and data integrity

    ❏   c. Personnel safety and network connectivity

    ❏   d. Personnel security and network connectivity

4. Which person should make short-term recovery decisions just after a disaster?

Quick Answer: **218**
Detailed Answer: **225**

    ❏   a. The nearest person to the accident or incident

    ❏   b. A person who has been earmarked as the disaster recovery manager

    ❏   c. The network administrator

    ❏   d. A person working directly for the chief operations officer for disaster recovery

Objective 5.3: Business Continuity

1. A reliable disaster recovery plan is an important component of the organizations Business Continuity. Which of the following is the most critical item for this to be successful?

Quick Answer: **218**
Detailed Answer: **225**

    ❏   a. They must be short and written with pictures or graphs

    ❏   b. They must have management support

    ❏   c. They must have IT buy in

    ❏   d. They must be budgeted to within reason

2. Which of the following should be seen within a solid business continuity plan? (Select all that apply.)

Quick Answer: **218**
Detailed Answer: **225**

    ❏   a. A business impact analysis

    ❏   b. A risk analysis

    ❏   c. Integration and validation

    ❏   d. Maintenance and training

Objective 5.3.1: Utilities

1. You may want to shield your network with an Uninterruptible Power Supply (UPS). Which of the following describes a surge?

   ❑ a. A burst of power that is above normal voltage
   ❑ b. A prolonged power supply that is below normal voltage
   ❑ c. A prolonged high voltage that is above normal voltage
   ❑ d. A momentary low voltage

Quick Answer: **218**
Detailed Answer: **225**

2. You may want to shield your network with an Uninterruptible Power Supply (UPS). Which of the following describes a sag?

   ❑ a. A burst of power that is above normal voltage
   ❑ b. A prolonged power supply that is below normal voltage
   ❑ c. A prolonged high voltage that is above normal voltage
   ❑ d. A momentary low voltage

Quick Answer: **218**
Detailed Answer: **225**

3. You may want to shield your network with an Uninterruptible Power Supply (UPS). Which of the following describes a spike?

   ❑ a. A burst of power that is above normal voltage
   ❑ b. A prolonged power supply that is below normal voltage
   ❑ c. A prolonged high voltage that is above normal voltage
   ❑ d. A momentary low voltage

Quick Answer: **218**
Detailed Answer: **225**

4. You may want to shield your network with an Uninterruptible Power Supply (UPS). Which of the following describes a brownout?

   ❑ a. A burst of power that is above normal voltage
   ❑ b. A prolonged power supply that is below normal voltage
   ❑ c. A prolonged high voltage that is above normal voltage
   ❑ d. A momentary low voltage

Quick Answer: **218**
Detailed Answer: **225**

Objective 5.3.2: High Availability/Fault Tolerance

1. Which of the following networking activities best maintains data in a high state of availability?

   ❑ a. Firewall software implementation
   ❑ b. Security auditing
   ❑ c. IDS monitoring
   ❑ d. RAID implementation

Quick Answer: **218**
Detailed Answer: **225**

2. Which of the following terms is the meaning of RAID?

❑   a. Redundant Array of Intelligent Disks

❑   b. Remote Administration of Internal Doctors

❑   c. Redundant Array of Inexpensive Disks

❑   d. Ready Aids to Internetworking Devices

Quick Answer: **218**
Detailed Answer: **225**

Objective 5.3.3: Backups

1. When planning for business continuity, which backup method offers the most complete restoration?

❑   a. Incremental backup

❑   b. Differential backup

❑   c. Complete backup

❑   d. Full backup

Quick Answer: **218**
Detailed Answer: **225**

2. When planning for business continuity, which backup method has the fastest restore time?

❑   a. Incremental backup

❑   b. Differential backup

❑   c. Shortcut backup

❑   d. Full backup

Quick Answer: **218**
Detailed Answer: **225**

Objective 5.4: Policy and Procedures

1. Which of the following refers to the term Common Criteria?

❑   a. CompTIA's Common Security+ Objectives

❑   b. Internationally agreed upon IT Security Evaluation Criteria

❑   c. IEEE common standards for security training

❑   d. ITEF common standards for security evaluation

Quick Answer: **218**
Detailed Answer: **226**

2. When establishing policies and procedures, we should annotate which components are most important by a scale or weighted system. If management has determined that software has a value of 3, server performance has a value of 6, and email has a value of 5, what is the correct order to prioritize your efforts?

❑   a. Server performance, software, then email

❑   b. Software, server performance, then email

❑   c. Email, server performance, then software

❑   d. Server performance, email, then software

Quick Answer: **218**
Detailed Answer: **226**

Objective 5.4.1: Security Policy

1. Which of the following explains the requirements needed to protect an organization's network data and computer systems?

Quick Answer: **218**
Detailed Answer: **226**

- ❑ a. The IT weekly security bulletin
- ❑ b. The organization's security newsletter
- ❑ c. The business continuity plan
- ❑ d. The company's security policy

Objective 5.4.1.1: Acceptable Use

1. Which of the following policies clarify "users" roles and limitations when using network equipment, hardware and software, as well as email and Internet access?

Quick Answer: **218**
Detailed Answer: **226**

- ❑ a. The organization's security newsletter
- ❑ b. The acceptable use policy
- ❑ c. The disaster recovery plan
- ❑ d. The company's security policy

Objective 5.4.1.2: Due Care

1. What is the security term for the requirement of senior management to ensure that specific security protection is provided to the organization?

Quick Answer: **218**
Detailed Answer: **226**

- ❑ a. Hierarchical security
- ❑ b. Due Care
- ❑ c. Linear supervision
- ❑ d. Separation of Duties

2. You are reviewing your organization's security policy and procedures guidebook and come across the term Due Care. Which of the following best explains this term?

Quick Answer: **218**
Detailed Answer: **226**

- ❑ a. Actions taken to reduce the probability of damage or injury
- ❑ b. Preventative measures taken to reduce the probability of liabilities
- ❑ c. Actions taken to secure loose cabling and prevent theft
- ❑ d. Preventative measures taken to reduce the cost of sick time taken

Objective 5.4.1.3: Privacy

1. Which of the following company documents is designed to ensure that employees are aware of their rights and limitations when it involves use of organizational computers and any organizational employee auditing procedures?

   ❏ a. Health Insurance Portability and Accountability Act (HIPPA)
   ❏ b. Privacy policy
   ❏ c. Due Care policy
   ❏ d. Separation of Duties policy

Quick Answer: **218**
Detailed Answer: **226**

2. You are establishing company IT policies and procedures. Which of the following should you consider important to include when planning for email, downloading of unauthorized software, and your Web site data?

   ❏ a. Due Care policy
   ❏ b. Privacy policy
   ❏ c. Need to Know policy
   ❏ d. Separation of Duties policy

Quick Answer: **218**
Detailed Answer: **226**

Objective 5.4.1.4: Separation of Duties

1. Your company plans to implement a security policy that uses Separation of Duties as a main theme. What characterizes this Separation of Duties concept? (Select all that apply.)

   ❏ a. Tasks are divided among different employees
   ❏ b. Each employee works on a section of the overall task
   ❏ c. No one employee is able to complete the task alone
   ❏ d. Only the supervisor has complete control of all tasks

Quick Answer: **218**
Detailed Answer: **226**

2. Which of the following relates to the concept of Separation of Duties?

   ❏ a. Day shift and night shift
   ❏ b. Two-man control
   ❏ c. Partner efficiency
   ❏ d. Buddy-buddy system

Quick Answer: **218**
Detailed Answer: **226**

3. Which of the following is the term that is used to ensure that no single individual is able to compromise a system?

   ❏ a. No Nonsense Networking (NNN)
   ❏ b. Separation of Duties
   ❏ c. Due Diligence
   ❏ d. Due Care

Quick Answer: **218**
Detailed Answer: **226**

Objective 5.4.1.5: Need to Know

1. One of your employers has only been given the minimum information required about the network system to complete his assigned task. Which security policy relates to this concept?

  ❑   a. Acceptable Use
  ❑   b. Due Care
  ❑   c. Privacy
  ❑   d. Need to Know

Quick Answer: **218**
Detailed Answer: **227**

Objective 5.4.1.6: Password Management

1. When considering password management within a security policy, which of the following is generally considered the minimum length for a strong password that should also be able to withstand a Dictionary or Brute Force attack?

  ❑   a. 6
  ❑   b. 8
  ❑   c. 10
  ❑   d. 14

Quick Answer: **218**
Detailed Answer: **227**

2. Which of the following is the strongest password?

  ❑   a. Basketball001
  ❑   b. CharleyBrown
  ❑   c. Shouldn'tB4gotten
  ❑   d. MY1STpassword

Quick Answer: **218**
Detailed Answer: **227**

Objective 5.4.1.7: SLA

1. What do the letters SLA stand for as applied to network security?

  ❑   a. Single Authentication
  ❑   b. Security Level Administration
  ❑   c. Service Level Agreements
  ❑   d. Secure Linked Access

Quick Answer: **218**
Detailed Answer: **227**

Objective 5.4.1.8: Disposal/Destruction

1. One of your coworkers has just deleted this morning's audit files and folders to make more space. What impact does this have if those files contained information about a cracker's hacking attempts?

Quick Answer: **218**
Detailed Answer: **227**

❑ a. It has no significant impact because there is a backup tape from yesterday

❑ b. It's likely that this will slow down the network

❑ c. It's likely that this will speed up the network

❑ d. It's likely that the cracker will not be prosecuted

2. Which of the following terms relates to the effective destruction of data on magnetic media, such as floppy disks or backup tapes?

Quick Answer: **218**
Detailed Answer: **227**

❑ a. Tape disposal

❑ b. Magnetizing

❑ c. Degaussing

❑ d. Erasing

Objective 5.4.1.9: HR Policy

1. Which of the following company documents deals specifically with an employee status or change in status and must include the requirements to notify IT personnel of any employee status changes?

Quick Answer: **218**
Detailed Answer: **227**

❑ a. New Hire policy

❑ b. HR policy

❑ c. Security policy

❑ d. IT policy

Objective 5.4.1.9.1: Termination—Adding/Revoking Passwords, Privileges, etc.

1. Because disgruntled employees pose the greatest threat to the internal network security, what is one preventative measure that can be taken when considering terminating such an employee?

Quick Answer: **219**
Detailed Answer: **227**

❑ a. Revoke his or her password and privileges prior to termination notification

❑ b. Revoke his or her password and privileges during termination notification

❑ c. Place his or her password and privileges on hold during termination notification

❑ d. Leave his or her password and privileges intact until termination notification

Objective 5.4.1.9.2: Hiring—Adding/Revoking Passwords, Privileges, etc.

1. One of the greatest Human Resources (HR) challenges is to ensure that new hires have limited, but appropriate access to authorized network resources. Which of the following groups should HR coordinate with to ensure that passwords and privileges are appropriate? (Select all that apply.)

   ❑   a.   The HR supervisor
   ❑   b.   The IT staff
   ❑   c.   The new hire's supervisor
   ❑   d.   The CIO

Quick Answer: **219**
Detailed Answer: **227**

Objective 5.4.1.9.3: Code of Ethics

1. Which of the following general policies provides employees with ethical guidelines and clarifies expected behavior?

   ❑   a.   Acceptable Use policy
   ❑   b.   Ethical Use policy
   ❑   c.   Behavioral Guidelines policy
   ❑   d.   Code of Ethics

Quick Answer: **219**
Detailed Answer: **227**

Objective 5.4.2: Incident Response Policy

1. Which of the following organizational policies provides employees the guidelines, or the who, what, where, when (and maybe why), in cases of a physical disaster, network disaster, or security attack?

   ❑   a.   Emergency disaster plan
   ❑   b.   Disaster recovery plan
   ❑   c.   Incident response policy
   ❑   d.   Emergency response policy

Quick Answer: **219**
Detailed Answer: **227**

Objective 5.5: Privilege Management

1. Which of the following privilege management concepts gives individuals only those permissions to perform their assigned tasks?

   ❑   a.   Separation of Duties
   ❑   b.   Mandatory Access
   ❑   c.   Least Privilege
   ❑   d.   Management by Objectives

Quick Answer: **219**
Detailed Answer: **228**

. . . .

2. One of your users has only been given the minimum access required on the network system to complete his assigned task. What security concept does this relate to?

Quick Answer: **219**
Detailed Answer: **228**

- ❏ a. Acceptable Use
- ❏ b. Least Privilege
- ❏ c. Privacy
- ❏ d. Need to Know

Objective 5.5.1: User/Group/Role Management

1. Network administrators will find managing network security much easier if they adhere to which of the following concepts?

Quick Answer: **219**
Detailed Answer: **228**

- ❏ a. Assign user permissions by individual job functions
- ❏ b. Assign user permissions based on group roles or assigned jobs
- ❏ c. Assign roles to individuals and give them individual permissions
- ❏ d. Assign roles to groups and assign separate permissions to each user

2. A commonly known administrative procedure is to assign users permission to recourses. One frequent way to assign permissions may be based on the UGLR-Permission rule. Which one of the following is an effective way to allow many users access to centralized files and folders?

Quick Answer: **219**
Detailed Answer: **228**

- ❏ a. Users are Given Local access to Resources Permanently
- ❏ b. Users are Granted Local access to Resources when requesting Permission
- ❏ c. Users are Granted Local access to Resources with assigned Permissions
- ❏ d. Users are placed into Groups, which are placed inside of Local groups that have access to Resources with specific Permissions assigned to those resources

Objective 5.5.2: Single Sign-on

1. Which of the following technologies allows you to browse multiple directories with one logon?

Quick Answer: **219**
Detailed Answer: **228**

- ❏ a. Application Anywhere
- ❏ b. Group Logon
- ❏ c. VPN
- ❏ d. SSO

2. Which of the following methods are used to employ SSO? (Select all that apply.)

   ❑ a. Through use of authentication servers

   ❑ b. Through use of NAT servers

   ❑ c. Through use of encrypted authentication tickets

   ❑ d. Through use of scripts that replay the users' log-ins

Quick Answer: **219**
Detailed Answer: **228**

3. Although a benefit to valid users, Single Sign-on (SSO) can pose a security threat as well. Which of the following is a security concern when using SSO?

   ❑ a. Anyone can use it at any time

   ❑ b. Access to other network resources is unlimited after logon if a set of credentials with full access to all resources is obtained

   ❑ c. Initial logon is difficult

   ❑ d. Access to other network resources is extremely limited after logon

Quick Answer: **219**
Detailed Answer: **228**

4. Which of the following poses the greatest security threat if an administrator's password was disclosed when using SSO?

   ❑ a. A cracker would have unauthorized access to the administrator's server

   ❑ b. The administrator would loose his job

   ❑ c. The cracker would delete user accounts on the administrator's workstation

   ❑ d. A cracker would have maximum unauthorized access

Quick Answer: **219**
Detailed Answer: **228**

Objective 5.5.3: Centralized Versus Decentralized

1. When are user accounts and passwords stored on individual servers?

   ❑ a. In a hierarchical, domain-like environment

   ❑ b. In a local area network with peer-to-peer workstations

   ❑ c. In a centralized privilege management environment

   ❑ d. In a decentralized privilege management environment

Quick Answer: **219**
Detailed Answer: **228**

2. You have a growing networking department and you are wondering whether you should select a centralized or decentralized method of storing your servers. Which of the following offer the advantage of fault tolerance?

   ❑ a. Centralizing servers and decentralizing IT staff

   ❑ b. Decentralizing servers and centralizing IT staff

   ❑ c. Centralize your servers in secure server room

   ❑ d. Decentralize your servers to support remote departments

Quick Answer: **219**
Detailed Answer: **228**

Objective 5.5.4: Auditing (Privilege, Usage, Escalation)

1. Which of the following situations applies to privilege escalation?

   ❑ a. After executing a program in admin mode, the user was able to perform administrative functions
   ❑ b. After executing a program in user mode, the user was able to perform administrative functions
   ❑ c. After executing a program in user mode, the user was able to perform group functions
   ❑ d. After executing a program in admin mode, the user was able to perform group functions

Quick Answer: **219**
Detailed Answer: **228**

2. Although computer performance may be an issue, auditing is an important security feature that must be carefully planned. Which of the following should you monitor and examine as part of an internal networking audit? (Select all that apply.)

   ❑ a. Network resources for appropriate privilege assignments
   ❑ b. Success or failure of user logons
   ❑ c. Use of accounts at irregular hours
   ❑ d. Escalation of user privileges

Quick Answer: **219**
Detailed Answer: **228**

3. As part of a network security audit team, you are pretending to be a cracker and perform a penetration system test. What tasks are you trying to accomplish? (Select all that apply.)

   ❑ a. You are testing for system weaknesses
   ❑ b. You are trying to break through access control lists
   ❑ c. You are trying to unscramble encrypted data
   ❑ d. You are trying to identify and use passwords

Quick Answer: **219**
Detailed Answer: **229**

4. You are a member of a forensic team that is investigating a possible cyber attack. Which of the following terms refers to the gathering of network information, such as authorized and unauthorized user access to the network, folders, or files?

   ❑ a. Penetration
   ❑ b. Audit trail
   ❑ c. Forensic search
   ❑ d. Auditing

Quick Answer: **219**
Detailed Answer: **229**

Objective 5.5.5: MAC/DAC/RBAC

1. Which of the following access control methods requires defining the specific classification for subjects and objects and is
   used in a military environment, where users have specified
   clearances?
   - ❏ a. Discretionary access control
   - ❏ b. Role-based access control
   - ❏ c. Identity-based access control
   - ❏ d. Mandatory access control

Quick Answer: **219**
Detailed Answer: **229**

2. Which of the following access control methods is a type of
   Discretionary access control?
   - ❏ a. Mandatory access control
   - ❏ b. Nondiscretionary access control
   - ❏ c. Role-based access control
   - ❏ d. Identity-based access control

Quick Answer: **219**
Detailed Answer: **229**

3. Which of the following access control methods is a type of
   nondiscretionary access control?
   - ❏ a. Mandatory access control
   - ❏ b. Discretionary access control
   - ❏ c. Role-based access control
   - ❏ d. Identity-based access control

Quick Answer: **219**
Detailed Answer: **229**

Objective 5.6: Forensics (Awareness, Conceptual Knowledge, and Understanding—Know What Your Role Is)

1. You notice that one of your networked rooms is being
   attacked. What should you *not* do? (Select all that apply.)
   - ❏ a. Alert the incident response team
   - ❏ b. Shut down all networked computers
   - ❏ c. Log your computer off the network
   - ❏ d. Observe and take notes

Quick Answer: **219**
Detailed Answer: **229**

2. Instead of modifying data on a machine that has been under a cyber attack, you remember to make a duplicate to protect data integrity. How can you verify that you have an exact data duplicate?

  ❑ a. Copy the folders and set permissions to Read only after the copy is complete

  ❑ b. Use Ghost software to duplicate the hard drive

  ❑ c. Configure RAID 1 to duplicate the hard drive

  ❑ d. Run a Cyclic Redundancy Check with a checksum

Quick Answer: **219**
Detailed Answer: **229**

3. You are the first responder from the IT team at the scene of a potential cyber crime. Which of the following are *not* appropriate actions to take? (Select all that apply.)

  ❑ a. Keep the servers and workstations running, even if this allows a cracker continued access

  ❑ b. Turn off all servers and workstations to prevent a cracker from further damage

  ❑ c. Allow network users to return to their workstations

  ❑ d. Allow forensics personnel access to the room

Quick Answer: **219**
Detailed Answer: **229**

Objective 5.6.1: Chain of Custody

1. Which of the following relates to the term Chain of Custody? (Select all that apply.)

  ❑ a. To preserve evidence it must go up the chain of command

  ❑ b. Unfortunately, evidence must be tampered with, but only by forensic personnel

  ❑ c. Evidence should *not* be altered or tampered with

  ❑ d. Evidence should be logged for possession and length of possession

Quick Answer: **219**
Detailed Answer: **229**

2. Which of the following guidelines minimizes loss of data during collection of evidence?

  ❑ a. Protect the weakest link

  ❑ b. Remove the weakest link

  ❑ c. Respond to an incident within one hour

  ❑ d. Follow the Chain of Custody guidelines

Quick Answer: **219**
Detailed Answer: **229**

3. Which of the following defines the term Chain of Custody?

  ❑ a. A group of crackers caught and incarcerated

  ❑ b. A single cracker caught and incarcerated

  ❑ c. The forensic handling and control of evidence

  ❑ d. The record keeping used to imprison criminals

Quick Answer: **219**
Detailed Answer: **229**

Objective 5.6.2: Preservation of Evidence

1. After a computer crime has been committed, evidence must be preserved. Which of the following actions will help your forensic team in the preservation of evidence? (Select all that apply.)

   ❑   a. Seal evidence in tamper resistant containers
   ❑   b. Turn off the power supply to that section of the building to stop changes in network activity
   ❑   c. If possible, take snapshots of displayed monitors
   ❑   d. At a minimum, write down any messages that are displayed on the monitors

Quick Answer: **219**
Detailed Answer: **230**

2. To maintain data and equipment integrity, which of the following is the best course of action after a cyber crime has occurred?

   ❑   a. Confiscate all evidence, hard drives, CDs, and floppies
   ❑   b. Search individuals in the room for data
   ❑   c. Preserve all evidence
   ❑   d. Ask for all user logon information to review their data

Quick Answer: **219**
Detailed Answer: **230**

Objective 5.6.3: Collection of Evidence

1. After a computer crime has been committed, evidence must be collected, tagged, bagged, and inventoried. Who is responsible for this action?

   ❑   a. Forensic technician
   ❑   b. IT technician
   ❑   c. First responder
   ❑   d. Anyone who works in the office

Quick Answer: **219**
Detailed Answer: **230**

2. One of your employees is suspected of a cyber crime. Which of the following would you need to coordinate with before collecting physical evidence from this employee? (Select all that apply.)

   ❑   a. Human Resources
   ❑   b. CIO
   ❑   c. CEO
   ❑   d. Legal department

Quick Answer: **219**
Detailed Answer: **230**

. . . .

Objective 5.7: Risk Identification

1. What is the primary goal when managing security risks?

   ❑ a. Minimize the risks to a financial level
   ❑ b. Minimize the risks to an acceptable level
   ❑ c. Maximize the risks to a minimal financial standard
   ❑ d. Maximize the standard to a minimal financial risk

Quick Answer: **220**
Detailed Answer: **230**

2. Which of the following is a business function that determines which threats pose a danger to an organization so that proactive measures can be implemented?

   ❑ a. Risk assessment
   ❑ b. Risk identification
   ❑ c. Vulnerability assessment
   ❑ d. Vulnerability identification

Quick Answer: **220**
Detailed Answer: **230**

Objective 5.7.1: Asset Identification

1. Which of the following tasks is a critical component of organizational risk assessment, in that it lists and places a value on network and computer components?

   ❑ a. Threat identification
   ❑ b. Component identification
   ❑ c. Vulnerability identification
   ❑ d. Asset identification

Quick Answer: **220**
Detailed Answer: **230**

Objective 5.7.2: Risk Assessment

1. Which of the following risk analysis formulas is a useful tool that is based upon these three concepts: Single Loss Expectancy, Annualized Rate of Occurrence, and Annual Loss Expectancy?

   ❑ a. SLE + ARO = ALE
   ❑ b. SLE × ARO = ALE
   ❑ c. ALE – ARO = SLE
   ❑ d. ALE – ARO = SLE

Quick Answer: **220**
Detailed Answer: **230**

2. Which of the following explains the acronym SLE?

   ❑ a. Security Loss Expectancy
   ❑ b. Single Latent Exam
   ❑ c. Security Latent Exam
   ❑ d. Single Loss Expectancy

Quick Answer: **220**
Detailed Answer: **230**

3. You are conducting a risk assessment for your network department to determine the Annualized Rate of Occurrence (ARO). Where could you go for assistance with your project? (Select all that apply.)

   ❏ a. Financial and historical records

   ❏ b. Another network administrator from a similar company

   ❏ c. Your insurance company records

   ❏ d. Police department records

Quick Answer: **220**
Detailed Answer: **230**

4. After conducting a departmental risk assessment, you share the results with your supervisor. Which of the following would be the most realistic objective?

   ❏ a. Work to totally eliminate the most expensive risks first

   ❏ b. Work to totally eliminate the least expensive risks first

   ❏ c. Work to take action on all risks to reduce the external threats

   ❏ d. Work to take action to minimize the problems associated with identified risks

Quick Answer: **220**
Detailed Answer: **230**

Objective 5.7.3: Threat Identification

1. You are new to the company and are surprised when you read the results of a threat identification and risk analysis. Which of the following would be the source of greatest threat?

   ❏ a. Crackers are primarily found working at the ISP

   ❏ b. Crackers are primarily security students

   ❏ c. Crackers are employees from competitive companies

   ❏ d. Crackers are primarily disgruntled employees

Quick Answer: **220**
Detailed Answer: **230**

2. Which of the following threats will most likely produce a risk that affects confidentiality, integrity, and availability?

   ❏ a. Fraud

   ❏ b. Natural disaster

   ❏ c. Physical theft

   ❏ d. Terrorism

Quick Answer: **220**
Detailed Answer: **230**

Objective 5.7.4: Vulnerabilities

1. Which of the following security terms best explains vulnerability?

Quick Answer: **220**
Detailed Answer: **231**

- ❑ a. A network weakness that leaves the computer systems exposed to a threat
- ❑ b. A computer weakness that leaves the network systems exposed to a loss
- ❑ c. An organizational weakness that leaves the employees exposed to a virus
- ❑ d. An employee weakness that leaves the organization exposed to a risk

2. When security administrators desire to perform a risk assessment to determine vulnerabilities, they may employ penetration techniques. Which of the following are common examples of such techniques? (Select all that apply.)

Quick Answer: **220**
Detailed Answer: **231**

- ❑ a. Sniffing
- ❑ b. Scanning
- ❑ c. Spoofing
- ❑ d. War dialing

3. Bill saw another employee copy down a user's password and later use it. Instead of reporting this as a violation or vulnerability to the network, he spoke to the individual, who explained the act as a prank. When this action or vulnerability is ignored, what is the probability of the threat occurring again with possible dangerous consequences?

Quick Answer: **220**
Detailed Answer: **231**

- ❑ a. If action is *not* taken, the probability of the threat occurring will decrease
- ❑ b. If action is *not* taken, the probability of the threat occurring will increase
- ❑ c. If action is taken, the probability of the threat occurring will remain unchanged
- ❑ d. If action is taken, the probability of the threat occurring will increase

Objective 5.8: Education—Training of End Users, Executives, and HR

1. One benefit of training end users in system development, business goals, and physical security countermeasures is the concept of Buy In. Which of the following refers to this concept?

   ❑ a. Advancements in technology and physical security

   ❑ b. Accomplishment of organizational objectives

   ❑ c. User involvement and acceptance of organizational changes

   ❑ d. Employee financial contributions to company stock

Quick Answer: **220**
Detailed Answer: **231**

2. Most organizations ensure that the networking IT department receives certification training, new equipment, and software training. What other efforts should be made to ensure security? (Select all that apply.)

   ❑ a. Training on security policy and procedures for HR staff

   ❑ b. Executive training on security policies

   ❑ c. Social engineering training for end users

   ❑ d. Software installation and configuration training for the CEO

Quick Answer: **220**
Detailed Answer: **231**

Objective 5.8.1: Communication

1. Which of the following are reasonable methods of communication between end users and the IT department to improve the overall quality of service and be able to respond to a security incident?

   ❑ a. Have IT establish work hours 24 hours a day

   ❑ b. Contact IT through email whenever needed

   ❑ c. Have IT use pagers to respond to every call immediately

   ❑ d. Establish a tracking system for routine networking events and a pager system for emergencies

Quick Answer: **220**
Detailed Answer: **231**

2. Which of the following methods of communication are used by many large organizations to assist them in their networking support efforts?

   ❑ a. Dedicated IT staff member for every 10 end users

   ❑ b. On-call IT staff member for every 10 end users

   ❑ c. Help Desk personnel, guidelines, and equipment

   ❑ d. A required office visit and audit every month by dedicated IT personnel

Quick Answer: **220**
Detailed Answer: **231**

Objective 5.8.2: User Awareness

1. What is the benefit of providing scheduled user awareness training on social engineering?

❏ a. Increases user interest in your organization

❏ b. Increases user interaction with others socially

❏ c. Provides the best offense for creating social engineering responses

❏ d. Provides the best defense against socially engineered attacks

Quick Answer: 220
Detailed Answer: 231

2. What are the results of increased user awareness about security rules and requirements? (Select all that apply.)

❏ a. End users will more likely be able to comply with security guidelines

❏ b. End users will more likely desire to comply with security guidelines

❏ c. End users will more likely complain that they should comply with security guidelines

❏ d. End users will less likely complain that they should comply with security guidelines

Quick Answer: 220
Detailed Answer: 231

Objective 5.8.3: Education

1. What is the primary method of ensuring end users are aware of security requirements and possess the skills to take appropriate action?

❏ a. Classroom lecture

❏ b. Education through hands-on training

❏ c. Group meetings

❏ d. Open discussions

Quick Answer: 220
Detailed Answer: 231

Objective 5.8.4: Online Resources

1. Which of the following is one of the best sources of network security information for the largest group of end users?

❏ a. Online resources

❏ b. Documentation

❏ c. Posted policies

❏ d. IT staff visits

Quick Answer: 220
Detailed Answer: 232

Objective 5.9: Documentation

1. Which of the following should be retained as part of the system's permanent documentation?
   - ❏ a. Hardware installation tests
   - ❏ b. Software test plan and results
   - ❏ c. Printed audit logs
   - ❏ d. User configuration files

Quick Answer: **220**
Detailed Answer: **232**

2. Which of the following is a critical component of forensics, that assists in the conviction of a networked cyber terrorist?
   - ❏ a. Verbal discussion
   - ❏ b. Written documentation
   - ❏ c. Third-party hearsay
   - ❏ d. Macroscopic fingerprints

Quick Answer: **220**
Detailed Answer: **232**

Objective 5.9.1: Standards and Guidelines

1. You have all kinds of personnel and clients that may have access to your company network, including end users, programmers, and vendors. Which of the following terms relates to a quality of excellence that you expect from these individuals?
   - ❏ a. Guidelines
   - ❏ b. Standards
   - ❏ c. Policies
   - ❏ d. Procedures

Quick Answer: **220**
Detailed Answer: **232**

2. Which of the following terms applies to maintaining a certain level of performance, which can be used to evaluate network equipment as well as personnel?
   - ❏ a. Standards
   - ❏ b. Policies
   - ❏ c. Procedures
   - ❏ d. Guidelines

Quick Answer: **220**
Detailed Answer: **232**

3. Which of the following terms relates to identifying the actions to take to maintain a quality of excellence from equipment and end users?
   - ❏ a. Standards
   - ❏ b. Policies
   - ❏ c. Procedures
   - ❏ d. Guidelines

Quick Answer: **220**
Detailed Answer: **232**

. . . .

Objective 5.9.2: Systems Architecture

1. You may have heard an IT professional state that he inherited a mess. What is he probably referring to?

   - ❏   a.   Systems architecture
   - ❏   b.   Network cabling
   - ❏   c.   User passwords
   - ❏   d.   Computer types

   Quick Answer: **220**
   Detailed Answer: **232**

2. Which of the following should be established as a baseline and held in confidence within the IT department?

   - ❏   a.   Hardware requirements
   - ❏   b.   Software requirements
   - ❏   c.   Email accounts
   - ❏   d.   Systems architecture

   Quick Answer: **220**
   Detailed Answer: **232**

Objective 5.9.3: Change Documentation

1. What should you add to the systems architecture to keep it current?

   - ❏   a.   Initial inventory
   - ❏   b.   User passwords
   - ❏   c.   Any change documentation
   - ❏   d.   Current audit documentation

   Quick Answer: **220**
   Detailed Answer: **232**

2. You find that the software service pack has had a negative impact on other components of your network. Where can you go to trace your path and return to the previous settings?

   - ❏   a.   Security logs
   - ❏   b.   Event logs
   - ❏   c.   Initial inventory
   - ❏   d.   Change documentation

   Quick Answer: **220**
   Detailed Answer: **232**

Objective 5.9.4: Logs and Inventories

1. What should you use to maintain a record of software and hardware within your network?

   - ❏   a.   Logs
   - ❏   b.   Tabulations
   - ❏   c.   Inventories
   - ❏   d.   Manufacturer lists

   Quick Answer: **220**
   Detailed Answer: **233**

2. You have the requirement to establish security logging for a short period of time. Which of the following statements about logging are true? (Select all that apply.)

- ❑   a. Your business demands that you can trace all events back to a specific user
- ❑   b. Logs must be modified to collect and document the data
- ❑   c. Logs should be centrally located for analysis if at all possible
- ❑   d. Logs should provide enough data to be comprehensive or meaningful

Quick Answer: **220**
Detailed Answer: **233**

3. Your IDS has given you warning that an attack is occurring and you are now reviewing the log files. Which of the following applies to this situation?

- ❑   a. You are performing a baseline analysis
- ❑   b. You are performing a passive detective analysis
- ❑   c. You are performing active detection
- ❑   d. You are performing passive detection

Quick Answer: **220**
Detailed Answer: **233**

Objective 5.9.5: Classification

1. Your end users are allowed to create and share documents within their departments. You want to ensure that these documents are *not* shared outside of their own departments. Which of the following will help you accomplish this task?

- ❑   a. Documentation
- ❑   b. Classification
- ❑   c. Registration
- ❑   d. Notification

Quick Answer: **221**
Detailed Answer: **233**

2. Which of the following tasks are critical to the understanding of various classifications? (Select all that apply.)

- ❑   a. Obtain management support and clarification
- ❑   b. Provide classification classes to all end users
- ❑   c. Audit and review folders for proper classification and make corrections
- ❑   d. Adjust user permissions, denying them the ability to classify folders

Quick Answer: **221**
Detailed Answer: **233**

Quick Check ✓

Objective 5.9.5.1: Notification

1. Whom do you call when a cracker has jacked into your network and started poking around? Where should the answer to this question be?

Quick Answer: **221**
Detailed Answer: **233**

- ❑ a. Updated in your alert response book
- ❑ b. Written in your notification documents
- ❑ c. Posted on the IT wall
- ❑ d. Posted in the users' cafeteria

Objective 5.9.6: Retention/Storage

1. You should establish a policy that clearly specifies the length of time that folders, files, and other data should be stored before destroying them. Which of the following documents pertains to this policy?

Quick Answer: **221**
Detailed Answer: **233**

- ❑ a. Logging policy
- ❑ b. Auditing policy
- ❑ c. Retention policy
- ❑ d. Destruction policy

2. You've reached the date the stored data should be removed from a backup server. Where would you find the policy that allows you to verify this date before destroying the backup?

Quick Answer: **221**
Detailed Answer: **233**

- ❑ a. Auditing policy
- ❑ b. Retention policy
- ❑ c. Destruction policy
- ❑ d. Logging policy

Objective 5.9.7: Destruction

1. Which corporate policy requires you to shred or burn your office paperwork before leaving for the day?

Quick Answer: **221**
Detailed Answer: **233**

- ❑ a. Auditing policy
- ❑ b. Retention policy
- ❑ c. Destruction policy
- ❑ d. Logging policy

Quick Check Answer Key

Objective 5.1: Physical Security

1. a, b, c, and d.

2. a, b, and c.

3. a, b, and c.

Objective 5.1.1: Access Control

1. b.

2. b.

3. a, b, and d.

4. b.

5. a, b, c, and d.

6. a, c, and d.

7. b, c, and d.

8. c.

Objective 5.1.1.1: Physical Barriers

1. c.

2. b and d.

Objective 5.1.1.2: Biometrics

1. c.

2. c.

3. d.

Objective 5.1.2: Social Engineering

1. c.

2. d.

Objective 5.1.3: Environment

1. a.

2. c.

Objective 5.1.3.1: Wireless Cells

1. b.

Objective 5.1.3.2: Location

1. c.

2. b.

Objective 5.1.3.3: Shielding

1. d.

2. c.

Objective 5.1.3.4: Fire Suppression

1. d.

2. b.

3. c.

4. a and c.

Objective 5.2: Disaster Recovery

1. c.

2. a and b.

Objective 5.2.1: Backups

1. b.

2. a, c, and d.

3. c.

4. b.

5. b.

6. c.

Objective 5.2.1.1: Off Site Storage

1. a, b, c, and d.

2. b and d.

3. a, b, and c.

5.2.2: Secure Recovery

1. b.

Objective 5.2.2.1: Alternate Sites

1. a and b.

Quick Check Answer Key

Objective 5.2.3: Disaster Recovery Plan

1. b.

2. b.

3. a.

4. b.

Objective 5.3: Business Continuity

1. b.

2. a, b, c, and d.

Objective 5.3.1: Utilities

1. c.

2. d.

3. a.

4. b.

Objective 5.3.2: High Availability/Fault Tolerance

1. d.

2. c.

Objective 5.3.3: Backups

1. d.

2. b.

Objective 5.4: Policy and Procedures

1. b.

2. d

Objective 5.4.1: Security Policy

1. d.

Objective 5.4.1.1: Acceptable Use

1. b.

Objective 5.4.1.2: Due Care

1. b.

2. a.

Objective 5.4.1.3: Privacy

1. b.

2. b.

Objective 5.4.1.4: Separation of Duties

1. a, b, and c.

2. b.

3. b.

Objective 5.4.1.5: Need to Know

1. d.

Objective 5.4.1.6: Password Management

1. b.

2. c.

Objective 5.4.1.7: SLA

1. c.

Objective 5.4.1.8: Disposal/Destruction

1. d.

2. c.

Objective 5.4.1.9: HR Policy

1. b.

Quick Check Answer Key

**Objective 5.4.1.9.1:
Termination—
Adding/Revoking
Passwords, Privileges,
etc.**

1. a.

**Objective 5.4.1.9.2:
Hiring—Adding/Revoking
Passwords, Privileges,
etc.**

1. b and c.

**Objective 5.4.1.9.3: Code
of Ethics**

1. d.

Objective 5.4.2:
Incident Response
Policy

1. c.

Objective 5.5:
Privilege
Management

1. c.

2. b.

Objective 5.5.1:
User/Group/Role
Management

1. b.

2. d

Objective 5.5.2:
Single Sign-on

1. d.

2. a, c, and d.

3. b.

4. d.

Objective 5.5.3:
Centralized Versus
Decentralized

1. d.

2. d.

Objective 5.5.4:
Auditing (Privilege,
Usage, Escalation)

1. b.

2. a, b, c, and d.

3. a, b, c, and d.

4. b.

Objective 5.5.5:
MAC/DAC/RBAC

1. d.

2. d.

3. c.

Objective 5.6:
Forensics
(Awareness,
Conceptual
Knowledge, and
Understanding—
Know What Your
Role Is)

1. b and c.

2. d.

3. b and c.

Objective 5.6.1:
Chain of Custody

1. c and d.

2. d.

3. c.

Objective 5.6.2:
Preservation of
Evidence

1. a, c, and d.

2. c.

Objective 5.6.3:
Collection of
Evidence

1. a.

2. a and d.

Quick Check Answer Key

Objective 5.7: Risk Identification

1. b.

2. b.

Objective 5.7.1: Asset Identification

1. d.

Objective 5.7.2: Risk Assessment

1. b.

2. d.

3. a, b, c, and d.

4. d.

Objective 5.7.3: Threat Identification

1. d.

2. b.

Objective 5.7.4: Vulnerabilities

1. a.

2. a, b, and d.

3. b.

Objective 5.8: Education— Training of End Users, Executives, and HR

1. c.

2. a, b, and c.

Objective 5.8.1: Communication

1. d.

2. c.

Objective 5.8.2: User Awareness

1. d.

2. a, b, and d.

Objective 5.8.3: Education

1. b.

Objective 5.8.4: Online Resources

1. a.

Objective 5.9: Documentation

1. b.

2. b.

Objective 5.9.1: Standards and Guidelines

1. b.

2. a.

3. d.

Objective 5.9.2: Systems Architecture

1. a.

2. d.

Objective 5.9.3: Change Documentation

1. c.

2. d.

Objective 5.9.4: Logs and Inventories

1. c.

2. c and d.

3. d.

Quick Check Answer Key

Objective 5.9.5: Classification

1. b.

2. a, b, and c.

Objective 5.9.5.1: Notification

1. b.

Objective 5.9.6: Retention/Storage

1. c.

2. b.

Objective 5.9.7: Destruction

1. c.

Answers and Explanations

Objective 5.1: Physical Security

1. **a, b, c, and d.** All items listed provide some degree of physical security to your network.

2. **a, b, and c.** Examples of physical security controls include, but are not limited to, a double-locked server room, night watchmen, and storing backups of critical files.

3. **a, b, and c.** The purpose of implementing physical security is to prevent theft, prevent unauthorized disclosure of data, to prevent physical damage, and to maintain system integrity.

Objective 5.1.1: Access Control

1. **b.** This situation is an example of a physical security risk known as piggybacking.

2. **b.** The fail-soft door provides a safer employer environment, allowing employees to exit in case of emergency.

3. **a, b, and d.** Implementing technical access controls that are detective in nature include using a honey pot, auditing, and intrusion detection system.

4. **b.** The high cost of maintaining security guards is a potential concern.

5. **a, b, c, and d.** All of these statements are true for a transponder.

6. **a, c, and d.** Locks, iris scans, and security guards are examples of physical access controls.

7. **b, c, and d.** Typically, users only have access to data on a need-to-know basis; users who perform specific group tasks may be assigned group rights; and No Access is a tighter control than partial access with limited permissions.

8. **c.** No one should have unrestricted access to production programs.

Objective 5.1.1.1: Physical Barriers

1. **c.** Think about securing or hardening the ceiling and floor, as well as the walls when considering a physical barrier for the server room.

2. **b and d.** Reasonable alternatives to a separate or centralized server room include use of a locked cabinet or secure rack.

Objective 5.1.1.2: Biometrics

1. **c.** Biometrics relates to control of user access to critical information using physical characteristics.

2. **c.** False Acceptance Rate, Type II error, also known as False Positive, allows unauthorized access to an imposter.

3. **d.** The following order of biometric methods lists the most accurate to least accurate methods: iris scan, fingerprint, and voice verification.

Objective 5.1.2: Social Engineering

1. **c.** This is an example of social engineering.

2. **d.** Social engineering takes advantage of weakness in human behavior.

Objective 5.1.3: Environment

1. **a.** Environmental fluctuations in room temperature may cause chip creep.

2. **c.** The best environmental range for operating your computers is 40–60% relative humidity.

Objective 5.1.3.1: Wireless Cells

1. **b.** The reasonable tasks when employing Wireless Cells in a building include shielding walls and ceilings for greater security.

Objective 5.1.3.2: Location

1. **c.** Locate your department on the third or fourth floor.

2. **b.** Decreased visibility is a primary goal.

Objective 5.1.3.3: Shielding

1. **d.** Servers should have priority for protection.

2. **c.** A building that is free from outside electricity can be called a Faraday's cage.

Objective 5.1.3.4: Fire Suppression

1. **d.** Type C fire extinguishers are designed for electrical fires.

2. **b.** CO_2 systems are effective fire suppression systems.

3. **c.** A Clapper valve stops the flow of water.

4. **a and c.** CO_2 and Halon, if not banned, are the preferred ways to suppress an electrical fire.

Objective 5.2: Disaster Recovery

1. **c.** You should start the least critical process first.

2. **a and b.** Recording change levels and any revisions are critical requirements for disaster recovery.

Objective 5.2.1: Backups

1. **b.** Of the items listed, tape backup is the *best* way to protect data against disaster, corruption, or loss.

2. **a, c, and d.** Only incremental backup, full backup, and differential backup are methods of tape backup.

3. **c.** Full backup is the best method of tape backup.

4. **b.** Incremental backup does *not* track deletions, thereby increasing the storage requirements.

5. **b.** Incremental backup and full backup are used together most often.

6. **c.** Choose differential when you want to copy only files that were modified since the last full backup.

Objective 5.2.1.1: Off Site Storage

1. **a, b, c, and d.** All items listed are required for a hot site.

2. **b and d.** Cold sites are least expensive, but they are the most difficult to test.

3. **a, b, and c.** Electricity, air conditioning, and flooring are what you would likely see at a cold site.

Objective 5.2.2: Secure Recovery

1. **b.** Secure recovery should be the goal when planning for a disaster that affects your network.

Objective 5.2.2.1: Alternate Sites

1. **a and b.** Alternate secure recovery sites include hot sites, warm sites, and cold sites.

Objective 5.2.3: Disaster Recovery Plan

1. **b.** You must include a risk assessment plan when establishing a disaster recovery plan.

2. **b.** Ensure that noncritical systems are moved first from the alternate site back to the primary site.

3. **a.** Personnel safety and data security should be of primary concern.

4. **b.** A person who has been earmarked and trained as the disaster recovery manager should make short-term recovery decisions just after a disaster.

Objective 5.3: Business Continuity

1. **b.** They must have management support for these to be successful.

2. **a, b, c, and d.** All the items listed should be seen within a solid business continuity plan.

Objective 5.3.1: Utilities

1. **c.** A prolonged high voltage that is above normal voltage is a surge.

2. **d.** A momentary low voltage is a sag.

3. **a.** A burst of power that is above normal voltage is a spike.

4. **b.** A prolonged power supply that is below normal voltage is a brownout.

Objective 5.3.2: High Availability/Fault Tolerance

1. **d.** Implementation of Redundant Array of Inexpensive Disks (RAID) maintains data in a high state of availability.

2. **c.** RAID stands for Redundant Array of Inexpensive Disks.

Objective 5.3.3: Backups

1. **d.** Full backup offers the most complete restoration.

2. **b.** Differential backup has the fastest restore time.

Objective 5.4: Policy and Procedures

1. **b.** Common Criteria refers to the internationally agreed on IT Security Evaluation Criteria.

2. **d.** Server performance (6), email (5), then software (3) is the correct order to prioritize your efforts.

Objective 5.4.1: Security Policy

1. **d.** The company's security policy explains the overall requirements needed to protect an organization's network data and computer systems.

Objective 5.4.1.1: Acceptable Use

1. **b.** The acceptable use policy clarifies user's roles and limitations when using network equipment—hardware and software—as well as email and Internet access.

Objective 5.4.1.2: Due Care

1. **b.** Due Care is the security term for the requirement of senior management to ensure that specific security protection is provided to the organization.

2. **a.** Due Care refers to actions taken to reduce the probability of damage or injury.

Objective 5.4.1.3: Privacy

1. **b.** The privacy policy is designed to ensure that employees are aware of their rights and limitations when it involves the use of organizational computers and any organizational employee auditing procedures.

2. **b.** You should consider your company privacy policy when planning for email, software downloads, and Web site data.

Objective 5.4.1.4: Separation of Duties

1. **a, b, and c.** When establishing a security policy of Separation of Duties, the intent would be to prevent employees from completing the overall task alone.

2. **b.** Two-man control means that two users must review and approve each other's work, which is a Separation of Duty.

3. **b.** The term Separation of Duties ensures that no single individual can compromise a system.

Objective 5.4.1.5: Need to Know

1. **d.** Need to Know is the Security Policy that limits the employee's knowledge of the network system, but still gives them enough information to perform his or her assigned tasks.

Objective 5.4.1.6: Password Management

1. **b.** Strong passwords should contain a minimum length of eight (8) characters.

2. **c.** Of the passwords listed, Shouldn'tB4gotten is the strongest.

Objective 5.4.1.7: SLA

1. **c.** SLA stands for Service Level Agreements.

Objective 5.4.1.8: Disposal/Destruction

1. **d.** It's likely that the cracker will *not* be prosecuted.

2. **c.** Degaussing is the process of effective destruction of data on magnetic media.

Objective 5.4.1.9: HR Policy

1. **b.** The HR Policy deals specifically with an employee status or change in status and must include the requirements to notify IT personnel of any employee status changes.

Objective 5.4.1.9.1: Termination—Adding/Revoking Passwords, Privileges, etc.

1. **a.** One preventative measure is to revoke their passwords and privileges prior to termination notification.

Objective 5.4.1.9.2: Hiring—Adding/Revoking Passwords, Privileges, etc.

1. **b and c.** Generally, HR will coordinate with the IT staff and the new hire's supervisor.

Objective 5.4.1.9.3: Code of Ethics

1. **d.** A Code of Ethics provides employees with ethical guidelines and clarifies expected behavior.

Objective 5.4.2: Incident Response Policy

1. **c.** An Incident Response policy provides employees the guidelines in cases of a physical disaster, network disaster, or security attack?

Objective 5.5: Privilege Management

1. **c.** Least Privilege is a privilege management concept that gives individuals only the permissions to perform their assigned tasks.

2. **b.** Least Privilege is a privilege management term that limits the employee's access, rather than knowledge of the network system, but still gives him enough permissions to perform his assigned tasks.

Objective 5.5.1: User/Group/Role Management

1. **b.** Assign user permissions based on group roles or assigned jobs.

2. **d.** UGLR-P is my own shortcut for an industry standard, whereby Users are placed into Groups, which are placed inside of Local groups that have access to Resources with specific Permissions assigned to those resources.

Objective 5.5.2: Single Sign-on

1. **d.** Single Sign-on (SSO) allows you to browse multiple directories with one logon.

2. **a, c, and d.** Single Sign-on (SSO) can be employed by using Authentication Servers, scripts that replay the users' log-ins, or by using encrypted authentication tickets.

3. **b.** Single Sign-on (SSO) can pose a security threat because access to other network resources is unlimited after logon.

4. **d.** A cracker with maximum unauthorized access poses the greatest security threat if an administrator's password was disclosed when using SSO.

Objective 5.5.3: Centralized Versus Decentralized

1. **d.** User accounts and passwords stored on individual servers in a decentralized privilege management environment.

2. **d.** If your goal is to ensure fault tolerance, then decentralize your servers to support remote departments.

Objective 5.5.4: Auditing (Privilege, Usage, Escalation)

1. **b.** This situation is an example of privilege escalation.

2. **a, b, c, and d.** You should monitor and examine all these items as part of an internal networking audit.

3. **a, b, c, and d.** During a penetration system audit you try to accomplish all these tasks.

4. **b.** An audit trail refers to the gathering of network information, such as authorized and unauthorized user access to the network, folders, or files.

Objective 5.5.5: MAC/DAC/RBAC

1. **d.** Mandatory access control (MAC) requires defining the specific classification for subjects and objects and is used in a military environment, where users have specified clearances.

2. **d.** Identity-based access control is a type of discretionary access control.

3. **c.** Role-based access control is a type of nondiscretionary access control.

Objective 5.6: Forensics (Awareness, Conceptual Knowledge, and Understanding—Know What Your Role Is)

1. **b and c.** You should *not* shut down all networked computers or log off your computer from the network, but instead alert the incident response team and continue to observe and take notes.

2. **d.** Run a Cyclic Redundancy Check with a checksum.

3. **b and c.** You should keep the servers and workstations running, even if this allows a cracker continued access until computer forensics personnel can access the room.

Objective 5.6.1: Chain of Custody

1. **c and d.** Evidence should *not* be altered or tampered with, but instead should be logged for possession and length of possession.

2. **d.** Following the Chain of Custody guidelines minimizes loss of data during collection of evidence.

3. **c.** Chain of Custody is a forensic term that relates to the special handling and control of evidence.

Objective 5.6.2: Preservation of Evidence

1. **a, c, and d.** You should seal evidence in tamper-resistant containers, if possible, take snapshots of displayed monitors, and at a minimum, write down any messages that are displayed on the monitors to preserve evidence.

2. **c.** Preservation of evidence is the best course of action after a cyber crime.

Objective 5.6.3: Collection of Evidence

1. **a.** A forensic technician is responsible for collection of evidence.

2. **a and d.** Before collecting evidence against a suspected employee, you should contact your HR and legal departments.

Objective 5.7: Risk Identification

1. **b.** The primary goal when managing security risks is to minimize the risks to an acceptable level.

2. **b.** Risk identification is a business function that determines which threats pose a danger to an organization so that proactive measures can be implemented.

Objective 5.7.1: Asset Identification

1. **d.** Asset identification is a critical component of organizational risk assessment, in that it lists and places a value on network and computer components.

Objective 5.7.2: Risk Assessment

1. **b.** Single Loss Expectancy (SLE) times (×) Annualized Rate of Occurrence (ARO) produces (=) Annual Loss Expectancy (ALE).

2. **d.** Single Loss Expectancy (SLE) is a cost estimate (monetary value) for a single potential loss or risk.

3. **a, b, c, and d.** All items listed may be sources to help you in your project.

4. **d.** You should make it a goal to take actions to minimize the problems associated with identified risks.

Objective 5.7.3: Threat Identification

1. **d.** Crackers are primarily disgruntled employees.

2. **b.** Of the items listed, physical theft will most likely affect confidentiality, integrity, and availability.

Objective 5.7.4: Vulnerabilities

1. **a.** The security term, vulnerability, refers to a network weakness that leaves the computer systems exposed to a threat.

2. **a, b, and d.** Sniffing, scanning, and war dialing are common examples of penetration techniques.

3. **b.** If action is not taken, the probability of the threat occurring will increase.

Objective 5.8: Education—Training of End Users, Executives, and HR

1. **c.** User involvement and acceptance of organizational changes is greatly enhanced by employee buy in through training.

2. **a, b, and c.** Include your HR staff, executives, and other end users on all aspects of the organization's security policy, including social engineering.

Objective 5.8.1: Communication

1. **d.** Of the items listed, the most reasonable method of communication between end users and the IT department would be to establish a tracking system for routine networking events and a pager system for emergencies.

2. **c.** Help Desk personnel, guidelines, and equipment are used by many large organizations to assist them in their networking support efforts.

Objective 5.8.2: User Awareness

1. **d.** You may offer the best defense against socially engineered attacks by conducting user awareness training on social engineering topics.

2. **a, b, and d.** The results of increased user awareness about security rules and requirements includes end user buy in. End users will be less likely to complain that they should comply with security guidelines; They will more likely be able to, and desire to, comply with security guidelines.

Objective 5.8.3: Education

1. **b.** Education through hands-on training is the primary method of ensuring end users are aware of security requirements and possess the skills to take appropriate action.

Objective 5.8.4: Online Resources

1. **a.** Online resources are one of the best sources of network security information for the largest group of end users.

Objective 5.9: Documentation

1. **b.** A software test plan and results should be retained as part of the system's permanent documentation.

2. **b.** Written documentation is a critical component of forensics, that assists in the conviction of a networked cyber terrorist.

Objective 5.9.1: Standards and Guidelines

1. **b.** The term "standard" relates to a quality of excellence that you expect from others.

2. **a.** Standard applies to maintaining a certain level of performance, which can be used to evaluate network equipment as well as personnel.

3. **d.** Guidelines relate to identifying the actions to take to ensure a quality of excellence from equipment and end users.

Objective 5.9.2: Systems Architecture

1. **a.** He probably is referring to Systems Architecture.

2. **d.** Systems Architecture should be established as a baseline and held in confidence within the IT department.

Objective 5.9.3: Change Documentation

1. **c.** You should add any change documentation to the systems architecture to keep it current.

2. **d.** You can go to the change documentation to trace your path and return to the previous settings.

Objective 5.9.4: Logs and Inventories

1. **c.** You should use inventories to maintain a record of software and hardware within your network.

2. **c and d.** If at all possible, logs should be centrally located for analysis and should provide enough data to be comprehensive or meaningful.

3. **d.** You are performing passive detection.

Objective 5.9.5: Classification

1. **b.** Classification of shared documents will help you accomplish this task.

2. **a, b, and c.** Obtain management support and clarification; provide classification classes to all end users; and audit and review folders for proper classification and make corrections are critical to the understanding of various classifications. In essence this should be part of user education.

Objective 5.9.5.1: Notification

1. **b.** Your notification documents will vary based on your organizational needs, but they should answer the question, "Whom should I call?"

Objective 5.9.6: Retention/Storage

1. **c.** A Retention policy clearly specifies the length of time that folders, files, and other data should be stored before destroying them.

2. **b.** A Retention policy clearly specifies the length of time that folders, files, and other data should be stored before destroying them.

Objective 5.9.7: Destruction

1. **c.** Your company Destruction policy may require you to shred or burn your office paperwork before leaving for the day.

CD Contents and Installation Instructions

The CD features an innovative practice test engine powered by MeasureUp™, giving you yet another effective tool to assess your readiness for the exam.

Multiple Test Modes

MeasureUp practice tests are available in Study, Certification, Custom, Missed Question, and Non-Duplicate question modes.

Study Mode

Tests administered in Study Mode enable you to request the correct answer(s) and explanation to each question during the test. These tests are not timed. You can modify the testing environment *during* the test by selecting the Options button.

Certification Mode

Tests administered in Certification Mode closely simulate the actual testing environment you will encounter when taking a certification exam. These tests do not allow you to request the answer(s) and/or explanation to each question until after the exam.

Custom Mode

Custom Mode allows you to specify your preferred testing environment. Use this mode to specify the objectives you want to include in your test, the timer length, and other test properties. You can also modify the testing environment *during* the test by selecting the Options button.

Missed Question Mode

Missed Question Mode allows you to take a test containing only the questions you have missed previously.

Non-Duplicate Mode

Non-Duplicate Mode allows you to take a test containing only questions not displayed previously.

Random Questions and Order of Answers

This feature helps you learn the material without memorizing questions and answers. Each time you take a practice test, the questions and answers appear in a different randomized order.

Detailed Explanations of Correct and Incorrect Answers

You'll receive automatic feedback on all correct and incorrect answers. The detailed answer explanations are a superb learning tool in their own right.

Attention to Exam Objectives

MeasureUp practice tests are designed to appropriately balance the questions over each technical area covered by a specific exam.

Installing the CD

The minimum system requirements for the CD-ROM are

➤ Windows 95, 98, Me, NT4, 2000, or XP

➤ 7MB disk space for the testing engine

➤ An average of 1MB disk space for each test

To install the CD-ROM, follow these instructions:

If you need technical support, please contact MeasureUp at 678-356-5050 or email **support@measureup.com**. Additionally, you'll find Frequently Asked Questions (FAQ) at **www.measureup.com**.

1. Close all applications before beginning this installation.

2. Insert the CD into your CD-ROM drive. If the setup starts automatically, go to step 5. If the setup does not start automatically, continue with step 3.

3. From the Start menu, select Run.

4. In the Browse dialog box, double-click Setup.exe. In the Run dialog box, click OK to begin the installation.

5. On the Welcome screen, click Next.

6. To agree to the Software License Agreement, click Yes.

7. On the Choose Destination Location screen, click Next to install the software to `C:\Program Files\Certification Prepartation/`.

8. On the Setup Type screen, select Typical Setup. Click Next to continue.

9. After the installation is complete, verify that Yes, I want to restart my computer now is selected. If you select No, I will restart my computer later, you will not be able to use the program until you restart your computer.

10. Click Finish.

11. After restarting your computer, choose Start, Programs, MeasureUp, MeasureUp Practice Tests.

12. Select the practice test and click Start Test.

Creating a Shortcut to the MeasureUp Practice Tests

To create a shortcut to the MeasureUp practice tests, follow these steps.

1. Right-click on your Desktop.

2. From the shortcut menu, select New, Shortcut.

3. Browse to `C:\Program Files\MeasureUp Practice Tests` and select the MeasureUpCertification.exe or Localware.exe file.

4. Click OK.

5. Click Next.

6. Rename the shortcut MeasureUp.

7. Click Finish.

After you have completed step 7, use the MeasureUp shortcut on your Desktop to access the MeasureUp practice test.

Technical Support

If you encounter problems with the MeasureUp test engine on the CD-ROM, please contact MeasureUp at 678-356-5050 or email `support@measureup.com`. Technical support hours are from 8 a.m. to 5 p.m. EST Monday through Friday. Additionally, you'll find Frequently Asked Questions (FAQ) at `www.measureup.com`.

If you'd like to purchase additional MeasureUp products, call 678-356-5050 or 800-649-1MUP (1687), or visit `www.measureup.com`.

informIT

What if Que

joined forces to deliver the best technology books in a common digital reference platform?

We have. Introducing
**InformIT Online Books
powered by Safari.**

- **Specific answers to specific questions.**
InformIT Online Books' powerful search engine gives you relevance-ranked results in a matter of seconds.

- **Immediate results.**
With InformIt Online Books, you can select the book you want and view the chapter or section you need immediately.

- **Cut, paste, and annotate.**
Paste code to save time and eliminate typographical errors. Make notes on the material you find useful and choose whether or not to share them with your workgroup.

- **Customized for your enterprise.**
Customize a library for you, your department, or your entire organization. You pay only for what you need.

POWERED BY

As an InformIT partner, Que has shared the knowledge and hands-on advice of our authors with you online. Visit InformIT.com to see what you are missing.

informit.com/onlinebooks

Get your first 14 days **FREE!**
InformIT Online Books is offering its members a 10-book subscription risk free for 14 days.
Visit **http://www.informit.com/onlinebooks** for details.